A Process for Lighting the Stage

Ian McGrath

Illustrations by Barry Landy

ALLYN AND BACON

Boston   London   Sydney   Toronto

Copyright © 1990 by Allyn and Bacon
A Division of Simon & Schuster
160 Gould Street
Needham Heights, Massachusetts 02194

Library of Congress Cataloging-in-Publication Data

McGrath, Ian.
    A process for lighting the stage / Ian McGrath : illustrations by Barry Landy.
      p. cm.
    Bibliography: p.
    Includes index.
    ISBN 0–205–12043–1
    1. Stage lighting. I. Title.
PN2091.E4M35   1990
792′.025—dc19   89–30684
                                             CIP

Printed in the United States of America

10 9 8 7 6 5 4 3 2 1   93 92 91 90 89

To my students (1982–84) at the National Institute of Dramatic Art, Sydney, Australia, who demanded that I verbalise this process.

Would you care to share a rainbow with me?
Would you like to brighten cloudy skies?
There's more richness to be had,
Such colour to be felt
Than all the greys a lonely life inspires.

Contents

Illustrations

Figures

Preface

Why another book on stage lighting? And why am I the author of it? After all, I believe that I can give you no right or wrong answers, only solutions more or less suited to the production in question. But I also believe that there are principles to be understood before you can, with authority, bend them to your purpose; there are processes to comprehend before you can apply them to your method of working; there is an appreciation of the profession to be developed before you can realise what "artistic collaboration" will mean to you.

A course or time in the profession will help to bring this vast body of knowledge within your grasp; experience, practice, and experimentation will strengthen your grip; but, in my opinion, you are still *not* a lighting designer. You must develop the courage, the need, and the confidence to be unique—to try something new, to risk failure, to discover for yourself "artistic truth."

I doubt that these qualities can be taught. How, then, did I learn? By watching the good and the bad of those lighting designers who went before, my contemporaries, and—I am unashamed!—of those who follow; by seeing success and failure, differing ways to the same solution, and different applications of old methods. This form of plagiarism is accepted and encouraged in the profession because it ensures the continuation and expansion of the craft.

That's the reason for this book. It is to enable intermediate/advanced students and aspiring lighting designers to study the approach of one designer, extracting from it whatever they find beneficial and rejecting the unsatisfactory. There are already enough texts with a bias toward the mechanics of the craft. What I am emphasising is the sequence of processes that carry you to opening night.

Differing Phraseology

You will soon discover that within this profession phraseology is inconsistent from theatre to theatre and from country to country, often depending on the history and experience of the individuals involved. In order to save you repeated interruptions while you look up a glossary, I follow all terms that may be in dispute with alternate phraseology in brackets; for example, *gauze [scrim]* and *lantern [instrument]*.

Appreciation

I should like to express my gratitude to Rick Burchall and Barry Landy for their support, assistance, and encouragement while this book was being written. My thanks also to the National Institute of Dramatic Art, Sydney, Australia, for support and technical facilities.

Ian McGrath
Sydney, Australia
December 1988

CHAPTER 1

Introduction to the Functions of Lighting Design

You are reading this book because you want to become a lighting designer or, at least, to learn about the craft and how it affects you. I'll leave my congratulations until later and let you get into the subject matter immediately.

1.2 Historic Perspective

Stage lighting as a profession is fairly new, but the craft itself is as old as theatre. The Greeks used the best lighting in the world—the sun—but could not do much to control it except to direct its rays onto the stage with bronze mirrors. Also, they arranged their stages to catch the early-morning or late-evening light.

Of course, every caveman who ever performed a tale of the hunt used lighting; the campfire would have illuminated the audience as much as the performer. The best storytellers of that day would have stayed close to the light source, placing it between them and their audience. But they did not provide what today's audiences expect: lighting design.

The Italians and the French, as they developed purpose-built theatres, initially were not much more ingenious than the caveman. As Figure 11.1 shows, candlepower evolved to a sophisticated standard, but not until a brighter, cleaner source of light was devised did modern techniques begin to emerge.

1.2.1 Gas Lighting for Theatres

It was the nineteenth century before gas was exploited in theatres—and not to universal acclaim! Many considered it harsh and unflattering, certainly not the sort of thing one would have in one's home!

Control—for that was the major theatrical advantage of gas—was initially very basic. The follow-spot or "lime" operator sat on a bag of gas—heavily if he wanted bright light or very gingerly if he wanted dim light. He could not lift his weight completely. If he did, the flame would burn back into the bag, blowing up the operator, his "lime," and the theatre. That state of affairs could not and did not last for long.

Soon, very sophisticated control of gas lighting was available, based largely on plumbing skill. It was controlled much as we reticulate water or domestic gas today. With a series of pilot lights and a control position, where the operator's basic tool was a wrench, theatre lighting was not dissimilar from what we have today; many of the terms we still use (dips, footlights, dome) have their origins in gas. If you read *Theatre Lighting in the Age of Gas* (see Bibliography), you will see that many features of gas lighting can be rediscovered and adapted to modern use.

1.2.2 Advent of Electricity

Electric stage lighting is an infant barely older than the twentieth century, and within that short history it has developed spasmodically. In 1881 D'Oyly Carte introduced electricity to the British theatre, but the initial advances were technical—perfecting equipment, materials, and controls—rather than artistic. This was a setback for lighting design which had developed to sophisticated levels among gaslight technicians due to the demands of, for example, the actor-manager Henry Irving.

The development of equipment continued, consolidated, and reached a degree of stability by the early 1950s when, in England and America, specialised lighting designers appeared intent on making technology a servant to the artistic enterprise. Again, though, technology—now through rapid advances in computer control boards and in the range of lanterns [instruments] available— interfered with artistic development. What was neglected was the hallmark of the lighting designer: the purposeful application of craft and technology to the needs of a performance.

1.3 What Exactly Is a Lighting Designer?

Do we really need lighting designers? Would shows ever reach opening night without them? Yes, of course. While lighting designers are a bonus to productions, many high-quality productions would succeed without them. Almost anyone can switch on the worklights or hang a few lanterns, colour them, push up a fader, and serve the show extremely well. But this is "illumination"; it is not lighting design.

Simply stated, lighting designers work within their department in exactly the same way as do all other designers (such as wardrobe, set, and sound). They merge their department's skills, knowledge, and resources (both manpower and equipment) with the production concept (see chapter 4) in the service of the show for the benefit of the audience.

1.4 Relationship to Audience

"For the benefit of the audience" is a phrase that is too often forgotten. Lighting designers are, after all, in the entertainment industry; without an audience they have no purpose—they are engaged only in an expensive form of self-gratification.

Everything you do must be for the benefit of those who, in the long run, pay you; that is the responsibility of any craftsperson who wishes to survive. That is not to say that you are obliged to "give 'em what they want—muck!" but your service must be for their benefit.

The primary purpose of lighting is to allow the audience to see what the members of the company are doing. If, in the process, the lighting designer can assist in the interpretation, the clarity . . . the magic . . . of the performance, that is likely to be appreciated more by ourselves and our colleagues than those out front.

1.5 Relationship to Management

It has been said that, given enough typewriters and paper, monkeys will eventually reproduce Shakespeare's sonnets. The same could be said about stage lighting: with enough personnel, electricity, lanterns, and time, anyone can light a masterpiece. But so long as theatre must earn its own living and not rely entirely upon subsidy, a production cannot be treated as one vast enjoyable experiment. Theatres are expensive to run, and the producer is trying to reduce the time we keep the house "dark" (in this case, meaning without paying customers). He or she employs the lighting designer to sit at a desk and, from experience and knowledge, create on paper what the monkeys would produce in the unlimited time!

Thus, you are responsible to the management for the *efficient* lighting of the show; somewhat more peripherally, the *effectiveness* of the lighting will also concern management. The director and the collaborative team wish to create magic, and they require the lighting designer to give conceptual support to their production concept. Hence, designers have divided loyalties created largely by budgetary considerations and, as you read on, you will discover more about this dichotomy.

1.6 General Points

There are a couple of general points to be made before ending this introductory chapter.

1.6.1 In Which Theatrical Genre Are You Working?

The material on the stage you are to light may be from any one of the lively arts. To what degree will you need to vary your lighting techniques to suit? The principle behind this book is that the principles and performance standards it discusses can and must be applied regardless of the genre. Of course, you will find it advantageous to bend and vary your approach to suit the material, but the principles of good design should be applied equally to puppet shows, dance, drama, rock and classical concerts, opera, musical comedy, or product promotion.

Introduction to the Functions of Lighting Design

1.6.2 T.V. and Film Lighting

Although this book is about stage lighting, many of its principles apply equally to T.V. or film and even to the lighting of buildings. The techniques, however, may not be directly applicable; you will need to study elsewhere for specific skills in related fields.

1.6.3 Is the Lighting Department Sexist?

Let me apologise now; I may refer to the lighting designer as a "he," largely because I'll be referring to myself. This is not to imply that lighting design is the exclusive domain of men—quite the opposite.

1.6.4 Professional versus Amateur

I refer to myself as professional (I am fortunate enough to be paid for what I love to do); this is not to exclude the amateur practitioners of the craft. One of the Dames of the British theatre said, "An amateur can be occasionally brilliant but a professional must be consistently good." The distinction becomes a question of attitude—not salary! There are some very professional amateurs and some very amateur professionals.

CHAPTER 2

Scheduling Your
Responsibilities

Assume that you have had an offer to light a show; the first thing you need to do—even while you are on the phone—is to check your calendar. The importance of a diary to a lighting designer cannot be stressed too highly; we're not referring to a "Dear diary" but to a clear record of your commitments and appointments. One of the greatest crimes you can commit is to double-book yourself; your diary should help avoid that embarrassment, and your accountant will also find it valuable.

If you find yourself committed elsewhere during what we'll call Section C in the schedule below, it would be inadvisable to accept the new commission; you'll be unable to devote your whole attention to the job in hand. However, during Sections A and B it's common practice (and from a financial viewpoint, necessary) to mix shows, scheduling them so as to avoid clashes. A busy free-lance designer can be working three or more shows in different cities at any time.

Once you have ascertained that time is available, quickly discuss with the producer the other personnel involved, the show itself, theatre and performance space, and money (both fee and budget). Assuming, for our purposes, that this is a medium-to-large show being produced by a subsidised company, the usual rehearsal schedule would be five weeks. The schedule below lists major events in the production process, your responsibilities as lighting designer (Lx Des.), when each task should be completed, and the time involved. You need to produce something similar as an aid to organisation, but remember that what you see below is merely an example; *yours must be adapted to suit the show, theatre, company, time span—all the multitude of variables.*

This example will serve as a broad structure for the entire book, which will remind you in each chapter where you are within the schedule. It also indicates the chapters that discuss each item. Study the draft schedule carefully so that you will always be aware of the time frame, even when many pages are spent on a process that, in real time, must be completed quickly.

Many of the terms that appear in the following table may be unfamiliar to you; try not to let that concern you too much at this stage—the relevant chapter will clarify them when you reach it. The purpose of this table is to provide an overall view of the task ahead of you and impose a time frame.

Section	Weeks to Opening	Rehearsal Room	Departmental Action	Reference Chapter
A Preproduction Period	Variable up to twelve months	Nil	Formulation of production concept; time for art, ideas, and dreaming in close collaboration; a period to watch, listen, advise, contribute.	3, 4
B Early Rehearsal Period	Six	Nil	Set and costume design presented to management. Budget and logistic estimations and planning. Casting finalised and theatre confirmed. Minor involvement by lighting designer and crew.	5
	Five	Presentation of set and costume design. First reading. Rehearsals commence.	Set and costume design accepted. Lighting designer: in-house familiarity—meet in-house staff; time-in-lieu [compensatory time]. Experiments. Special effects manufacture and orders begun. Information collection. Attend production meeting.	6, 7
	Four	Rough blocking	Experiments with model and theatre. Prepare documentation and complete information collection. Equipment and stock checks (colour and spares). Lighting design evolution: attend rehearsals; basic cue synopsis evolution. Department rounds—costume fittings, set workshop. Attend production meeting.	7, 8
	Three	Finer blocking	Continue lighting design evolution. Final synopsis conference. Place orders, etc. Department rounds. Attend full run with board operator if possible. Attend production meeting.	9–14
C Documentation and Production Weeks	Two	Drilling, fine tuning; performance values.	Prepare plan, colour and stock lists, lantern schedule, and patch lists; deliver to head electrician by a.m. Thurs. Update cue synopsis; prepare state-of-the-board sheets, rough cue sheets, and information for plotting [dry tech.]. Finish special effects manufacture. Ensure orders arrive. Complete equipment (colour) preparation. Attend final run with board operator; final conference to check details and changes. Attend production meeting.	15

Section	Weeks to Opening	Rehearsal Room	Departmental Action	Reference Chapter
	One	Fine tuning; transfer to theatre	Production week (ch. 16 for details). Rig, focus, plotting. Technical rehearsal. Dress rehearsals, final check. Opening Tuesday or Friday.	16 17–21

2.3 Lighting Department—Individual Responsibilities

This book will detail every function of the lighting department. But as to what person has the responsibility for a particular function will depend upon the organisation of the production company. At times it will be the lighting designer alone, but sometimes the distinction between tasks usually performed by the head electrician and/or the designer may be unclear. Only by working as a team, discussing the details, and allocating tasks to those best suited to them can you achieve your goals without placing undue stress on any individual. No situation will be the same, regardless of whether you're on the staff or a free-lancer.

2.4 Time Commitment

I'll give here a very rough estimation of the minimum time required to achieve a satisfactory result. Again it could vary wildly, depending on many factors ranging from your own experience to the style chosen for the production; however, the following could be considered minimum for a medium-to-large show.

Section A—The Preproduction Period. As a general rule three working days comprising discussion, research, and the like is sufficient for this preproduction period; concepts involving research and development need special consideration. Keep in mind that this process could occur up to a year prior to the production and cover a period of months (for example, a major opera). In other companies it may never happen or is fitted into the coffee breaks once rehearsals have commenced. This last kind is regrettable and should be discouraged.

Section B—The Early Rehearsal Period. Your involvement should average out to two working days for each of the four weeks. This will comprise time here and there, depending upon the amount of manufacturing required and the staff available to you.

Section C—Documentation and Production Weeks. During both these weeks you will be heavily involved; hence, you cannot do much with other shows. Documentation of your lighting design in a form accessible to your crew (e.g., plan, cue sheets, etc.) generally takes four working days; anything less than that probably means that your paperwork and crew preparation are incomplete.

Your production week schedule depends largely upon that of the production manager, but a major show usually needs a minimum of twelve hours each for rig, focus, plotting [dry tech.], and rehearsals.

2.5 *Late Involvement of Lighting Designer*

What happens if, when you're offered the job, you discover that opening night is only two weeks away, with the set nearly constructed and rehearsals well under way? Do you accept the job?

The first thing to realise is that the company is probably not looking for a lighting designer but for an "illuminator." Many have not had the opportunity to work with anything but an illuminator and do not understand what a lighting designer offers. Others desire nothing more than illumination and expect to pay accordingly. It is also possible that their lighting *designer* has dropped out, but usually this will be presented as a special request.

In this profession you tend to be known and judged by your most recent work; thus, if you enter into a contract knowing that you will approach opening night ill prepared, you are risking a great deal. If you spend extra time gathering the background of which you have been deprived, you may not be ill prepared, but you will need to set your fee accordingly; this is likely to be too high for companies that are seeking only illumination. If you accept the commission, whenever possible point out the refinements that are missing because you were not involved from conception.

CHAPTER 3

A Collaborative Affair

For years I limited my comments about working with others to "I learned a lot and I'd like to work with them again" or "I choose not to work for them again." Somehow I had evolved a vague philosophy that demanded I work *with* people, not *for* them; I was unable to extend my ideas further. I then had the pleasure of reading *The Magic of Light* by Jean Rosenthal (see Bibliography); I quote from that book:

> Collaboration flourishes when there is an understanding on the part of each member of the team that the others involved are to be respected and their authority fully recognised. The motions of carrying out the collaboration, the different techniques each group will require because of the personalities involved, make collaboration a hope, not always an achievement.

I've not been able to improve upon that as a concise statement of the ideal attitude toward theatrical endeavor.

According to the *Oxford Dictionary*, *to collaborate* is "to work in combination at a literary or artistic production"; alternatively, "to cooperate treacherously with the enemy." Although you may have experiences that incline you toward the latter definition, accept the first. And you should extend the concept beyond the usual director/designer/lighting limits to include any individual involved in the production. Some contributions will be minor; others will be so indispensable as to alter the nature of the show. But remove any one endeavor and the production, as a whole, diminishes.

3.2 Cooperative versus Collaborative

I am talking of collaboration, not cooperation. These two very different approaches to theatrical enterprise tend to create radically different products and appeal to different audiences. Those who prefer cooperative ventures need not stop reading now, but they should realize that my frame of reference, particularly in these earlier sections, involves a single unifying vision and authority that is projected to, and serves, the audience. In recent times that vision has been embodied in the director; in the not-so-distant past it was in the actor/manager.

It may be an individual talent that commands the attention of the audience—perhaps Miller's plays or the Joan Sutherland/Richard Bonynge approach to opera—but behind each is an individual with a unique viewpoint to project. It is the director who chose the piece, who has cast it in the hope that it will achieve success and who will, in time, choose the next production, and so on. This does not belie my assertion that theatre must be a collaborative function, for intelligent directors realise that the range of skills involved in a major production is beyond them alone; their talent rests in selecting people who will serve their vision well and present it in the best possible manner.

Wise directors are something like benevolent dictators. They encourage their team to deliver their best by creating the atmosphere and sense of freedom the team requires. That's the benevolent side! Then they filter every idea, judge it against their vision, and reject the unsuitable (but in such a way that the idea's creator requests the pleasure of working with that director in the future). That's the dictator!

Directors, though, cannot always be expected to supply the energy and sense of accord that enables the various departments to work together; instead, they must engender the interdepartmental collaboration mentioned in 3.1. Some cast and select for this ability above all others, accepting a possible lowering of standard as a pay-off for calm and rational behaviour; others select temperaments that clash both on and off stage, creating the conflicting energies necessary for performance—their energies are largely expended in maintaining sufficient peace to allow the show to survive the length of the run. Whichever approach they choose, directors must accept most of the responsibility for the success or failure of the collaborative effort; they must become the arbiter not only of taste but also of temperament.

3.4 Examples of Collaboration

Because not everyone believes strongly in the need for collaboration, let me give you some examples from my own experiences that point out how important collaboration is in reality.

3.4.1 Director, Designer, and Lighting Designer

Because this relationship is so important, it requires a chapter of its own (chapter 4).

3.4.2 Choreographer

In a ballet company the choreographer is equivalent to a director, but in opera and drama choreographers are departmental heads and their concerns are similar to your own.

The collaboration between choreographer and lighting designer should be close; you must know the choreography as intimately as you do the remainder of the staging before you can position specials (9.4.2) or appreciate how dangerous a wing cluttered with lighting equipment is to fast-moving dancers.

You cannot assume that the choreographer and the dancers will clearly appreciate all the ramifications of our endeavors. For example, we conceived a waterfall centre stage through which a dancer would make a spectacular entrance; all concerned discussed the effect in detail, and it was approved. At the technical rehearsal the fog generator behaved splendidly, the lighting was superb, the dancer stepped through—and fell flat on his back! I had forgotten to mention that CO_2 deposits a slippery film of water on the stage.

Besides eliminating possible catastrophes, collaboration can lead to happy resolutions of problems. During the coffee break at rehearsal of the polonaise in Tchaikovsky's *Eugene Onegin*, the choreographer bewailed the fact that he was trying to fill a grand ballroom with a handful of dancers; the production could afford no more. Later, I noted a repeating pattern onstage (see Fig. 3.1). It occurred to me that, with distinctive lighting, we could arrange for the dancers to be constantly accompanied by their own shadow. In the eyes of the audience the number of performers onstage would be doubled. After discussion, the choreographer amplified the pattern; and, by the time we got to technical rehearsal, we had created a seemingly crowded stage.

3.4.3 Production Manager

The production manager is the individual charged with coordinating all physical aspects of the production—of which lighting is just a part—and sometimes must force compromises to accommodate the limitations of budget, safety, and efficiency. That is why the lighting designer needs collaboration and careful exchange of information, especially during manufacture of the setting and when preparing production schedules. This will ensure, for example, that you have a reasonable share of the stage time available and that ladder access is as free as possible.

Often the function of the production manager is perceived as purely limiting—a frustrating necessity! Fortunately, this is not often the case. When working at his best, by means of regular production meetings and the like, the production manager may be the instrument whereby each department is encouraged to perform to its maximum.

3.4.4 Stage Management

The individuals in stage management are responsible for the efficient control of the rehearsal space, the running of the show, and its maintenance once the production team has moved on. In some smaller companies the stage manager is also given the responsibilities of production manager, technical director, and workshop manager; the deputy stage manager may assume responsibility for the

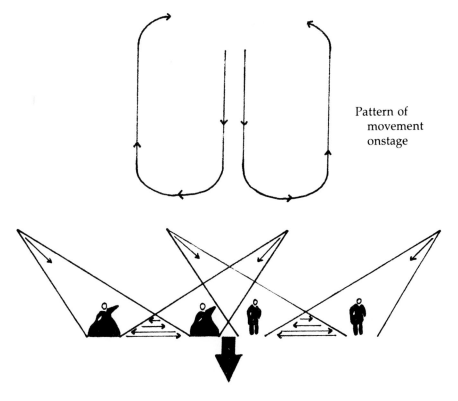

Pattern of
movement
onstage

Figure 3.1
Polonaise from Eugene
Onegin

rehearsal room and for calling the show. Whichever organisational structure is used, communication is of paramount importance.

As a free-lance designer, you cannot be in rehearsal all the time, and yet that is the major source of your information; stage management will be able to inform you when major events are occurring so that you use your time effectively. Your cue synopsis is as much for the benefit of stage management as for anyone else; it tells when a director, in evolving a scene, deviates from what was originally visualized. Moreover, your cue synopsis enables calling the show to be planned ahead—perhaps even rehearsed while still in the relaxed atmosphere of the rehearsal room. Most important of all, it is the people in stage management who maintain the show to the standards you set; if you are able to clearly communicate your intention, they can maintain and protect your reputation.

3.4.5 Sound/Music Department

There is a tendency in drama to ignore the increased power that is generated when sound and light work together. Musical theatre and opera use it as the foundation of their art; the music adds substance, encourages suspension of disbelief, and gives license to the emotions. But drama can be equally effective, especially since it has a far greater freedom in its choice of effects.

Of course, both the lighting and sound departments will have their particular tasks, but a close cooperation, with single intent, of both designers will offer solutions to many problems that neither department could solve as effectively alone. If you can make the audience associate lighting (increase the keylight) and sound (a jackhammer in the distance) with the first few entrances of a character, you not only comment strongly on the character but also establish a range of subliminal triggers. You are able to remind the audience of the character even when not on the stage.

Or, say, you have the *King Lear* storm sequence to create on a small budget. If the sound department concentrates its efforts on the storm aided by the few lighting effects available, you can get on with the important job of lighting the actors. In the minds of the audience the storm will still be raging!

At the other end of the spectrum of collaboration is the orchestra pit that blazes more light than your front-of-house (F.O.H.) bridge, a continuing problem for both of us. It is as difficult for the lighting designer to balance a delicate moonlight scene with a blaze of white light from below as it is for the orchestra members to create the music when they can't see their scores. To cope with this problem, I have given an especially cooperative musical director a small desk to control the light output from the pit; during sensitive scenes he took the light down to a mutually satisfactory level.

3.4.6 Cast Members

Too often, lighting designers become embroiled in lighting a set; they forget that the important canvas upon which they are painting is the cast and, if the actors through lack of attention to precise staging detail are in a different place each night, your problems are insoluble. However, when next you meet this problem, before shouting, get onstage and remind yourself how difficult it is to appreciate the whole picture when you are part of it.

Perhaps the most important thing you can do is to remind the cast, particularly those less experienced, of the range of factors in which you are both interested, for example, make-up. If your cast is aware that you, too, are working to project their characterisation in the best light possible, they will generally be most cooperative; but your criticism must be constructive—you must not condemn their efforts without being able to suggest improvements; you must know as much about make-up as they (see Corson, *Stage Makeup* in the Bibliography).

3.4.7 Wardrobe

As the range of colours and textures available from wardrobe is vast, the only way to find out what your lights do on the particular selection is to experiment. Ask the supervisor, as they're cutting each costume, to keep a small section, such as 50 × 100 mm [2″ × 4″], of each material; you can experiment with this in the same way you play light on a set model.

Don't forget that costumes are designed as carefully as your lights are designed; an actor's characterisation and movement are particularly influenced by the "frocks." A panel may be inserted into a gown to give a Brünnehilde-type figure a waist; if you mis-colour that scene so that the panel blends into the remainder of the costume, poor Brünnehilde re-appears en masse.

A continuing problem for lighting designers is hats; they effectively define a character but, equally effectively, keep light off the actor's face. If you visit the millinery workshop during the manufacture of a scene's hats, you may be able to point out that the lighting direction will be from prompt [stage left]; then the milliner might be able to lift the hat on that side, allowing you to get your light in and under.

3.4.8 Set Workshop

Similarly, you can show the set workshop how it and the lighting department can help each other. The workshop can construct scenery sufficiently strong to support not only itself but also your lights or may be able to leave a hole upstage in a column where you can hide a light. It will be easy for the workshop to select a scaffolding compatible with lighting equipment and just as easy for you to leave space on a bar where you know bulky scenery is going to fly very close. What is important is that you are all aware. Frequently, the workshop will manufacture pieces into which special effects must be fitted; without your input it can't know how much access you need to the interior for electrical wiring and may glue and screw so securely that the piece must be nearly destroyed once you are ready for it—a waste.

But, most important of all, you may find that frequent visits to the workshop help you realise the true dimension of the set far better than any model or drawing the designer is able to produce.

3.4.9 Everybody Else

There are so many involved in a production that I cannot give examples from each; some are too easily forgotten: the cleaners who are forced to fit around late rehearsals or the publicity officer who is told that rehearsal pressures make it impossible for the principal attraction to give an interview.

And don't forget the stage doorman, who can either ignore the message he has received, or, alternatively, go looking for "that lighting fellow who introduced himself"; that message could be the offer of your next job!

3.5 In Summation

A head mechanist I know said: "Fun!? Theatre is never fun! It's either difficult or bloody impossible!" I don't necessarily agree with him, but I know that, without collaboration, it most certainly will be bloody difficult!

CHAPTER 4

The Production Concept

Before you consider practicalities, there is one more philosophical area to explore. It's the relationship between the director, the set/costume designer, and the lighting designer. Again, I'll be presenting a personal viewpoint, which may be open to dispute from every direction. Just keep in mind that it is intended as a point of departure from which you may be able to develop a unique method of working within the profession.

4.2 The Function of the Director

Figure 4.1 attempts to define the purpose of the director and also illustrates methods of achieving that end. The purpose of the venture is the projection to the audience of a unified viewpoint or interpretation. It's known by many different names: Strasberg referred to the spine of the play; Stanislavsky created the metaphor of a set of guiding rails that led to the centre of a lake called Inspiration. It

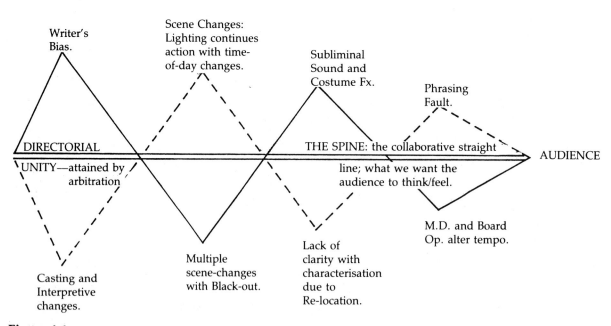

Figure 4.1
Directorial Purpose

doesn't matter what you call it so long as you and all concerned understand its function.

Perhaps the greatest ability that directors can develop is objectivity, the ability to recognise elements at deviance with their vision. In Figure 4.1 the single solid line represents what the director considers to be deviations from the spine, while the broken line indicates the steps our director may choose to correct these distortions. If the director can clearly define the problems, departmental heads may suggest ways their skills might best solve those problems, or the director may request particular action. In the final assessment the responsibility rests with the director to define the problem and to choose the method and degree of correction.

Consider some of the examples suggested in Figure 4.1. The director perceives a bias in the writing; and, since, for whatever reason, the playwright cannot rewrite, the production must compensate. Let's say that the playwright indicates the intent as dramatic but that the director, conceiving this to be incorrect, decides to interpret the play as a comedy. This may be achieved in part by casting unusually and/or imposing a bizarre style on set and lighting.

Many older plays were written with a multitude of scenes and intended to be played with blackouts between. Modern audiences expect from film, T.V., and theatre alike a stepped-up pace; subsequently, they will not work at maintaining their attention during long changes between scenes. A frequent solution to this problem is to continue the time framework by means of lighting through what otherwise would have been a blackout. I recently did a 1920s three-act play; a modern audience no longer expects a third act, so we chose to play acts 2 and 3 together, using lighting to indicate a time lapse between. The original intention was to continue this style into the presets for the acts; this, however, did not work out in the plotting [dry tech.] session. I still believe the principle was correct; a continuous flow of time would have created a consistent lighting style.

For the next example, consider a relocation in time. It seemed that we were not totally successful in adapting a miracle play to modern costume. In the original the character Death was easily represented carrying a scythe; however, in this production's relocation into a motorcycle gang, the skull and crossed bones on the back of a leather jacket had an entirely different connotation. Solution: Add to the distinctive sound of the jacket—the squeak of leather against leather—a distinctive sound to the boots—a steel tip that rings on the stage floor. To both these sounds add suitable music and distinctive lighting; then, every time the dialogue turns to death, use the combination to establish for the audience an association between those effects and Death.

And for a final example, think about a musical whose finale seems to work against the desired phrasing; it finishes with a whimper, not a bang! The solution may rest with the musical director's upping the tempo; when punctuated by the lighting-board operator and the flyman operating the house curtain, the situation will improve enormously.

The types of situations in these examples represent assessments that the director can make at any time during the production process. Keep this in mind as you continue in the book, which often says that you must remain flexible; the examples above are the first indication of how important that can be.

4.3 Personal Integrity

One school of thought maintains that, as a professional, you should be able to apply your skills to any spine. You are, however, making life difficult for yourself if you accept a commission to work on a show whose moral conviction is contrary to your own. There existed for a long time in Paris the Théâtre du Grand Guignol, whose purpose was to incite pleasurable horror from rape, murder, and the like. If your convictions are like mine, you won't be able to work effectively for that end.

4.4 Types of Directors

When students were asked to describe the director they would most like to work with, one presented the graphic given as Figure 4.2. Here the flow of concepts through the director describes well the function of a collaborator; he is a channel by which ideas can be moulded, sieved, discarded, generated, blended, unified, and returned-to-sender for modification. The illustration represents a benevolent dictator who trusts and respects the talents of those working with him and acknowledges the power of the unified whole over the individually brilliant. To maintain the significant heart-shape, the artist included only two supporting designers, but the director may engage as many as necessary. The set designer is always there, the lighting designer only in more recent times; but the production manager, sound designer, choreographer, and many others may be involved.

Notice the direction of the arrows, indicating the flow of ideas and information; the set designer may grasp upon a suggestion of the lighting designer or vice versa; both may supply an idea to the director, who tests it against the spine and accepts or rejects; unacceptable material can be trashed or modified. Clever directors rarely trash the idea themselves but return it in such a manner that designers willingly discard it, developing something that may incorporate the essence of three or four discarded ideas and surprising everyone with ingenuity and aptness.

Of course, all this would be in the "best of all possible worlds," where collaboration is the norm rather than the exception. In the real world directors, like lighting designers, come in all shapes, sizes, temperaments, and persuasions. (As Jean Rosenthal said, collaboration is hoped for, not always achieved, because of the personalities involved.) If you are to survive in the real world, it may help to be aware of some of the extreme variations you may meet. Such extremes are rare, just as a pure type is rare; most are a little of each,

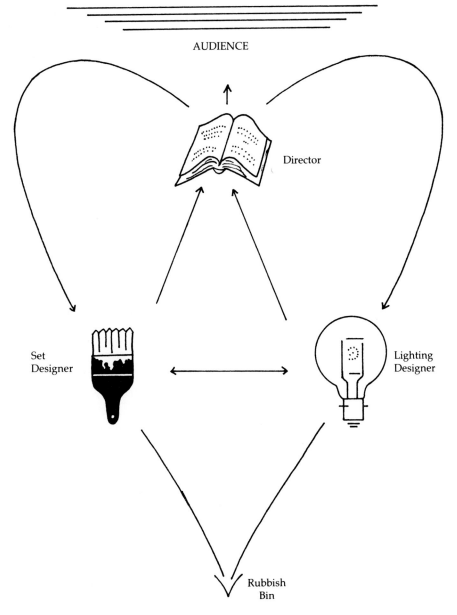

AUDIENCE

Director

Set
Designer

Lighting
Designer

Rubbish
Bin

Figure 4.2
The Triangular Trilogy

depending on the time of day, lateness of rehearsal, and proximity of opening night.

There are the dictatorial directors, who know exactly what they want and will accept nothing else. This single-mindedness ensures they are clear, precise, and easy to comprehend, but they don't really need a lighting designer as a creative influence—a head electrician is quite capable of translating this direction into practicalities. There's a variant style who will accept only those elements of a design that precisely coincide with their ideas, rejecting all compromises or alternate methods; production managers tend to find this type difficult when budget restrictions are tight.

There's another type who disclaim all technical knowledge; these people genuinely feel inadequate when talking to technicians and frequently avoid them. But here comes the catch; they know what they want when they see it! It is a common problem (not only among directors) and is based on an inability to visualise. You must use every available device to present information in such a way as to generate feedback and prevent the design process from degenerating into a costly, time-consuming lucky-dip.

The third extreme can be very easy to work with, but very unchallenging! Desperate not to impose, they try too hard to be pleasant. The resulting lack of feedback makes it difficult for the designers to perceive precisely what is required. Flood this director with a myriad of choices, force a reaction, and you may be able to extract enough information to impose upon yourself a set of priorities. You'll need to develop your skills for gleaning every scrap of information there is to be had. The most important source is the rehearsal room; most directors communicate well with actors though they may feel uncomfortable, even unwelcome, in technical fields. The speed of a cue may be hidden in an actor's gesture, or the mood may be defined by the conflict between characters. You must learn to interpret information directed to artists other than yourself and take every opportunity to ease direct communication.

4.5 Set Designers

It must be difficult to conceive a complete picture (which necessarily—even if subconsciously—includes lighting), then to lose control of the element that is the means whereby the remainder becomes visible to the audience. To spend hours, days, weeks, conceiving and creating an item, to have housemaid's knees and paint under the fingernails to prove it . . . and then suffer a lighting designer's toning that item down to highlight some other element of the whole must be heartrending. But there's also joy to be had in this relationship when you discover through another's eyes elements you never imagined in your work.

Each department has a specific responsibility to the production; and, on occasions when conflicts arise, all concerned must learn to trust the objectivity of the director. You may not agree with individual decisions, particularly when it affects your creations, but you must have faith that the end result has a unity and integrity beyond your individual viewpoint.

Throughout, this book details examples of the interaction between set and lighting designers. Study them carefully, for this is a most important relationship, and upon its successful conclusion will depend far more than individual reputations.

4.6 Lighting Designers

They, too, can be categorised into the four types—though few would disclaim technical skills. A dictatorial lighting designer would rarely be employed, though I have known this department to hide behind the union's skirts and claim lack of time available to make a change—that's not the union's fault!

There are a number of the pleasant-persons type among lighting designers: "Just tell me what you want . . ." and they deliver the standard rig minimally adapted to give the impression of a purpose-designed show. Then it's too late, and the director is forced to accept something unsuitable.

Lighting collaborators are a recent development; because of our fits-and-starts recent history, the more established directors and set designers may have difficulty accepting the lighting designer as an equal artist. To some the term *lighting designer* implies merely an illuminator and their past experience backs that up. They are familiar with the technician who first appears just before transfer to the theatre—a token gesture—to discover if any colours need changing in the standard rig. If you believe that lighting design entails a great deal more than this, you must be prepared to sell your skills, to evangelise, and to convince the others that you are a constructive member of the team.

4.7 Free-lancers versus Teams

Given the need for this blending of three or more individuals (with all the difficulties that have only been hinted at so far), it's understandable when we see a director's and designer's name linked in show after show. And, more recently, set and lighting designers have formed teams. These teams ensure productivity and stability without the need to forge new channels of communication. Expecting high standards from one another, members can get on with the job without having to worry about the diplomacy involved in a new relationship.

To achieve the best results for each show, the producer/entrepreneur must select and match the complete range of behind-the-scenes personnel for their appropriateness for the particular job, particularly those artists who form the design team. This suggests a strong bias of mine towards individual free-lancing; the risks can be high but I believe that, if the design team are carefully chosen as much for their ability to collaborate as for their individual skills, the rewards can be higher still.

4.8 Formulating the Concept

From what you have already read, you will appreciate it's impossible to impose a structure on this process. It depends greatly upon the individuals involved, the time available, and the limitations of the material. This section can only formulate some guidelines and perhaps warn of pitfalls.

4.8.1 Research

As a lighting designer, you must research; you cannot do too much. The text is the basic source, but you should also research the period, the writer, associated music, theatrical conventions—anything you can lay your hand on that pertains to the piece. For example, when approaching Puccini's *Suor Angelica*, you'll note with interest that his sister was a member of the religious order for whom Puccini first gave a performance. You cannot but wonder how similar Angelica was to Puccini's sister.

You will also find it helpful to break material into its components; for example, you could consider the words and the music of *Suor Angelica* as two simple entities before eventually considering the whole.

It's imperative that you also study the performance space and its facilities; detail can be researched later but you need to know now what's feasible. The best you can expect from this research is a sheaf of notes and some intuitive reactions. Many rational arguments can be firmly based upon a subjective reaction, tempered by objective experience.

4.8.2 Communication

Each team will develop its own methods and aids to interaction: period photographic collections, a cartoon storyboard, a suitably selected bottle of wine—but whatever you use, if no one listens, it's a waste of time! Listening is a skill that all believe they have naturally, but too often people edit what they hear to fit their own preconceptions.

Take notes. Remember that the objective of these meetings is not only to formulate the concept but also to reach a clear understanding that enables all teams to go their separate ways without losing sight of common objectives.

4.8.3 Why? Why? Why?

Try to achieve mutual understanding of the answer to three questions: Why are we doing this particular piece? Why now? Why for this audience? The answers could be quite pedestrian: Why this piece?—it was a success last time and we need the money. That may be a reasonable argument for management; but, if the artistic team go no further, they are likely to create a production as pedestrian as the answer.

Find an answer to each *why* that is satisfying artistically, professionally, and morally for each member of the team. Then you will give yourself a high degree of motivation, define goals, and answer many questions regarding relevance.

4.8.4 Defining the Style

If you study books of theatrical theory, you can list a frightening number of *isms:* naturalism, surrealism, realism, symbolism, heightened naturalism, and so on. For the benefit of the unenlightened such as myself (needing to clutch a dictionary throughout such discussions), attempt to establish the style in terms that everyone can understand. Better that you define *Annie* in such terms as "always seen through the eyes of the character Annie" than try to find the right *ism* and hope that all agree on the definition. Such a simple statement of intent can easily be applied by each department; for example, the costumes and set may take on a cartoon quality, with the adult characters being larger than life.

The same statement suggests to me that Miss Hannigan, the evil administrator of the orphanage, should be seen by the kids as monstrous; perhaps you can light Hannigan and her cronies from the footlights so that they cast vast shadows onto the backdrop. These monsters truly are of monstrous proportions when "seen through the eyes of Annie."

As a theatrical piece usually requires a character to change with time, you may choose to develop the style along with the character; perhaps the later scenes of *Annie* can adopt more naturalistic proportions.

4.8.5 Interpretation

Though closely associated with style and frequently confused with it, interpretation must be considered separately. Style is defined as "the manner of writing or doing," whereas to interpret is "to bring out the meaning of or render by artistic performance." With style you are concerned to create a consistent, clear approach and appearance, but with interpretation you may be concerned only with the content of a moment.

An example will better illustrate the point. Frequently, opera is ridiculous to an audience not familiar with its conventions; thus, you may choose to reinterpret in the hope of improved reception. Consider Bizet's *The Pearl Fishers*, act 3, part 2, scene 4, where the sight of the hero staggering about the stage singing superbly as he dies is often difficult for a modern audience to swallow. With opera you cannot enter into radical changes unless the music supports the premise, but studying Bizet's score closely gives you some license. You can hear the stab's impact: the orchestration changes, with a dreamlike quality emerging that allows for the introduction of the love theme from Leila and Nadir.

Now you could suggest to the director that perhaps the narrative, in real time, ends with the stab; Zurga dies almost instantly. If you invert the lighting in some way and, at the same instant, freeze everyone involved with the real time (the assassins), you then have the license to bring back Nadir and Leila as figments of Zurga's imagination. They can appear in an idyllic setting, and the audience can join Zurga as he exults in the success of his sacrifice. With Zurga's last words we return to real time, the images in his mind fade, and lighting returns to state. Zurga falls in death, and the assassins continue stabbing as the curtain falls.

This can be only a suggestion; it requires full cooperation from the director and the set designer in addition to approval in principle from the musical director. But it is the sort of idea a true collaboration will encourage, treat with respect, and measure objectively; it may end up in the trash, but it may also receive an enthusiastic reception. Everyone needs to develop the strength, confidence, and resilience to attempt such a presentation.

4.8.6 Time, Location, and Apparent Source of Light

Before you can profess to understand the concept, you must be able to define precisely how these three factors vary scene by scene, moment by moment, throughout the whole piece. Further, when seeking clarification, you may introduce to the director and/or designer a potential for lighting they may not have perceived.

Time. Particularly in a naturalistic production, the lighting designer must define every moment in the piece, time of day and, if possible, the date. Combined with the location, this determination may indicate apparent sources (sunlight, moonlight) or quality of light. It could justify a long twilight if the place is set in a high latitude or indicate the type of lighting (candle, gas, or electricity).

Location. Using the floor plan, obtain a consensus regarding the points of the compass. In a naturalistic production, this will indicate the direction of the sun's travel and ensure consistency. Too often the audience sees the sun rise and set through the same window! If there is no indication in the script where the points of the compass lie, the team may choose to orient the stage plan in whichever way best suits the production. They could arrange for the wedding couple to enter with the golden glow of dawn upon their expectant faces, whereas the shadowy and ambiguous villain enters backlit by a blood-red sunset. (These are obvious examples, but your collaborative efforts will find more subtle variants that serve your production concept well.)

Apparent Source of Light. This phrase is the most important in the vocabulary of a lighting designer. It may be expressed differently (lighting motivation); but, whatever you call it, it is the pivot upon which your design depends. A clear understanding of it for each scene will indicate quality, directionality, colour, and intensity, irrespective of style.

When an apparent source is undefined, a collaboration, by choosing what and where the source should be, may enhance the stage picture enormously. For example, if the script indicates a moonlit scene, you could relieve the oppressive mood by placing a street lamp so that it lights the shadowed side of the actors' faces. This allows you to balance the stage for colour, mood, and intensity.

4.8.7 Practical Considerations

The range of details you must consider while formulating the concept is vast; this section includes only a sampling.

Currently, there is a tendency to ignore the space in which the piece is being played. Often, it seems that the production concept demands space and facilities far in excess of what is available within the stagehouse, *but* the production goes ahead regardless! The secret of foreseeing problems rests in your knowledge of the theatre and your ability to communicate its limitations to the remainder of the team. It's very easy to overemphasise difficulties and gain a reputation for pessimism; it is equally easy to ignore the basic laws of gravity and physics in the heat of the creative moment.

It's not just extravagant flights of fancy you will need to limit; as the concept develops, you must be able to make an educated guess as to your requirements. Roughly how many cues do you foresee? Are they feasible within the time available? Do you have sufficient dimmers, and is the control desk suitable? If the cyclorama is to feature, do you have lighting position at the correct distance from the cyc? If actors are staged up to the cloth, do you have equipment and space to backlight the cyclorama, and is it of suitable material? Is the budget for additional equipment going to be prohibitive?

The range of educated guesses you must make and the short time allowed in which to decide frequently make this an exhausting process, but it is only through your active involvement as lighting designer that the feasibility of the concept is ensured and facilities are used effectively.

4.9 The Concept—What Do You Have to Show?

The process is drawing to a close; all those involved have reached an understanding of the concept. The designer has produced a model and costume sketches for everyone to study and comment upon. Perhaps three or four models were destroyed and the final version created from its component ideas—but at least there is something solid. What can the lighting designer produce? Nothing! . . . at best some rough sketches hinting at mood and directionality with a note concerning colour.

At this stage of the production's development you have insufficient information to develop a lighting design; all you've done is to establish parameters—and to take careful notes! You know the style, understand points of interpretation, and have defined time/location/apparent source of light for each moment . . . but you need to gather much more information before you can sit down at the drawing desk. You are among the last of the designers to go concrete; most of your work occurs at a rush once the actors' staging is complete. Your ability to remain flexible until quite late sometimes requires you to find solutions to problems not of your own making.

4.10 How Rigid Is the Concept?

Depending upon the company and how far in advance it works, there is the possibility the concept will evolve and develop in unforeseen ways (particularly when you consider the number of individual talents yet to become involved).

Generally, the set and costume designers will formalise their ideas very quickly so that these can be budgeted and construction commenced. The director, however, is less bound, as, during the rehearsal process, the performers bring to the concept their ideas and limitations that may force a deviation from the original (remember Fig. 4.1?). Everyone must appreciate the ramifications for other departments if these variations are too extreme. It may be that an excellent idea from the cast is impossible, since it would involve reconstruction of the set and a blowout of the budget; but perhaps another department can use its skills to introduce the essence of the idea. Whatever the result, the solution will be found through the communication, trust, and understanding established during the formulation of the production concept.

CHAPTER 5

Design Presentation to Managements: Budgets

It's six weeks to opening night and the countdown has begun. Some companies who work well in advance may have already budgeted; but most production managers try to locate budget activity as close as possible to the commencement of construction. In times of inflation and spiraling labour costs, to budget too far ahead is asking for trouble.

5.2 Presentation

The entire production concept is now presented to management—in particular, the physical aspects of it (the set, costumes, and properties)—so that costs can be determined. For the remainder of this week frantic activity will occur in the set and props workshops, wardrobe and, in a minor way, the electric's department. Your task as lighting designer is to develop cost details and to get them to the production manager.

The form the presentation takes will vary from company to company; what is important is to meet the deadlines that have been imposed to assure a complete presentation to those who desperately need the information. The function itself will probably be quite brief. It may be attended by the general manager, but the important people involved include the production manager, director, and designer; it is not always necessary for the lighting designer to be present or even become involved in the discussion unless there is an abnormally high proportion of special effects (SpFx) or lighting; however, your moral support will help the designer and mollify the production manager. If your schedule demands your presence with another production at this time, you must arrange with either the designer or the production manager how you can be reached.

This is a week of particular pressure for the designer, as it was on the design that the deadlines were imposed. It is also pressured for the production manager, who has a week—no more—in which to estimate materials and labour required in the manufacture of every artifact; to cost any specialized services; and to make necessary compromises—all this before final approval can be obtained from management.

Chapter 4 suggested that the production manager be invited to join the production concept discussions; the advantages of that should now be obvious. Instead of compressing their work into one week, the production manager may be able to complete some of it beforehand. That, however, is a bonus; the major advantage lies in reducing the number of surprises for both the designer and production manager. The presence of both at the concept meetings encourages curtailing extravagance or creating compromises as painlessly as possible.

5.3 Estimation or Guesswork?

Chapter 4 finished by saying that, at this point, a lighting designer has insufficient information to embark upon the design. Yet, perhaps only moments after the formulation of the concept, you will be asked to estimate precise costs. A frequent reaction to this pressure is to overestimate; for example, you cannot know what colour you require, so you order everything you could possibly desire. Although such behaviour is understandable, it could be self-defeating. "But," I hear you say, "what does it matter if the millinery department is forced to work with reduced materials or if the set designer must cut a gauze [scrim] so long as the lighting department gets what it wants?" If that is your argument, you need to reread chapter 4 if you consider it valid.

It is the responsibility of every department head to estimate as accurately as possible materials and services—then to deliver the product at or below that figure. Of course, you'll make mistakes, but if you are honest and open with your estimations, management will appreciate the genuine nature of your mistake and assist you in whatever way it can. Those departments who deliver under budget will subsidise those who slip over, and the burden is shared around; but you must have credit before expecting assistance.

5.4 Estimating Materials and Services

The only way you can accurately predict the cost of materials, hiring charges, and services is to maintain an up-to-date catalogue of all suppliers, their contact details, and most recent price lists. With this information at hand and a realistic estimate of what's required, you should be able to supply the production manager immediately with outside estimations and follow up with competing written quotations.

There will be a number of suppliers who will quote for the items you require. In addition to dollars-and-cents you must also consider quality and, in this regard, professional gossip. Your own experience and the opportunity to compare products (at trade shows and the like) will be valuable.

Finally, no one can quote accurately unless you supply sufficient detailed information—not only catalogue numbers but also delivery dates, and so on. If your specifications are vague, suppliers may be forced to overquote, and that does neither of you any good.

There are ways of keeping your options open; for example, you may order an effects projector and leave the size of the objective lens "to be advised," or you may detail two possible lenses. The phrase "to be confirmed" is frequently used and is the reason for the repeated reference to orders in your schedule of work (see chapter 2).

5.5 Estimating Human Resources

When you work with union personnel, your task of estimating labour costs is relatively straightforward. From the production concept you make an educated guess about the size and complexity of the show; add to this a factor that considers the difficulty of working within the space; and, using the rough rule-of-thumb rates for rig, focus, and so on (see 15.3), you calculate the total time, personnel, and, finally, wages required. You need to retain on file the current award (pay rates), which the union will gladly supply. These calculations will usually be done in conjunction with the production manager, and at the same time you should commence discussions regarding the draft production schedule (see chapter 16).

It is in situations where the union is not in evidence that you must be particularly careful of your human resources. It doesn't matter whether this is in an amateur organisation or a house that uses staff (fixed wages); the risk of abuse is high. No one should ignore the fact that human resources are as much a cost in real terms as they are in money; a labour force cannot be abused to compensate for lack of budget. To request that an individual build an effects projector from jam tins during many sleepless nights, then to expect him or her to operate the board accurately and with sensitivity is foolishness. Undoubtedly, the greatest resources in the theatre are the talents of its individuals; no one has the right to endanger the fabric of the profession by abusing them. If any of you are being abused or will be, remember that no show is worth physical or emotional damage.

5.6 Rejection

No one likes to have pet projects rejected; but, if your flights of fancy soar out of control, you may have to get used to some rejections. You may be told to cut certain items; or the production manager, stating that the budget must be cut by a certain amount, may ask you to volunteer items you can give up. Perhaps you can afford to lose nothing without rendering the concept ineffective; then the production manager has no choice but to request a new design that will fit within the budget. However, when pruning is called for, departmental heads are likely to be very protective of those elements that are their responsibility; in that case, the director may be required to make an objective assessment of those items whose loss will cause least damage to the concept, and that decision must be respected by all. Don't forget, however, that every element is interrelated; if one item is cut, others may go automatically. For example, if a gauze [scrim] is cut, logically you must cut effects projectors designed to play upon the gauze. Try to select one group of associated items so that all cuts are effected with least damage to that whole.

Within the profession there is a phrase, "guesstimation," which illustrates the knife's edge upon which all are attempting to balance during this important week. Like most of the skills required of a lighting designer, guesstimation becomes easier with experience, but two factors, if ignored, will cause your enterprise to fail. First is the quality and reliability of the information you collect together. The second is attention to detail; a tiny component overlooked or a decimal point misplaced can be disastrous. Conversely, playing things too safely never generates the excitement that is the essence of theatre.

CHAPTER 6

The First Reading and Early Rehearsals

It's five weeks to opening night—and there's more to be achieved in this week than the material covered in this chapter alone. From this point on, time becomes a force that relentlessly accelerates to opening night. At the first reading you'll see a number of new faces, each representing an expense, and suddenly the overheads sky-rocket. Soon management must see some return on its investment, so all concerned must bring the process to fruition quickly. These are the cold, hard, unartistic facts of commercial theatre, and sub-sidised theatre is only slightly less pressured.

6.2 Design Presentation

The first rehearsal call for the company of performers is frequently used to introduce as many of the behind-the-scenes staff as possible. It's a time to meet one another, learn names and responsibilities, establish routines (is the rehearsal room open or closed?—that is, may you attend at any time or only by invitation?). Further, it's an opportunity for the company to view the design (set and costumes), that has now been approved by management.

6.2.1 Lighting Department Involvement

Whenever possible, the lighting designer should attend with as many of your staff as possible, in particular the board operator. If you're working in a leased theatre, the in-house staff will be working the current show and won't be available. With free-lance staff, man-agement usually regards rehearsal attendance as a large expenditure with no apparent return; in a staff situation, however, attendance should be encouraged. Whichever circumstance applies, there is a strong argument for the board operator to attend because the cast, stage management, and board operator need to become familiar with one another and the show as soon as possible.

6.2.2 Lighting Designer's Involvement

Generally, you have no specific responsibilities at this meeting. You will be introduced (and you should introduce other members of the department), but what interests the company are the designer's model and the costume sketches. You may be able to support the designer's presentation, particularly if this show calls for heavy lighting; but, at this early stage, details of lighting will be totally lost on the company. The more important function is to open communication. Too often, lighting designers are unknown to the company until the technical rehearsal, when an utterly unfamiliar voice is heard from the darkened auditorium.

Depending on the approach of the director, the social functions will be dispensed with quickly, and, for the first time, the company will read the script together. This can take up to two days, since a host of questions will be asked, background and research material will be made available, and the director will often clarify the style that has been decided on.

It's an important time for the lighting designer if the director is of the type who finds it difficult to talk to technicians. During this time you will begin to form an impression of each of the performers; you may notice strengths and weaknesses that will need watching as rehearsals develop. Let's say that an actor is weak vocally; you may consider concentrating attention on him (a tight special—perhaps a head-and-shoulders pin spot) during a long monologue. To reiterate: this is not the time to make decisions but to gather information for future development.

6.4 What Has Light to Do with Stage Management?

If you have not already done so, this is the time—at first reading—to establish communications with stage management (stage manager and deputy stage manager). This should be *communication* (both ways), not *information* (one way). Frequently, stage managers are expected to feed the lighting designer information without receiving anything in return. On the other hand, many lighting designers choose to leave stage management in the dark until the plotting [dry tech.] session, when minimal time will be given to positioning of the cues in the prompt copy. This may be feasible in a small show; but, in one with many cues involving different departments, the earlier you can give prompt copy information to the deputy stage manager (even if it's only rough), the sooner he or she will comprehend the complexity of the show's call and will start preparations (even to the point of calling tight sequences during the later stages of rehearsal).

The following sections (6.4.1 and 6.4.2) tell briefly about some areas of communication.

6.4.1 Rehearsal Schedule

This document, generally prepared daily by the deputy stage manager, details what is intended for rehearsals next day. It is frequently revised and, because of rehearsal room pressures, may not always

---

be adhered to; the deputy stage manager may be able to inform you of changes before they happen so that you effectively use your time.

6.4.2 The Watchdog Function

The lighting designer cannot be at all rehearsals, yet these are the greatest source of current information (changes, modifications, restaging, new ideas); without the assistance of the deputy stage manager you may be the one to be left in the dark! As the lighting designer you must supply basic information (see 8.12) which you must take the time to explain carefully so that the deputy stage manager is aware of the intentions for the lighting, can perceive deviations, and will pass information back to you as soon as possible.

6.5 Further Attendance at Early Rehearsals

Directors work in many different ways; some will have the piece roughly blocked within two days; others will spend ten days around a table discussing the script word by word. You should discover your director's approach prior to rehearsals so that you can organise your time. Keep in mind as well that your appearance at a rehearsal may have a double purpose; the most important is the gathering of information, but you may choose to attend rehearsals of a particular scene or sequence because it is considered difficult. I have found myself talking aloud through a complex sequence of lighting changes in order to familiarise all of us there and to ensure that we are working toward the same end.

6.6 In Summation

You have seen how important these first rehearsals are in terms of future communication with cast and crew alike. Always keep in mind what fountains of information rehearsal rooms are, and don't become the type of lighting designer who would not be recognised by the company.

CHAPTER 7

Mulling Over the Design

This activity is part of the fifth week prior to opening night in conjunction with the material covered in chapter 6. Almost certainly it will continue into the following week and meld into the activities covered in chapter 8.

You are about to embark upon a process in which you do a great deal of nothing; yet, without this process, your work may be safe and mundane or rushed and risky. It is a process that many ignore or underplay. There is no need to formalise the activity in the manner about to be described; you can do it in bed, or on the beach, or in the park awaiting "Symphony under the Stars" (where I did some work on this chapter). The important thing is to ensure that it does happen, that you allow yourself time to absorb a vast quantity of information, much of which will not be specific but will come as intimation, atmosphere, or hunch. Take it all in, allow it to ferment and solidify, allow time for investigation and rejection . . . and be content with just a few good ideas.

These ideas may give the solutions to specific problems or may merely suggest difficulties yet to be solved, but all will merge with the aims and ideals of the company, since they are based on information emanating from the production process.

7.2 Suitable and Sympathetic Surroundings

During this period I need a comfortable space that becomes my base of operations (and notepaper and pencil beside my bed at night). The space may be as small as a briefcase or as large as an office; whatever its size, it's designed with a single purpose in mind: to get information you need down on paper before an idea escapes you or you're distracted into other paths. The notepaper and pencil beside the bed is for that all-important inspirational moment that invariably occurs to me just before I slip off to sleep; unless I note it then, I can never remember it next morning. This is a time for ideas, and you must create for yourself an environment that encourages their formation.

7.3 Information

On my pinboard I have everything that pertains to the show; much of it (such as the theatre plans) remains throughout the process, but other items appear only while they remain relevant. Here (7.3.1 to 7.3.8) are some of the items you could gather there.

7.3.1 Theatre Dimensions

Obtain up-to-date small-scale drawings from theatre management; both plan and section will be required. However, it's rare to find drawings that are completely accurate; at times they are dangerously deceptive. Satisfy yourself that they are reliable during a visit (see 7.4), and be sure to note all obstructions (for example, air-conditioning ducts) that may render certain positions useless.

7.3.2 Plan and Section of the Set

The set designer will produce drawings (scale 1:25 metric, 1:24 imperial) for each scene, but sometimes they leave the section (a view through the centreline of the theatre on a vertical plane) for the lighting designer to compile (see chapter 10). Sections are usually taken through the centreline, but it may be useful to have available drawings based upon other axes; for example, Figure 7.1 illustrates how a section across stage will aid tremendously when positioning sidelighting. Alternatively, if there is a complex item of set that is aligned diagonally, it may be worth obtaining a section through that item, as illustrated in Figure 7.2.

7.3.3 Flying Plot

The flying plot details the purpose to which each of the flylines will be put for the show; for example, masking, lighting, items of scenery, cyclorama, etc. As this document becomes available from the production manager, check it against the designer's section; in particular, note how it varies by scene. Chapter 10 will discuss this in more detail, but be aware of its importance as a record of the in-

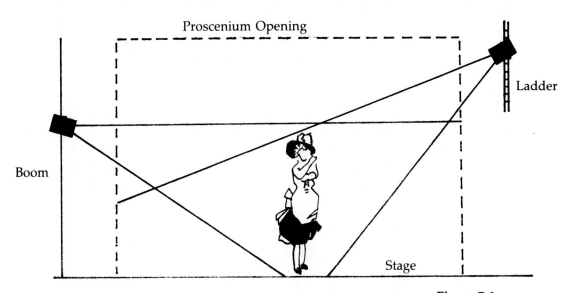

Figure 7.1
Across Stage Section

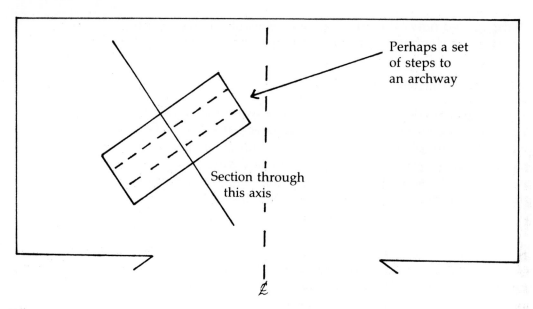

Figure 7.2
Section through Set

terrelationship between lighting bars [pipes] and masking. What clearance is there? Can you backlight without the borders' causing obstruction?

7.3.4 Stock List

This will normally be supplied by the head electrician of the theatre. Try to get an idea whether the equipment is thoroughly maintained or if you must cope with some items having been removed from service. Also discover if there are sufficient spare parts in stock. Unless you are pressured unreasonably for equipment, try not to use the entire stock of any one lantern [instrument] type; this ensures that, if you do meet trouble, you have a spare.

7.3.5 Patching Details

The head electrician will also supply information that details the equipment installed to aid in connecting lanterns to dimmer—known collectively as a patching system. Again, you should check its serviceability. Use the head electrician's knowledge to find traps involved in this particular system—all have them! Remember, this individual is the one most familiar with the space. You would be short-sighted to ignore the advice or safety rules of the head electrician. Chapter 15 will discuss patching in detail but, for now, ensure that you obtain all available documentation.

7.3.6 Control Desk and Dimmer Details

Again, these details will be available from the head electrician, but, if possible, talk to past or current board operators to obtain information regarding the quirks of the control desk. You need dimmer numbers and capacity, type of dimmer (less important with most modern systems), and desk type, together with details of any modifications the desk may have received. There is no point in designing lighting sequences that the board is incapable of handling; that's not design—it's pigheadedness!

7.3.7 Script

In addition to having a script by your side at all times, you may choose to use extracts containing important lighting sequences. A cartoon storyboard is one of many ways to supplement your script.

7.3.8 Anything Else

Information in just about any form may have a place on your pinboard during the production. For example: material swatches from the wardrobe supervisor; paint samples the designer used in the model and intends using on the set; a sample from the designer on a piece of cardboard half a metre [18″] square perhaps, that indicates what is intended regarding texture and colour on the floor; equipment specifications for units you intend hiring, together with quotations and a copy of the order . . . just about anything that could have bearing on the production!!

7.4 Theatre Familiarity

Much of the information mentioned above can be comprehended only after a visit to the theatre and discussion with the staff. The design team may have visited during formation of the production concept, but now you need a purely electrical tour.

This is the time to get to know the theatre's staff as individuals with particular faults and talents against the background of conditions and equipment with which they work. The obvious people to meet are the head electrician and board operator, but try to include the crew: head mechanist, stage doorman, house manager, and so on. Once you have gathered information on a theatre, retain it on file and continue to update it; this will save time when next you work that theatre.

7.5 Stationery Preparation

During early rehearsal there is not a great deal of pressure upon the lighting department—you will make up for it later (see chapters 9 through 21). You can, however, make that rushed period a little less frantic by preparing now. One way to ease the load is to prepare sufficient quantities of specialised stationery (cue synopsis, lantern schedules, state-of-the-board sheets, 1-100 [$\frac{1}{8}″$:1′] scale drawings, and so on). Future chapters will detail the need for these documents—the note here is just a reminder.

Because there may not be a great deal for the staff to do during this period, you might allow them time-in-lieu [compensatory time] of the extra hours they will be required to work in production week. This time must not be at the expense of necessary preparation, nor at the risk of having them unfamiliar with the show.

7.7 Specialised Items for Manufacture

You may not be able to join the crew relaxing on the beach; you may need to produce detailed drawings and wiring diagrams for equipment they must manufacture on their return. Or you may have a list for the set/props workshops so that they can complete items on schedule.

This is all more complex than it seems, since the remainder of the lighting design is still fluid; you may be forced to make these isolated ideas concrete to give sufficient time for manufacture. It's a time for educated guesses; should your guess be too far off, you may involve your staff in hours of labour that will be seen as useless when the effect is cut during the technical rehearsal. You need to have close communication with the designer regarding these items.

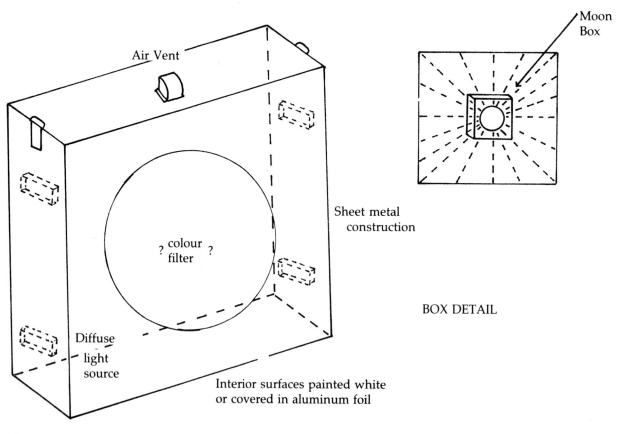

Figure 7.3
Moon Box

For example, you intend to back a painted cloth of the sun with a moon box. (Now there's a contradiction in terms!) Figure 7.3 and further discussion in Chapter 14 will explain what that means. Obviously, you and the designer must get together to ensure that both your sun images are the same size. Alternatively, you may need to discuss in detail the power source to be included in an apparent source of light (such as, a street lamp) so that the props workshop can manufacture it to the designer's specifications but also include access for electrical wires.

7.8 Experimentation: Are You a Designer or a Monkey?

As stated early in the book, the principle behind your employment is to ensure results without expensive trial-and-error techniques. Just the same, you now need some experimentation. Hence the question: are you a lighting designer or one of that band of literary monkeys? Although there is a fine line to be negotiated, you should realize that you can do a considerable amount of experimentation that is not expensive or time-consuming. The set designer's scale model is central to this process; it, together with swatches of materials from wardrobe and, perhaps, the floor sample mentioned in 7.3.8, will enable you to experiment in the workshop for colour choice and lantern [instrument] placement. Set up a small system similar to that illustrated in Figure 7.4 in an area you can black out. Six or eight small lanterns and, perhaps, three dimmers will be sufficient, but select the lanterns carefully.

If you are working with a 1 kw Fresnel (see 11.8) as a basic onstage unit and you experiment using that lantern on a 1:25 metric/1:24 imperial scale model, you are likely to gain impressions of effects that will be impossible to re-create; you would require a 25/24 kw lantern [instrument] of vast proportions to create the same effect in the theatre. Similarly, dimming down the lanterns will give you equally confusing distortions since the colour temperature will be quite wrong (see 13.4, 13.10), and the resultant colour on the model will be strongly biased toward the red end of the spectrum.

Use the hand-held lantern to experiment for side, back, and any other sort of light that may be of use; discover three of four colours that, singly or in combination, will give you all the tonings the show demands on the cyclorama. Similarly, you can discover colours and angles that make individual costumes or set elements stand out, using the front washes.

Scaling down effects and projections is risky; a strobe or ripple machine is quite difficult to miniaturise and you may select an effect that, when transferred to the theatre, lacks the dynamics and spectacle you created on the model. If the theatre is available, you may be able to experiment in full scale. This may not be an option and is usually expensive in time and personnel; but, if you are inexperienced, you will find it invaluable. Try one onstage lantern and one front-of-house (FOH) lantern; then use that experience as a guide for selecting all the lanterns you may need. Another method is to

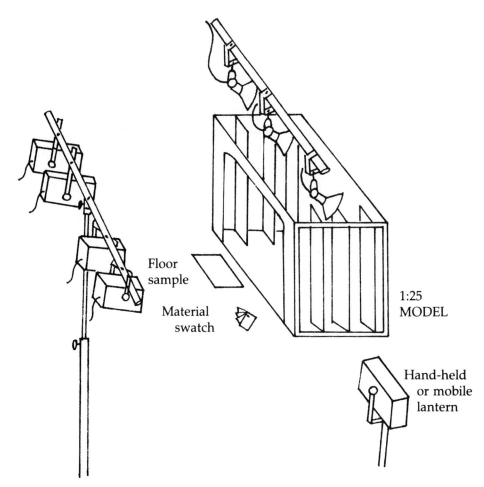

Figure 7.4
Lighting the Model

plagiarise a bit if the theatre is currently operating. You can see what the other lighting designer chose; by attending a performance, you'll be able to gauge its usefulness or how it may be adapted to your own purposes.

7.9 Consultation

Once you have completed your experiments but before you become settled in your mind, invite the designer and director to view the results. You may find that new questions are raised or that your definition of "hot and diffuse" is different from that of both the director and designer.

Be careful to point out the problems of scale and to ensure that all understand they are viewing an indication of results, not a demonstration of fact. In a similar vein, you may be able to impress upon the designer the need for exact matching of the paint used on the model to the paint on the full-scale set. You might follow this up by suggesting that you install (in the paintshop) lanterns with the decided-on colours so that the designer can compare results with the model.

In summary, let me reiterate: this technique is a two-edged sword. Results are inconclusive, and you may create expectations that are impossible to fulfill; however, this process can ease the problems of communicating your intent for the show's lighting.

Whatever your degree of experience, you will probably find that there is only one place to get a true indication of what you intend: the stage itself. Go there armed with the results of your experimentation and all the great ideas you've conceived; stand onstage in worklight and let your imagination fill in the details. You may find that some of your ideas are impossible; perhaps the box boom (see Fig 12.13) is not in the position you envisaged or something obstructs the position you intended using.

Both your inspiration and solutions will be moulded by the locale itself, perfectly matching the ambience. For example, in a Mozart opera I was lighting, the soprano mentioned at rehearsal her embarrassment at the facial contortions she was obliged to use for proper vocal results in a fiendish aria. Added to this, I knew her staging. I realised that she had most expressive hands and that her costume was dark-blue velvet with elbow-length sleeves. All this information did not come together, however, until I stood in her position onstage and tried to see myself from the audience's viewpoint (see Fig 7.5). She would need to incline her head towards centre to see the musical director and to deliver the lyric upstage to the tenor. Lighting from the orchestra bar would reveal the facial contortions and, possibly, catch the proscenium arch; however, from the low position in the prompt [stage left] box boom, I would be able to catch those expressive hands of hers, highlight them against the background of the dark dress, and, possibly, cast shadows of

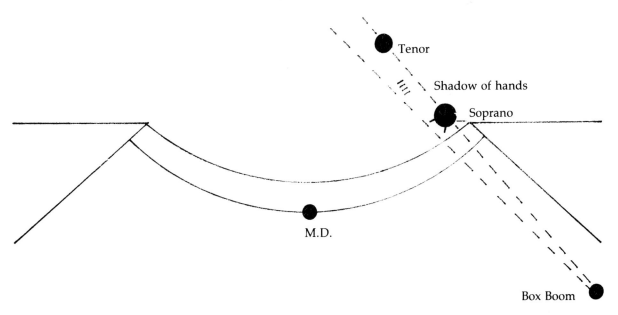

Figure 7.5
Lighting a Mozart Soprano

the grasping hands on the tenor; that's not to say her face would be in black, but in reduced light, which would make it easier for her to see the musical director without squinting.

7.11 In Summation

As the end of this week draws near, you may not have a great deal to show—perhaps some careful notes regarding colour, together with some indication of position and type of lantern. There may be added notes from rehearsals and production meetings you've attended or details you've picked up during visits to the various workshops. These important responsibilities must not be neglected during this week but should continue in parallel with the mulling over! Your subconscious will be working overtime on this accumulated information. With a little pressure in the week to come, it will present you with the essence of a design that serves the show, falls within budget, and suits the locale.

CHAPTER 8

Formulating a Basic Cue Synopsis

There are four weeks to opening night. Now it's time to commit your thoughts to paper so that others may see what you intend.

In most rehearsal processes the actors will, by now, be rough blocking; entrances and exits, together with the broad staging of each scene will be established. (But, remember no one can guarantee that these will remain the same as rehearsals progress.) You will be able to see a rough shape for the piece, pinpoint centres of focus for each scene, and gain an idea of the relationships between characters. (The personalities of the cast will, by now, have had an influence.) We'll be working on a full-scale markup with crates to represent major elements of the set and substitute props/costumes. As the original concepts may have changed in some minor way, each change must be evaluated, incorporated or rejected by all those who took part in the initial production concept formulation.

Remember that many of the items of set, props, and costume are well under construction and cannot be changed without a major change in budgeting; however, now that you see flesh and blood embodying your ideas, you may need to capitalise upon some moment of characterisation or inspiration—it's called remaining flexible. The meetings and discussion need not be formal but may occur spontaneously during coffee breaks or in talking with the designer and production manager, perhaps at a costume fitting.

The costume sketches are often prepared using the production concept and script as a basis without any knowledge of individual performers who will fill those costumes. Often, the leading man is not the Adonis visualised but is considerably more human, with the sort of disproportions we would expect from you and me. The costume must be adapted to cope with these frailties, and the production concept will need to bend a little in order to incorporate them. Perhaps he is not as tall as had been hoped and will need to stand upon added rocks, boxes, or tree stumps to get his head up among the clouds the production concept demands. To keep the audience unaware of the trickery, the lighting designer should avoid lighting the actor's feet. All departments must be aware of these minor changes—with their effects upon each department—so that all continue to work towards the same end. Now it's time for a little lighting Art!

There are many who would say that the process you are about to embark upon is the lighting design, but this is not really the case. As you read more of this discussion up to and including opening night, you will understand why.

Right now you are defining an outline of what you hope the lighting design may achieve; you are not concerned with *how* to achieve the various effects, but only with listing *what those effects should be* and with communicating your intention to all concerned with their implementation; for example, board operator, director, and technical director/stage manager. Before beginning, quickly refresh your memory with notes taken during the production concept discussions, and reread the script to ensure complete familiarity.

The potential for light will be influenced by the space and the designer's set; there's no point in attempting to achieve an effect another department can do better, but you may be able to clarify some element of the whole in addition to being the primary source of others. Consider (8.3.1 to 8.3.7) a few examples; later you'll be able to add some of your own.

8.3.1 Vision

Your major responsibility is to ensure that the audience has sufficient light to perceive the stage picture clearly and without distraction. This generally entails taking out the house lights and raising the stage lights until every detail of performance, set, costume, and staging is clearly visible.

8.3.2 Focus

Taking the simplistic concept of vision further, light can be used to direct the audience's attention where you choose by means of isolation and intensity.

8.3.3 Period

Using colour, perhaps movement, and a clear indication of apparent source of light, the lighting designer can help to define the period in which the piece is set. For example, you can re-create the effect of gaslight or, perhaps, of naked flame. These, together with the contributions of set and costume, will suggest the era strongly.

8.3.4 Location

Again, by such means of colour, direction, and apparent source of light, you can assist in locating the piece. You can expect the audience to recognise interior or exterior, forest glade, or burning desert from lighting alone. Setting the scene by means of lighting makes for relatively cheap and quick scene changes.

8.3.5 Time

Colour, direction, and apparent source are the most important considerations for determining the time of day. Lighting is capable of representing moonlight or sunlight, sunrise or sunset, and, further, of indicating a passage of time with a transition from one state to another.

8.3.6 Mood

Any of the above representations can be enhanced by the superimposition of texture, colour, and so on, to create another dimension: mood. Our leafy glade from 8.3.4 may be given a fetid, rotting dimension or be overlaid with an ethereal calm using backlight.

8.3.7 Atmosphere

How atmosphere differs from mood is a matter of interpretation; I consider it as an integral element of the scene that originates from without it. For example, your leafy glade can be further varied as the smoke from a nearby bushfire drifts across. It's a fine distinction but one that may aid you in creating scenes with multiple dimensions.

8.4 So, What Were You Mulling Over?

You have, of course, considered the above questions before this time. They have formed a considerable proportion of your prior deliberations—but in a somewhat random fashion. It is now time to organise all the facts that have been mulling around in your subconscious so that they can be brought together as a cohesive whole. You will be surprised at how many decisions you will make simply by sitting down with the script and blank cue synopsis forms. Out of your imagination you will draw all the half-formed ideas, possibilities, and moments of inspiration; the process of writing will transform them into a unity of thought and intention from which you can start creating a lighting design.

8.5 What Is the Purpose of a Cue Synopsis?

Your purpose is to formulate a lighting concept for each moment in the theatre with visions flowing from one to the next, taking the audience from beginning to conclusion, from fetid gloom to ethereal brilliance, from morning to following day, from character's childishness to maturity—wherever the script and the production concept demand.

It is important that you look for a flow, one vision for every moment that demands it. A moment may last the length of a scene or a few seconds; it may change as characters enter, exit, or move from place to place. A moment may exist in only one character's mind or in the atmospherics surrounding them all, but it must originate in the prior moment and lead to the next!

As you formulate this vision, you should not limit your imagination; your only restraints are the parameters of the production and the ambience of the theatre and set. You should not be bound by what you've done in the past or by what is conventional; your only guide must be the needs of the show! At this stage don't worry too much about equipment or time. You can compromise in those areas *after* you have discovered what the piece demands; in this way you will serve the production without allowing limitations to dictate results. Give yourself freedom to try something innovative and risky. Perhaps you may apply conventional techniques to unconventional ends (drama could be lit balletically)—anything that is within the parameters of the production concept.

Your basic cue synopsis should contain little or no lighting jargon but should be descriptive and evocative, liberally spiced with emotive words that clearly encapsulate the end results you foresee. The document is for the benefit not only of the lighting designer but also of everyone concerned with the lighting process. Other departments must be able to understand clearly this first document issued from lighting; all need to ensure that they are working towards the same end, complementing one another—not clashing. Most important of all is that the director be assured the visions of all departments are, in essence, the same.

8.6 Classification of States and/or State Changes

As yet it's too early to be talking about cues, since the cue synopsis is little more than a statement of intent. There may be additions right up to opening night; and, if you allow your imagination to run free, there will be compromises forced by limitations of equipment and time. Since you have no idea at this stage of each dimmer's purpose, you cannot predict how many cues may be required to effect a state change—all reasons for thinking in terms of states, not cues. Most states can be classified in one of the following ways (8.6.1 to 8.6.4) or in some combination of them.

8.6.1 Theatrical States

These are basic theatrical devices for interfacing between real time and dramatic time, such as taking house lights down and stage lights up with the curtain. Generally these states have little artistic comment to make; they mark beginnings, ends, pause for scene change, and the like. Since these practices are so basic, many productions of late seem to ignore their potential for preparing an audience and for "punctuation." Those who complain about the tardiness of audiences (and the inability of front-of-house personnel to shift them into the auditorium on time) ignore the enormous potential of lighting and sound. They could be phrasing carefully selected music, fading house lights, and building curtain warmers to awaken the patrons' anticipation.

Similarly, technical effects can punctuate endings (for example, to save a laugh that would be killed by a late or slow fade to black). And everyone has experienced those rare and beautiful shows where, in the instant after the curtain descends, there is a hush as the audience savours the show's last moments before bursting into spontaneous applause. Mistiming the house lights or curtain call may shatter that pause and force spectators into applause against their will. Almost certainly, the response will be less warm than it would have been had the ending been handled more sensitively.

8.6.2 Naturalistic States

Almost invariably, these states are associated with an apparent source of light. Changes are justified directly from the script (for example, sunsets or roomlights switched on), or they may be demanded by staging (for example, a door opens, spilling artificial light across a moonlit exterior).

8.6.3 Effect States

These states are firmly based upon parameters of style and interpretation. (Section 4.8.5, the *Pearl Fishers* illustration, is a perfect example.) They may be used to vary phrasing, to change focus, or to make a comment. Not intended to be subtle, they are apparent to the whole audience.

8.6.4 Subliminal States

All the variables available to the lighting designer (such as colour, direction, movement, and shape) can be used to create these subliminal states, which are intended to work upon the subconscious of the audience (with only a few being aware of the manipulation). Perhaps in a murder mystery you could amplify the "red herrings" by means of a sinister quality—maybe a heavily shadowed face with dark areas gently filled with green or magenta—for a character known to be sweet and innocent; or, in a melodramatic piece, you may choose to add colour to make the wife's lover "evil," since he will be the justification for the husband's killing them all. Alternatively, you could use a rosy pink if you intend fostering adultery among your audience—it all depends upon the production concept.

States will rarely fall cleanly into a particular category; delineation is often fuzzy in practice (for example, a naturalistic change can justify a subliminal statement). I am frequently requested by directors to "pass a cloud over the sun" as a comment upon the action onstage. To achieve this, I can reduce directional light and substitute a suitable diffuse colour. Perhaps the director will ask you to establish the quality of fear. Every time the script mentions fear, you can pass a cloud over the sun and substitute a smoky-pink wash (the leafy glade wanes as the bushfire approaches). When the character representing fear (an arsonist?) arrives onstage, you can build this subliminal statement, thus strengthening the association. At the finale, when fear has taken control, you may flood the stage with smoky pink and overlay it with a flame effect. Thus, the audience associates fear with colour, flame, and character by a progression of states that phrase to an end-point. Note the development from a naturalistic/subliminal state, through a subliminal/effects state, to a strong effect state with naturalistic overtones. None can be clearly classified, but the classifications assist in formulating the progression.

8.7 Consistency

Perhaps the most important consideration at this stage is to maintain a consistent style throughout the whole piece. You will often be involved in establishing almost Pavlovian responses in an audience, then in using the expectation in a payoff later. But if you forget— and a mention of, say, fear occurs without the associated subliminal trigger—you may impede development of expectation, confuse the audience, and ruin the payoff.

8.8 Balance of Cues within the Piece

Don't be too concerned about trying to distribute the cues throughout a piece evenly; it's very unusual in practice. Most productions follow a pattern: they cluster cues around the opening, establishing style and dynamics to gain the attention of the audience; subliminal cues laying the groundwork for later payoffs may then begin.

In places, the action is flowing along nicely with the interest in the characterisations and the conflict between the characters, you may need very few other cues, at most a slight shift of focus to follow action around the stage. At the close of the first act, there will be a flurry of activity designed to punctuate and to encourage a feeling of anticipation. The opening of act 2 will have cues designed to regain the audience's attention and after that, in most plays, relatively few cues until the finale. Those who follow this pattern— it's not a rule—will see that they are not obliged to keep the board operator busy, whether the show needs it or not.

8.9 What the Show Needs

Remember, be guided in your choice of states and changes by what is demanded by the production. You are in the service of the production and must not use it to serve your own ends.

One purpose of the cue synopsis is to enable other departments to see what lighting is intended and to ensure that the production does not get trapped into overproduction. If, for example, both the lighting and sound departments intend making comments on the entrance of a character, then the director may ask one department to leave it to the other, better suited to the task. Alternatively, you may be asked to alter the intent of your cue to ensure an ambivalent quality. Unless the style is highly melodramatic, most directors prefer that the villain not be entirely vile. They may ask the lighting department to emphasise the obvious while the sound department adds a softer touch—the monster may love butterflies! Conversely, the hero could be given a somewhat harsh, unyielding quality by means of a brittle backlight—that's ambivalence!

Coordination may also be the solution to other problems; for example, phrasing as the finale approaches. You anticipate that the available lighting may not have enough power to continue increasing lighting levels as the show draws to a close. The answer lies in choosing an opportune moment to drop light levels while the sound department covers with a change in music or increase in levels. Remember that wonderful number from the musical *Seesaw*, "It's not where you start, it's where you finish!" where the Tommy Tune character breaks across the flow of the song demanding a bigger finish? That may be the opportunity to drop general levels, add a special or follow-spot on him, and recommence the build.

8.11 Example of a Basic Cue Synopsis Sheet

A good example here would be the famous ballet sequence in Rodgers and Hammerstein's *Oklahoma!* Remember that you are writing the *basic* cue synopsis and much of the information, as yet, is undecided. You don't know cue numbers, and it's too early to impose them; cue lines, which position the call are, at best, ill defined; you may guess at types and timings for fades, but they are of minor importance at this stage. The column entitled Effect is what is central to the purpose of the document at this time. (See Figs. 8.1 to 8.3.; also note that *cue* can be abbreviated to *Q*, as in the headings there. *Lx* stands for *lighting*, and *MD* for *musical director*.)

If you are confused about the difference between the basic cue synopsis and the final or evolved cue synopsis, remember that the only real difference is time. The basic document details what you intend for the show's lighting. As you evolve the means of achieving those results—dimmers, cue numbers, cuing information—you update the *same* piece of paper as a means of recording those details. The document continues to evolve up to and during the plotting [dry tech.] session, after which it becomes redundant.

To this example, which demonstrates clearly the purpose of the basic cue synopsis, a few points should be added, as follows.

Production: OKLAHOMA!   Theatre: New Arts   Page: 12

LIGHTING Q SYNOPSIS

Q No	Stage Action/Line	Type	Time	Effect	Dimmers
	Laurey (singer) moves to bench O.P. [stg. rt.]	✕	Slow -allow exit	Isolate to green/gold deckle (as for A1/S1) special on Laurey (singer); fade all, including cyclorama to allow exit of chorus in black.	
	Laurey (dancer) enters u.s.O.P. behind singer Laurey.	↰		Dome pickup/follow, soft & warm. Board extend grn/gld deckle plus warm side to cover dancers – keep singer isolated. Cyc to blend from deckle to clouded sky used for "Beautiful Morning".	
	Wedding veil descends frm. flies	↰	Timed with flies.	Add bright downlight to cover veil & Laurey (dancer) centre; reduce remainder stage but retain singer isolated.	
	Laurey (dancer) exits O.P.	↰		Remove veil special; Dome follow to exit; retain chorus of dancers in deckle pool centre.	
	Curly(dancer) enters u.s.P.S.	↰		Build "Beaut Morn" dawn from O.P. boxboom bright. Must not include Laurey (singer) but emanates from her.	
	Laurey (dancer) enters – Wedding!	✕		Reduce dawn; increase deckle around couple centre (strong b/light); warm cyc adding halo below a rich sky; special on faces only – very loving! ....but isolated to avoid Jud's entrance.	

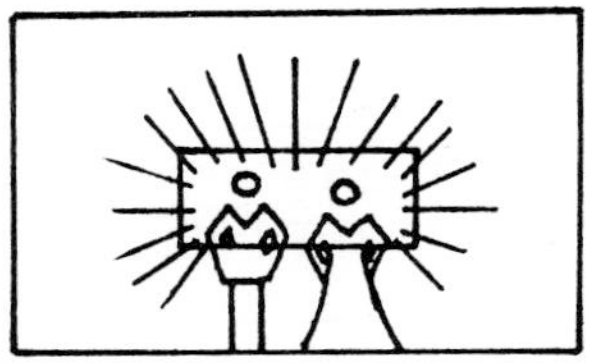

Figure 8.1 *Basic Lighting Cue Synopsis (1)*

Production: OKLAHOMA! | Theatre: New Arts | Page: 13

LIGHTING Q SYNOPSIS

Q no	Stage Action/Line	Type	Time	Effect	Dimmers
	Jud lifts veil – actor and Lx time with M.D.	 ✕	Snap	Instant change to cold and brittle front light – cyc a bleached echo of what it was, deckle now devoid of colour (o/w or steel tint?) Laurey (singer) also cools.	
	Laurey (dancer) moves to behind Laurey (singer).	 ⌐→	Fast but smooth	Fade stage and cyc to black; isolate to special on both Laureys – colder overlay shadows dancers face, reduced deckle still illuminates singer's.	
	Music Q – Jud & girls in position	Sequ	Snap then spread	Red/green special (coloured for costumes but based on shadows in Jud's smokehouse) onto Jud & girls u.s. centre with red/green parody of wedding halo on cyc, colours opposite to special (see sketch) THEN spread to alternate red/green coverage over stage + purplish parody of "Beaut Morn" sky (sick, distorted clouds – how?) for ballet.	

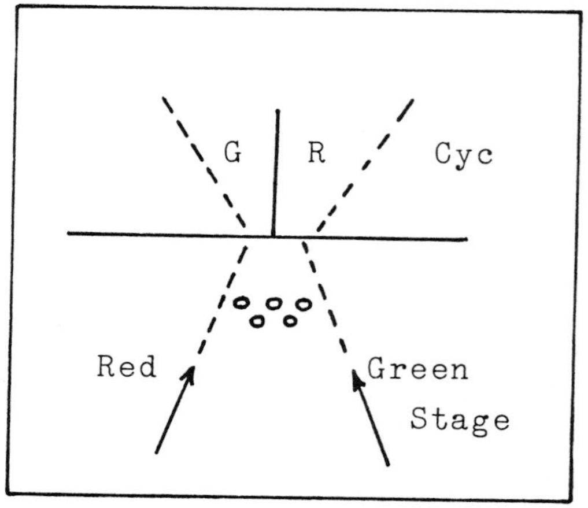

Figure 8.2 *Basic Lighting Cue Synopsis (2)*

		LIGHTING Q SYNOPSIS			
Production: OKLAHOMA!				Theatre: New Arts	Page: 14
Q no	Stage Action/Line	Type	Time	Effect	Dimmers
	Curly(dancer) & boys enter u.s.P.S.	 ✕ (crossfade)	Very slow	Reduce red/green effect; retain purple sky; isolate to cold A/A for fight. Dome cold & soft on Laurey (dancer). Effect is max by death of Curly (dancer).	
	Laurey (dancer) carried off u.s.P.S by Jud.	Prog?	Rapid	Fade to Dome and Curly highlights, then all out; retain only Laurey (singer) colder special	
	Laurey (singer) awakes.	 ✕ (crossfade)	Smooth & fast.	Return to state before sequence but with cold/ warm highlight from special on Laurey, warm on Curly and cold (red/green - ?) on Jud. N.B. very close to Q's before and after!	
	End of Act.	Prog	Fast	Fade to B.O. but retain highlights as long as possible.	

Figure 8.3 *Basic Lighting Cue Synopsis (3)*

8.11.1 Number of Cues

This example was derived from a production that used a manual control desk; with a computer I would have added more cues since the time for presets would not hinder operation.

8.11.2 Cuing Information

As time progressed and, in particular, during the technical rehearsal of *Oklahoma!*, I was able to be far more specific regarding the placement of cues. In the cue synopsis I try only to indicate how cues fit into the rough choreography.

8.11.3 Types of Cues

The symbols under Type heading generally indicate master fader movement (add, subtract, crossfade, sequential, and so on).

8.11.4 Reference to Prior State

I found it clearer to refer to previous lighting states (for example, "Beautiful Morning") and to suggest how they can be altered. Throughout the ballet I adapted material used subliminally in earlier scenes to develop effects.

8.11.5 Communication by Sketch

You may use whatever methods you choose to express your thoughts; often a thumbnail sketch will save many words (see Figures 8.1 and 8.2).

8.11.6 Neatness

So that you can clearly read the material, these examples are in type, but that is not necessary for your notes; they need only be neatly handwritten.

8.12 Distribution

Unfortunately, departments are very often limited in their photostat budget and cannot give a complete synopsis to everyone who may find it useful. As lighting designer you should select those who will benefit from this knowledge and ensure that the cue synopsis gets to them.

Generally, the director, deputy stage manager, yourself, and the technical director must receive a complete copy. If possible, the board operator, sound department, production manager, and designer should also receive a copy. If this is not possible, give them free access to yours.

It is important to remember that the process described in this chapter is not the design, but merely the outline of what you hope your design may achieve by opening night. The document should encompass every potential you see for lighting within the production, with only a passing regard for limitations of time and equipment—those compromises will be forced upon you later! It is an outline of the extent to which your design could serve the production, a document of intent—not a guarantee of results—that encourages coordination with other departments.

CHAPTER 9

Breaking Down Vision into Components

Now there are only three weeks until opening night; the time for "art" is finished! From here on, you must rely upon craft, cunning, experience, ingenuity, and the ability to compromise. There is still one relatively relaxed week during which you must gather up-to-date information and begin breaking vision down into components. It's easy to say, but it will require the following six chapters to discuss the principles involved and cover only a minor part of the associated craft.

Throughout the next six chapters keep in mind how little time is available in which to break down your vision; it may take you longer to study these chapters than you have for the process itself!

9.2 *The Purpose of the Breakdown*

This section will give an overall perspective of the process before considering it in detail; this may help you organise the mass of information to follow.

All you have to work from is the basic cue synopsis detailing the end results you hope to achieve. The breakdown involves reducing these changing visions into component parts, detailing each element precisely, and documenting how the parts fit together to form tools for re-creating your cue synopsis visions in full scale onstage.

Each vision is likely to require a couple of cues and a number of dimmers, each controlling a circuit that in turn will require a number of lanterns [instruments] grouped and positioned very specifically. You will choose each lantern for its ability to achieve specific results, and you must foresee for all lanterns the colour and accessories necessary for them to fulfill your intention. Without this detail you cannot draw your plan [plot], you do not know what equipment you require, you cannot predict how long each element of the reconstruction process will take, and you would be foolhardy to guarantee results.

The breakdown process is central to lighting design and yet cannot be learned from a book; the skills involved need to be gathered over time. The following chapters will point out principles and theory necessary for a clear understanding of the tools you will be using. They will describe some techniques developed for approaching the problems and, maybe, will pass on a few tricks of the trade;

however, only continued practice will arm you with the confidence and ability to achieve results consistently.

You must realise that the original vision is rarely achieved in total. On rare occasions you will surpass yourself, and these moments must compensate for the frequently painful and frustrating compromises needed to salvage what you can from your original vision. Need I say that this is no profession for a perfectionist?

9.3 First Stage; Synopsis to Circuits

Your initial task is to break down the basic cue synopsis into a list of circuits from which your visions could be reconstructed. Looking at each vision in turn, ferret out the individual groups of lanterns you will need as tools and estimate the power needed to achieve the results you visualise. Then, form one list from which the whole show can be serviced. That list will comprise a series of descriptive titles, plus explanatory notes, that summarise the purpose of each circuit.

Note that I talk about circuits, not dimmers. There is a fine, frequently confusing distinction. A circuit consists of one or more lanterns that must be considered an entity. The lanterns never behave independently of one another; they are always at the same relative intensity and, therefore, can be controlled by one dimmer (so long as that dimmer has the required capacity).

A circuit will be allocated to a dimmer for all or part of a show; however, by means of repatching, a single dimmer may be able to control one or more circuits at the same time (again with the power proviso); or it may handle a number of different circuits separately throughout the show. Example: a 1 kw profile [ellipsoidal] lantern forms a tight spot with a pair of backlight Fresnels in red and another pair in blue (all 500 w); each is a circuit; but, by switching or re-plugging at the patch panel, one 2 kw dimmer can control the spot with either red or blue backlight. You could never have half-red, half-blue backlight because once circuits are formed, they cannot be altered without rerigging.

Again, try not to be hampered by limitations of equipment; you will be reading about methods for rationalising the number of circuits, but that is an entirely separate function. For the time being, extract from your vision every element you desire to ensure complete flexibility at the plotting [dry tech.] session. If you see in your mind's eye fifteen components at different intensities that build up your vision of the cyclorama, you must list them all. In the extreme, the answer is simple; for every lantern rigged, it would be desirable to have a separate dimmer; however, with state-of-the-art technology, that is unlikely.

Special Note. In fact, a system already exists where the principle of "one lantern: one dimmer" is achieved. Recently developed, it is probably the basis of lighting installations of the future. At its core is a digital computer; at the extremities are lanterns plugging directly to appropriately sized dimmers; they connect by means of four pins directly to a trunking network throughout the theatre. The trunking supplies, through the usual three pins, the power to run the dimmer; the fourth pin supplies directions from the computer concerning the output level of the lantern. In principle this system differs little from current installations; it is merely a rearrangement of the components into more suitable positions and sizes, with the addition of a "call sign" that can be allocated to each dimmer/lantern so that it responds to the computer's instructions.

A variant system incorporates low-voltage lanterns (see 11.4) with dimmer and electronic transformer built into each lantern; however, this system is not generally available, and you will generally need to contain your number of circuits.

9.4 Circuits Considered for Purpose

It will help if you can organise your way of analysing the visions. To that end, the following breakdown will be helpful.

9.4.1 Acting Areas

These circuits are principally designed to light performers—hence the term *acting area*. (This can be abbreviated to A/A in your notes.) They ensure clear visibility for your audience. In addition, since they are relatively localised though unpredictable in shape and size, these circuits may focus attention in particular areas of the stage. Although they may be of any colour, generally each area will be covered by two complementary circuits (for example, blue and amber); this enables you to warm or cool the area to suit mood (see chapter 13). Section 9.5.1 will detail how to arrive at shape and size of acting areas, but, wherever possible, avoid lighting the set with acting areas (see 9.4.4).

9.4.2 Specials

These circuits are generally manufactured for one instant in time and for one spot onstage. They may be used alone as an effect or as a highlight in the midst of a more general state. Coloured, shaped, and located however necessary, a special will generally light performers although, occasionally, one is used on the set to draw the attention of the audience to some particular element. A follow-spot is little more than a mobile special, the qualities of which can be controlled from moment to moment.

9.4.3 Atmosphere

These circuits are designed to make emotive suggestions to the audience. They may be of any colour, size, or shape though often they are fairly broad, catching both the set and performing areas. There is no rule preventing you from creating an atmospheric circuit as localised as a special, however.

9.4.4 Set Dressing

These circuits are designed to present and use the set in the best possible manner, and it is important to restrict them to the set alone. Too often, lighting designers use broad circuits that light both set and actors. The problem is that if the set becomes too dominant and needs to have its intensity reduced, light on the actors will also be lost. By clearly separating set dressing and acting areas, you would have full control over balance, but this brings up a new problem. If either is designed poorly, the audience will perceive a distinct change between the two—they won't blend, and the overall picture will seem fragmented and lacking in unity.

9.4.5 Background/Ambience

Ambience is generally very broad and may use anything as a medium (such as a smoky atmosphere, cyclorama, or even blacks). All form a background against which both set and performers will be viewed, and, by controlling it, you add a further dimension to the stage picture. Frequently, specials will be buried within the ambience (such as clouds on the cyclorama), and the set dressing may overlap into it, but it must retain its own distinct qualities.

Figure 9.1 illustrates how the five groups of circuits just described may be scattered about the stage. As a general rule, they fall into three distinct zones (performance area, set, and background), but often the distinction or separation between each is narrow. For example, acting areas may extend well into the set to create an entrance (doorway); as was already noted, specials may be anywhere, and atmospherics generally include the set, though they should probably not include the background.

9.5 Circuits Considered for Type

Now you will find it practical to consider circuits not only for purpose but also for type. This includes such qualities as shape, isolation, and direction, which chapter 10 covers in greater detail. If you consider circuits in very broad terms, you will see that they can generally be classified as three separate types (9.5.1 to 9.5.3).

9.5.1 Areas

Section 9.4.1 discussed the purpose of these circuits; the criteria are rigid and force us towards a similarly rigid format. An area should be relatively isolated so that you can select focus, but it must also blend and join with other acting areas to form a continuous and smooth stage coverage. It should be well rounded so that the performer is clearly revealed to all members of the audience, and it may need to be duplicated in one or more colours. (In chapter 10 you will see how these restrictions may be loosened.)

Since areas are designed specifically to light actors, it is only from the rehearsal room and the basic blocking (actors' movements)

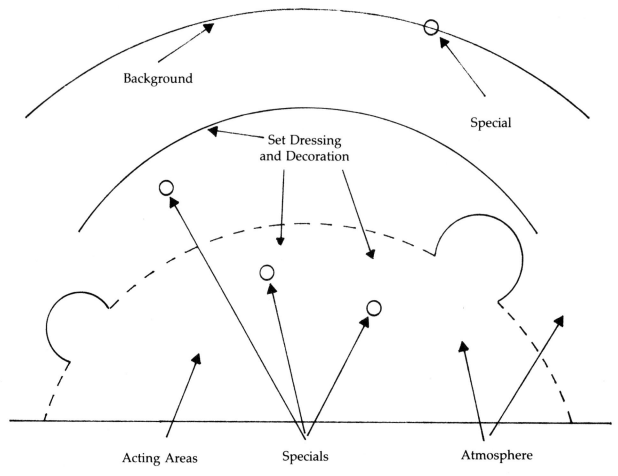

Figure 9.1
Positioning Circuits

that you can determine what shape the areas should be. Figure 9.2 illustrates an effective method for determining acting areas. Attend a rough blocking run of a scene with pencil and 1:100 [⅛":1'] scale sketch of the stage and set; follow the moves carefully, and indicate where a performer remains for more than, say, thirty seconds. Lines trace movement from point to point.

In this example (Fig. 9.2) he enters from O.P. [stg. rt.], pauses to deliver a line, moves to the steps, and calls her, then travels upstage while awaiting her arrival. She enters to the doorway, as he returns to the steps; both move to sit on the tree bench; she's feeling faint, so he gets her water from the fountain; refreshed, she flees downstage and he follows; she moves right and insists he move left—her father is coming! As the scene closes, both move centre and kiss good-bye; she exits into the house as he leaves downstage P.S. [stg. lft.].

Look at how the circles cluster. They indicate areas from which a great deal of dialogue and/or expression will be delivered. You need to ensure that performers are well lit during these moments; hence, they should be at the centre of acting areas. A study of these movement patterns and the layout of the set (Fig. 9.3) will indicate how the stage should be broken up.

This solution has some problems. There are two points onstage where four acting areas join. With too much overlapping, this point

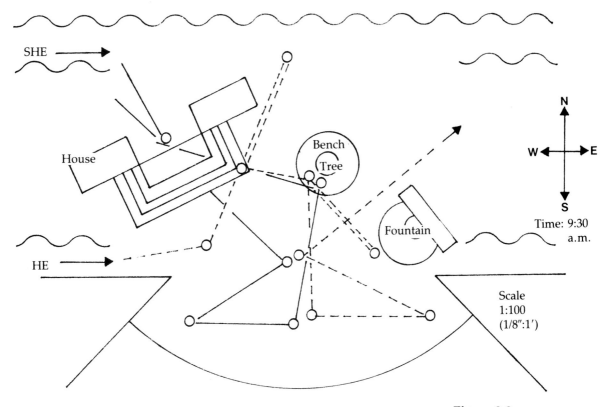

Figure 9.2
Defining Acting Areas

is likely to be very bright; but reducing the overlap will likely create a dead spot (chapter 10 discusses this, but in the meantime the second part of the figure may suggest a solution). There may also be problems in acting area 8 as "she" enters through the doorway; it might be difficult to focus into the doorway while avoiding the set (see 9.4.4). Since this is the moment when the audience first sees her, perhaps a special into the doorway will ensure that she gains attention. Similarly, since they are so long under the tree, perhaps a special on the bench forming a highlight within acting area 7 may be of benefit.

Note the convention when numbering most onstage items: downstage to up and prompt [stg. lft.] to O.P. [stg. rt.].

9.5.2 *Spots*

Specials, highlights, and the like (see 9.4.2) will often be referred to as spots; they frequently comprise only one lantern (but what happens if it blows?) and therefore have a strong sense of direction. Consider, however, a spot in-the-round designed to light an actor during a monologue; the performer cannot deliver the entire speech facing the light, since most of the audience will be deprived of his facial expression. Your spot must comprise a minimum of three lanterns at 120 degrees' separation. Remember, there are no rules!

Consider the two specials in section 9.5.1—first, the doorway. Given the information in Figure 9.2 concerning time of day and points of compass, the apparent source of light—the sun—will dictate the direction from which this special must come; that is, over

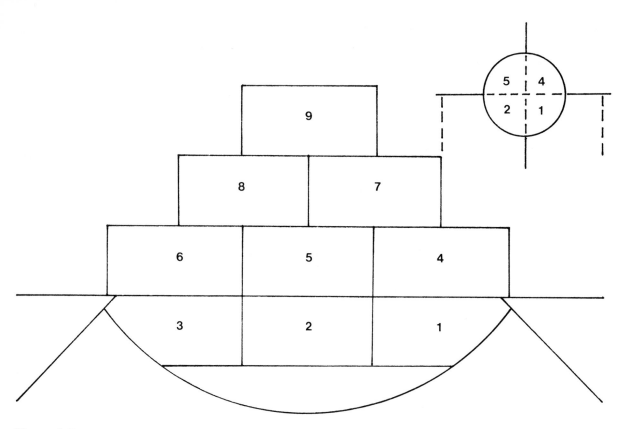

Figure 9.3
Layout of Acting Areas

the top of the tree from P.S. [stg. lft.]. It should not be a matter of luck but of good interaction between director, designer, and lighting designer that the staging dictates the female character face into the special.

The second special under the tree is more difficult, since the apparent source of light is the same. This beam of light must be parallel to the doorway special, and you must ensure that any realistic impression of the tree from the set designer does not obstruct the special. Further, she must sit well back and he a little forward so that he avoids her shadow's falling across his face. They will now both be strongly profiled from P.S. [stg. lft.], and acting area 7 will fill the remainder of their faces from O.P. [stg. rt.]. If not, you may have to add another element to be the special circuit. (*Note:* The foregoing imposes a strong naturalistic style that may not always be necessary.)

9.5.3 Washes

The term *wash* suggests a broader, more general type of light designed to convey any number of different qualities by means of colour, texture, directionality, and so on. In the Figure 9.2 example there may be a broad wash from P.S. [stg. lft.] representing parallel sunlight covering not only the stage but also the set. You need to be a little more selective and split the wash into at least two parts— one circuit for the set and one (perhaps two because of power considerations) for the remainder of the stage. The backcloth will obviously require a number of colour washes without any directionality, since you're looking for a soft, even coverage. The sun, as it passes through the leaves of the tree, will create a textured, deckle pattern—with, perhaps, some movement—on the right of the stage. If the scene elements only give a minimal representation of a tree, the lighting department will need to provide the textured wash over the house. (This may give the justification for splitting the sunlight directional wash.)

From low on the O.P. [stg. rt.] side you may choose to fill with light that, in a naturalistic sense, has been reflected back off the grass, giving a soft, low-intensity, greenish tinge. Why not allow your sunlight wash to reflect back from whatever the set designer has given you and leave it at that? Lighting designers require control of every source of light so as to use it selectively. For example, as our lovers separate to either side of the stage when the father's presence is suspected, you could raise the level of the green. (Sick with fear?) It's easy to scoff at, but, if it works, use it!

9.6 Combining Purpose and Type

Armed with this double description of circuits, you are better equipped to break down and define the elements from which your vision is constructed.

You should be able to describe each circuit succinctly so that its title encapsulates a sense of where it lies in the depth of field (such as foreground or midground), together with a clear idea of its purpose and an indication of the quality of light. For example, Blue Ambient Wash quickly describes a nondirectional blue wash well in the background; House-Deckled Wash or Doorway Sunlight Special will detail circuits already discussed.

9.7 Alternate Phraseology

In the phraseology used by lighting personnel you will find terms (for example, *keylight, fill, backlight, sidelight*) that further describe circuits with particular emphasis on purpose and direction. The phrases mentioned in sections 9.4 and 9.5 should not displace any of these; on the contrary, these classifications can amplify those terms and allow you to define more clearly the breakdown of your vision.

9.8 Breakdown Method

The question remains, how do you do it? The vision is in your mind; you can't represent it in any tangible form, yet you are required to pull it apart! As the prospect is a little daunting initially, it should be approached in easy stages.

I sit in my living room on a very pleasant Sunday around 2:00 P.M.; there are clear skies. Figure 9.4 represents a rough layout. Sunlight is bouncing off the wall of the flats next door before entering the windows of both the fawn-painted living room and the green room next to it. If I hold my hand up so that my palm faces west, the back of my hand is very clearly lit in strong, slightly diffused light that has a bias toward red; this is due to the sunlight (white) bouncing off a red-brick wall next door. The palm of my hand is softly lit by this same light bouncing off the western wall of my living room, where it takes on a fawn tinge.

As I turn my palm south, the quality of light changes on both surfaces. On the north side there is a strong directionality evident from the window light; but, in the shadows between my fingers, fawn light bounced off the walls forms a fill. My palm is lit from

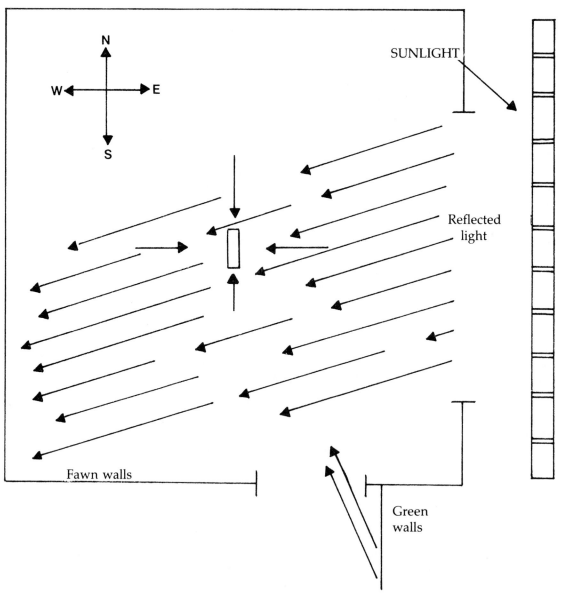

Figure 9.4
Analysing Natural Light

the southwest softly in fawn light; and from the southeast there is a hint of green, which is the bounce off the walls in the green room. If I turn my palm to the floor, the quality of light changes yet again. Because my dark carpet doesn't bounce light well, the light on my palm is deeper in tone and considerably less intense; the back of my hand also changes quality, since I have a white ceiling that reflects well.

To break down the vision, you must repeat this process in your mind's eye for every point onstage, particularly at points where performers must hold the attention of the audience.

But this is a pretty big jump, so, as an interim step, go to the Art Gallery. Start with the more naturalistic paintings and move through to the more stylised. Or pick up any glossy magazine or grab a handful of postcards—anything that presents you with a picture that may represent a stage. Try, in your imagination, to insert your hand into the picture; turn it north, south, east, west, up and down, and visualise how the light quality changes. What colour is it? What is its direction? Is it soft or hard? Does it have texture? How does intensity vary?

Traverse the whole imaginary stage and try to imagine how your actors will move within the picture; follow them around with your hand, taking notes of light variations. Now you're getting the idea! As you shift from old masters to more stylised works, the process remains the same, but the results will be heavily influenced by the style.

Return to your cue synopsis and repeat the process for each of the visions described. As you analyse the quality of light on your hand, give it a title: O.P. [stg. rt.] Directional Sun Wash, Bounce Backlight from Purple Drapes, Warm Fill from P.S. [stg. lft.]. Perhaps you can see, for example, a 1950s Hollywood special causing the eyes of the leading lady to glint? Call it the "Eyes" special.

A good check of your analysis is the shadows your hand casts. Are they consistent with the circuits you had in mind? If not, you've made a mistake. Shadows form such a strong image that often they give a clearer indication of source than if you tried to approach it directly.

Keep taking notes; don't worry about duplications (you'll rationalise them shortly); just ensure that you itemise everything you see in your vision. Sample notes that you might write are as follows:

> The cyclorama is not just a big sheet—it comprises a myriad of points, and each needs to be analysed. It's darker at the top; closer to the horizon the colour seems to bleach out.
> There are distant windblown clouds plus nearer ones that hint at a thunderstorm. Come back midstage: there's a storm brewing—is there any wind onstage causing movement? Perhaps there's rippling water throwing a reflection or a moving leaf texture?

If you want to practise lighting design, never stop this analysis. Look at the sky tonight as the sun sets; try, in your mind's eye, to break it down. How many gauzes [scrims], how many different circuits and colours? What colour is moonlight? How could we re-create stars onstage, the underglow on the clouds from the city or the moon reflecting off the sea? Constantly analyse your surroundings and compare nature's lighting designer to yourself—he's pretty good. Your aim should be to approach those standards as closely as you are able.

9.9 Simple Example

Figure 9.5 sketches an exterior rural setting at night; the shading on both the trees and background hills would place the moon on P.S. [stg. lft.] slightly upstage. A designer realising this idea onstage would likely execute a two-dimensional backdrop, a raked forestage (that is, the surface increases in height as it continues upstage) with some three-dimensional trees.

Should the designer ask my opinion, I could suggest a couple of ideas. Given that the intention seems to be the creation of those indigo country-night skies, the effect might be achieved by using a set of flat black velvet drapes well upstage with a two-dimensional painted outline of the hills. If possible, a black gauze just upstage of the rake (which also forms a ground-row cover for lighting equipment) will assist the sense of depth. With modern equipment I would need about 2 metres [6½ feet] between the gauze and the silhouette,

Figure 9.5
Night Scene with Trees

Breaking Down Vision into Components

and I'd like about 1 metre [3 feet] between the hills outline and the blacks. Figure 9.6 represents, in plan (part a) and section (part b), a possible solution. (Note that lighting bars are marked as "Lx.")

I would light the blacks from overhead upstage of the gauze in a deep-blue, very soft wash. But why light nothing? The answer is that the blacks will be dusty, and velvet reflects a certain amount of light; thus, a haze of blue, is created overhead, indicating the desired indigo sky, the ambience against which the scene will be presented. From the ground row I can evenly light the silhouette in whatever colour I choose (far lighter than the ambience blue); I'll use the same colour downstage for the blue directionality; but, since the silhouette will be viewed through a black gauze, the impression will be a distanced, diminished shade of blue.

Why the flat lighting for those hills; shouldn't their light have direction, too? It has been painted in; all the lighting designer needs to do is illuminate the hills so that the work of the scenic artist is apparent. Trying to light from upstage P.S. [stg. lft.] would just highlight all the irregularities in the surface and ensure that most of the light missed the object.

With gauze [scrim] the lighting designer needs to ensure that only intended light touches it. In this case where it is intended as

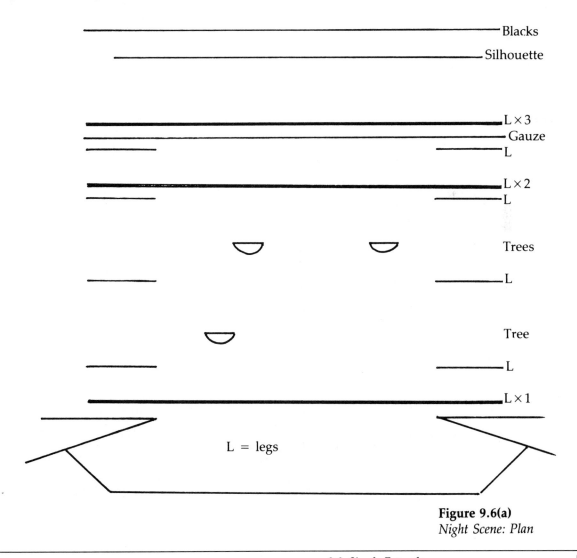

Figure 9.6(a)
Night Scene: Plan

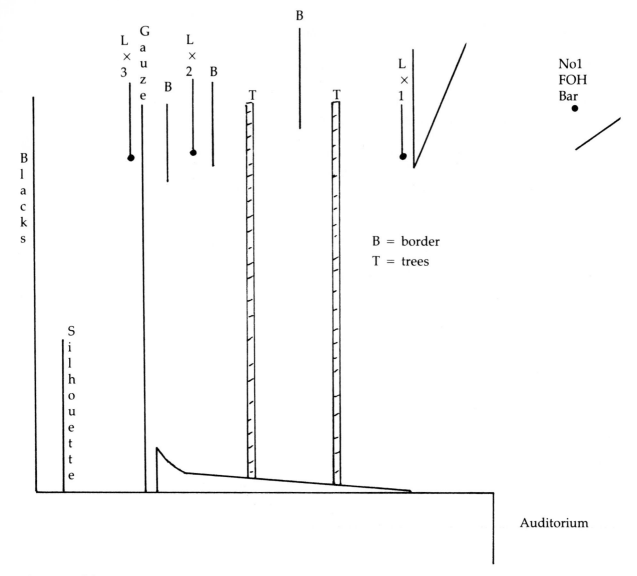

Figure 9.6(b)
Night Scene: Section

a distancing medium, it should have no light from both back and front—including as little bounce off the forestage as possible. Otherwise, the gauze will start to become opaque, with loss of clarity on the background. (When a gauze is being used to "reveal" scenes set behind, it needs light on the front to make it opaque.)

The downstage keylight will be parallel beams of light from P.S. [stg. lft.] upstage in whatever blue was selected; however, that's insufficient light in which to perform. The lighting designer must supply a fill from front and O.P. [stg. rt.] to round out the faces. This is the direction from which most of the audience will be viewing the scene and, therefore, requires more than low-level fill; it needs the equivalent of an acting area.

A common problem begins to emerge; lighting faces sufficiently may wash out the keylight. Don't fall into the trap of spiralling intensity (that is, edging up intensities of each circuit to compensate for the other), with the scene becoming overlit. This may be avoided by choosing deeper tones of blue than the keylight. That will main-

Breaking Down Vision into Components

tain sufficient light on performers while ensuring that keylight remains dominant.

Going back to Figure 9.5, insert a human figure into the picture. With a dark stagecloth, the eye will travel up to where there is more light and find the performer's face; however, if the trees are lighted evenly from top to bottom, the eye may continue to follow up the trunks from the actors. Remember, the lights are overhead, and it is more likely that the tops of the trunks will be brighter than faces.

The set designer will, almost certainly, paint the trunks down; thus, above head height the colours and texture will deepen so that the upper sections are less dominant. The lighting designer should follow this pattern and reduce the light also; perhaps the upper trunks are lit by moonlight through the leaves of the tree (unseen); the texture used to create this impression will break down the light and force the eyes of the audience back to the performers—but that calls for another circuit. Thus, from a single scene, you may end up with a list of circuits that could include:

Acting area centre, mid-blue—2 kw approx. P.S. [stg. lft.]

Moonlight wash, light-blue (directional P.S.)—5 kw?

Texture wash upstage, light-blue (directional P.S.)—2 kw approx.

Ground-row silhouette wash, light-blue (possibly another)—2 kw each

Overhead blacks wash, dark-blue (ambience)—5 kw?

Can you imagine how that list would rapidly increase if you were required to extend the scene through to dawn? (Just to keep the record straight, you could no longer suggest the black velvet background and would have to revert to a cyclorama.)

9.10 Rationalisation and Compromise

The process of itemising circuits entails a great deal of craft, but what follows depends more upon cunning, ingenuity, common sense, and, most of all, compromise. Let's say that you're working on a 60-way board (60 dimmers), 45 × 2 kw dimmers, and 15 × 5 kw dimmers; however, your analysis shows that you may have a list of 133 circuits that must somehow fit within the limits of the board.

It is important to realize that the major advantage of this rationalisation and compromise approach is to ensure that facilities don't dictate the lighting; instead, you construct tools needed for each show and use the facilities to their best advantage. The term, *saturation rig*, is frequently applied to this approach, since it demands a larger number of lanterns [instruments] than, say, a standard rig approach. But, remember, all are there to serve the show.

(*Note:* The following process should be done separately on both 5 kw and 2 kw circuits; of course, you may use a 2 kw circuit on a 5 kw dimmer, but not the reverse. Sort the 5 kw's out first, then use any remaining to assist with the 2 kw circuits.)

Listed below (9.10.1 through 9.10.5) are five ways to rationalise your 133 circuits to 60; they are listed in reverse order of difficulty. The first few will be easy to achieve; but, as you continue, the degree to which you must compromise will increase. Obviously, if you don't need to go beyond three refinements, don't!

9.10.1 Duplications

Search your lists for circuits that are duplicates in all respects—purpose, colour, direction, and the like; they are easily cut. There may be those with slight differences (for example, a blue front-of-house wash with and without texture and/or directionality). Return to the cue synopsis to ascertain which is the more important variation and how its inclusion in a state for which it was not intended may compromise the scene. Perhaps the blue wash need not be directional; this would make it useful in more than one scene, thus saving a circuit.

After a series of value judgments and a degree of reconstruction/compromise, you may be able to reduce your 133 circuits to, typically, about 85.

9.10.2 Overdesign

With your revised list of 85, return to the cue synopsis and ascertain how frequently each of those circuits is used. It's possible that when one scene grabbed your imagination you overindulged; perhaps the show demands a brief segment in a night club and you added eight circuits for atmosphere. Reconsider: is that scene so important? If the answer is yes, continue on; this may be the case in say, *The Tempest's* storm, where circuits create effects that are crucial to understanding the show. But you may be able to reconceive the effects so that they retain the essence of what you intended while using fewer circuits. Typically this process may reduce your list to 80 circuits.

9.10.3 Intensity Variations

Pinpoint those circuits remaining that always work in tandem but that you separated to maintain an intensity differential. You may have a 2 kw directional wash with another 2 kw circuit supplying the back fill; you expect the directional to be consistently about 20 percent above the fill. If you have a 5 kw circuit available, it's possible that with careful selection of lanterns to maintain the difference in intensity (for example, 650/w lamps in the directionals and 500/w in the fill, plus careful selection of colour), you may be able to combine these circuits. It is, however, a major compromise because flexibility will be lost and that could cause trouble in the plotting [dry tech.], but you may be able to reduce to 77 circuits.

9.10.4 Repatching

Section 9.3 talked about a highlight with two alternate backlights, a red and blue. Instead of having a dimmer for each circuit, you could save two dimmers by means of switching at the patch panel (by a floor lighting person). You must be sure that you don't overload your dimmer (you can never run all three circuits together on a 2 kw dimmer), and you must check to see if there is sufficient time and staff available to make the switch (see Fig. 9.7).

Alternatively, there may be circuits that are used for only brief periods; they are necessary to the design, but it's a waste of a dimmer to allocate them permanently.

Figure 9.7 illustrates a state-of-the-board (SOB) sheet; you will use the form for more important functions during the next weeks, but it's also useful now to plan how you can better use limited facilities by repatching.

As yet, you don't have dimmer or cue numbers; instead, use circuit titles and script page numbers to identify states. You need to indicate when a circuit is being used throughout the show. You won't need to examine every circuit; in Figure 9.7 the front-of-house (FOH) blue wash is so frequently used that there is no point in considering it for repatching; to do so would be foolhardy.

With the remaining seven circuits it might be possible to control both the P.S. [stg. lft.] spot and the centre highlight on the same dimmer, but that could be dangerous because there isn't sufficient time. There is a better opportunity to repatch both the O.P. [stg.

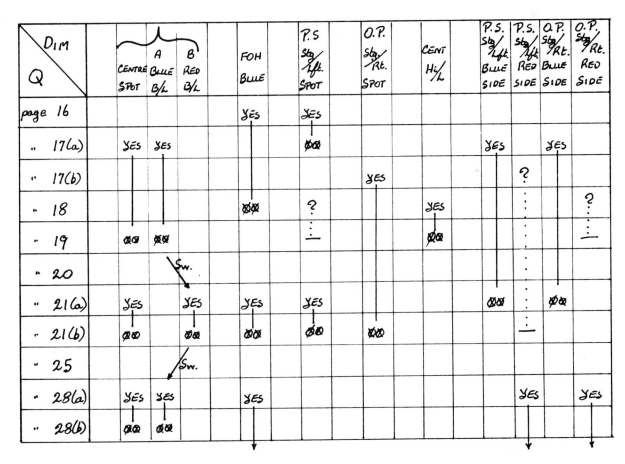

Figure 9.7
Board Plot to Consider Repatching

rt.] spot and the centre highlight with the P.S. [stg. lft.] and O.P. [stg. rt.] red side circuits; both could be changed during the, say, page 21 to 28 gap when the floor lighting person is already repatching the centre spot backlights.

I cannot overstress the need for accuracy and care when repatching and recommend that you not repatch unless it is imperative for the success of the show. Even the best floor lighting person may accidentally dislodge another circuit or make a mistake under pressure and poor worklight conditions. If at all possible, the process should be remoted from the panel by means of relays or by a nearby switch block (see Fig. 17.3). Choose moments for repatching that are without pressure, ideally during the interval [intermission] when you have time for checking.

By means of repatching and renaming circuits as A's and B's, you may be able to reduce your list of circuits to 63.

9.10.5 Cuts

There are still three circuits too many, and they must be cut. Which three must go? Remember that your primary business is to light actors; therefore, you should not consider an acting area. But you may be able to cut a highlight and compensate by raising the level of the associated acting area. A good general rule is to go looking for the most "artistic" circuit and question whether this has been designed for the benefit of the show or for yourself.

Early in this discussion of rationalisation and compromise you were cautioned that if you achieved necessary savings early, you shouldn't go any further—remember, a one-to-one relationship between lantern and dimmer is ideal. In rare cases you may find you have dimmers to spare; if so, you may choose to keep them in hand since there is still a long way to go before opening night and another special or a new idea might present itself. That will almost certainly be the case, whether you have dimmers to spare or not, and you may need to return to the process above if there is a need to fit something more into the rig. Alternatively, you may use that dimmer to satisfy a gnawing doubt. As you look through your final list of circuits over and over again, your gut says that something is not quite right; there doesn't seem to be enough green, or you have a feeling (a hunch, a gut reaction) that a downstage centre special may prove useful once you get into the theatre. In my own case, if the lanterns are spare, I often rig a couple of Fresnel units and a profile lantern but won't even bother to focus them. Since they are already in the air, they can quickly be brought into operation should the need arise during, say, the plotting [dry tech.] or technical rehearsal.

Despite the fact that part of your soul has gone into analysing the circuits, you must not be too rigid. Any or all the elements might change to suit the show as it evolves; you must remain flexible. But, because mistakes in the choice of circuits or omissions at this stage are irreparable without vast expenditure of time and personnel, you must be sure in your own mind that you have the whole show lit.

For this reason your gut reactions, hunches, and doubts should be acknowledged and considered very carefully.

You now have 60 dimmers and 60 circuits (with some A and B alternatives), and it may be convenient to allocate each circuit to a dimmer so that you can refer to it henceforth by number instead of the more clumsy title. Depending on the type of patching system (see chapter 15), this may be more difficult than it seems; however, the sooner you, as lighting designer, learn to recognise circuits and to call them by number from memory, the more efficient you will become. If by the focus or plotting [dry tech.] sessions (see chapters 18 and 19), you still need to refer to a piece of paper, you will be wasting time.

There is one further point: In a soft patch you have the ability to allocate circuits to dimmers with comparative freedom. It will be advantageous if you can group dimmers by purpose, frequency of use, or ease of operation; for example, it's easier to fade sequentially 1, 2, 3, and 4 instead of 15, 21, 16, then 2. You'll want to involve your board operator, who may have preferences; but it is likely that at this time you are the only one with sufficient information to make decisions.

It is time to pass on your information to anyone concerned, in particular to the director and the deputy stage manager. Again our purpose is two-way communication; if you welcome a reaction or warning from any source, that will be of benefit to you. Informed reactions will enable you to modify while still in the paperwork stage instead of in the theatre, where changes would be vastly more expensive.

You need to prepare (for your own benefit as well) three pieces of documentation (9.12.1 to 9.12.3).

9.12.1 Alphabetic List

This lists circuits alphabetically and gives the dimmer number associated with that circuit; thus, if you don't know the number, you can look it up quickly.

9.12.2 Numeric List

This lists numerically each dimmer and what circuit it is controlling; besides being a cross reference to the alphabetic list, it acts as an organisational aid and checklist which are both useful throughout the life of the show.

9.12.3 1:100 [⅛": 1'] Scale Sketches

These sketches, prepared for each stage setting, should indicate the coverage of each circuit (that is, the area within which an actor can stand and be lit by that circuit). There is no need to prepare one for each circuit; you may be able to fit them all on two or three sketches. For the rehearsal room the most important are those that detail spot positions and acting areas; washes and the like will mean very little to them. Figure 9.8 illustrates the example from section 9.5; note that it is little more than a combination of Figures 9.2 and 9.3.

9.13 Update Cue Synopsis

As you read earlier, the only difference between a basic cue synopsis and the final version is that you continually update the original document. Now that you have finalised the circuits for the show, it's time to update your synopsis with that information.

With your alphabetic list of circuits handy, go through the synopsis, and, in the final column entitled "Dimmer," *pencil* in—and I stress pencil—all those dimmers you believe will be necessary to achieve the results described. You may add or subtract at some later stage, but, for the time being, notate this first breakdown while it's still fresh in your memory. As yet, you have no idea of dimmer levels—that comes later.

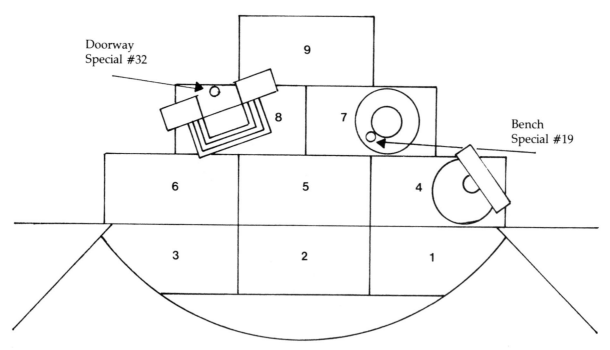

Figure 9.8
Acting Areas Superimposed on Set Plan

The process of breaking down into circuits is, of course, only a small proportion of the work to be completed at this time and must be fitted around other duties.

You should have arranged for and completed a check of stock (colour, spare lamps, and so on) so that, the moment you know what the show will require, you can make out orders. You may, even at this stage, be able to make an educated guess.

You must continue your rounds—to workshops, wardrobe, and, of course, rehearsals—ensuring that you remain in touch with the production throughout its evolution. It's far too easy to lock yourself away in your office completing wonderful paperwork for a design that no longer suits the production. Also make sure you remain in contact with your staff. Are the special effects being manufactured on schedule, or are your people having problems?

9.15 In Summation

You have made a giant step toward the completion of your lighting design; although there is a great deal to be achieved during the week, much of it is considerably more mechanical than the process of breaking down into circuits, just described. At this point on the schedule, major mistakes or omissions will lead to expensive and time-consuming repairs. That is why you should seek all possible feedback now to make sure you've covered every necessity of the show, with particular emphasis on lighting actors throughout.

CHAPTER 10

Continuing the Breakdown: Choice and Placement of Lanterns [Instruments]

This process should also be achieved during the third week before opening and follows immediately on the breakdown into circuits. The purpose of the process is to select the lanterns [instruments] you require, to discover an effective placement and colour for each, and to define the patching necessary to create your circuits. By the end of the process you should be able to confirm that the rig will be within limits of stock; further, you will have the information in a form which will enable us to draw up the plan [plot] quickly. This is achieved while still remaining flexible, able to incorporate quickly any changes that come to you from the rehearsal room.

This chapter will outline the process, and the next four chapters will go into details about the theory of light, lanterns, placement, and colour. This organisation is to establish a "need to know" that will encourage you to search for the theory and practice satisfying that need. Even after reading chapters 11 to 14, you will not have sufficient knowledge to embark upon a design; this book emphasizes the processes involved and deliberately limits the amount of basic theory to just four chapters that are nothing more than a summary.

If, as you read this chapter, you find your knowledge inadequate, skip on to chapters 11–14, and, after your refresher, return here and begin again.

10.2 Tools from Which to Create Tools

You have broken down your synopsis vision into circuits, which can be considered as purpose-built tools the lighting designer intends to create. To construct them, you must understand the properties of light and the manner in which it is manipulated by lanterns and equipment.

You start with light—that small portion of the electromagnetic spectrum perceived by the human eye. . . . . or do you? The object of design is to use tools *selectively* for a purposeful end-result. Without the complete *elimination* of light over which you have limited control, you are making your life as a lighting designer very difficult. From your viewpoint the theatre functions not only to support your equipment but also to ensure a blackout. Extraneous light (for example, orchestra lights, blues, prompt corner worklight) distorts the image you are trying to create; of course, you can't eliminate this light entirely, but you mustn't miss out on controlling it as much as you are able.

Can you itemise the ways in which light can be varied to serve your design? Note these properties in the list below, together with the chapters that discuss them more fully.

1. Shape/Feel   Ch. 11
2. Angle—vertical   } Ch. 12
    Angle—horizontal
3. Colour   Ch. 13
4. Movement   Ch. 14
5. Intensity   Ch. 18

Many beginners are amazed at how limited that list is; yet every natural or theatrical effect can be summarized in these terms. What is really amazing is the infinite number of variations they allow.

10.3 1:100 [⅛":1'] Scale Approach

Your task is to itemise how each of these variables is used in the circuits you have selected and, eventually, to produce a plan [plot] that will detail your decisions for the rigging crew. To commence with these five variables and your numeric list of circuits expecting to move directly to the scale plan is a daunting prospect. First, it's too early to become that rigid; you still have a little under a week before you must present the plan to the head electrician. Second, the magnitude of the task is beyond what you can reasonably expect of yourself.

At this stage, you will find it useful, as I have, to consider each circuit in isolation at a scale of 1:100 [⅛":1'], then to extrapolate whatever information is necessary to ensure that the full-scale product is feasible. You probably can cope with this amount of detail but extension beyond that only introduces ramifications leading to indecision. Of course, you need to keep in mind how the circuit interacts with others, but you can confine this to broad principles, which are easier to comprehend than the fine detail you must demand of yourself later.

There is a further advantage to limiting detail at this point, you are following the principle of approaching problems from the viewpoint of *what best serves the show*. Only when that has been determined do you consider how the equipment available can best be utilised.

You have already had reason to draw up 1:100 [⅛":1'] scale sketches for each stage setting (see sections 9.5.1 and 9.12.3); and, if you further modify them, they will form the basic documentation. Each sketch needs only sufficient detail of stage setting to enable you to locate yourself, but add an indication of all lighting positions (front-of-house bridges, onstage bars, booms, and so on). Don't become obsessed with accuracy—after all, you're working in a scale of 1:100 [⅛":1'].

Make enough photocopies to give you one page for every circuit, plus a few extras for those that need reworking/replacement;

then add to each page the dimmer number, its power capacity, and the title of the circuit (see Fig. 10.7). You can now proceed to consider each in turn. The order doesn't matter; do the easy ones first, if you prefer. It may be helpful to add any notes gathered from experimentation on the model or comments concerning compromises you have already made (see sections 9.10.2 and 9.10.3), but these are only reminders; you should be limited by nothing other than the circuits' purpose and power capacity of the dimmer.

Apart from a cursory glance, don't consider the stock list; you shouldn't even limit yourself to the lighting positions indicated on the sketches. If you need something more, detail it for checking later to see whether it's viable.

You have now gathered all the information pertaining to each problem in one place; but, before you go into particular examples, consider a few broad principles.

10.4 Rules Concerning Lantern [Instrument] Combination

There are no rules! Some lighting designers quite involuntarily restrict their choice of lantern [instrument] so that they combine only similar types into a circuit. Wrong! You may select any lantern (profile, Fresnel, flood, any wattage) and combine it in any way with any other type. For example, a soft but localised multidirectional area may include a pebble-convex highlight, a Fresnel backlight, and/or a directional profile texture. Or, acting areas may comprise both Fresnel and profile lanterns if you are hoping to create a very directional shape to the stage. In chapter 11 you'll find guidelines and recommendations regarding lantern usage (for example, only profile lanterns front-of-house), but even these can be contradicted if you are able to justify the need.

10.5 Lantern Size in Relation to the House

Earlier it was suggested that you need only a cursory glance over the stock list; that was to ensure that you were aware of the "size" house you were dealing with. You will quickly learn to categorise theatres in terms of "500 watt house," "1 kw house," "2 kw house," and so on; or you may wish to include an assessment of each position (2 kw front-of-house, 1 kw onstage). You are indicating the power of the average lantern you find in these positions; further, you are suggesting that their relative intensity is similar once they reach the stage. Taking this as a basis, you are able to vary either side in order to achieve the results you seek. Examples: For an intense spot in a "1 kw house" you may choose to allocate a 2 kw lantern to the task. Or, in a 500 watt house where you need a highlight, you could approach the problem in three ways; you may choose a 500 watt unit (but select a narrow beam lantern), increase the power of a standard lantern to 650 watts, or select a 1 kw instrument.

Be careful when, for instance, in a 1 kw house you produce a 500 watt show! Example: In the midst of the stage is an area that you require to divide into a number of localised acting areas; if you use the standard unit (1 kw) in each of these, you will certainly overlight the performers. You may hope to correct this by dropping intensity; but this underheats the lamp filaments, producing red-biased light (see section 13.4), and the colours you have chosen will not perform as expected—it will be very difficult to produce blue! The solution lies in using nonstandard 500 watt lanterns to light the areas.

Next, you need to determine a "feel" for each element within a circuit (for example, soft, hard, very soft, hard up/down, and soft side/side). Chapter 11 will consider the various lantern types and quality of light each produces.

At this point the summary below is intended only as a rough guide.

Flood	)	Very soft
	)	
Fresnel	)	)
		)
Pebble-convex		)
		)
Beamlight		) Soft
		)
Bifocal profile	)	)
	)	)
Plano-convex	)	)
	)	
Profile [ellipsoidal]	)	Hard

Differentiation between groups is not clear-cut, and you require much more information to reach a decision. For example, should you require a soft feel from front-of-house? Try a bifocal profile, since it provides both soft and hard shutters—the hard for ensuring minimal spill onto the proscenium and the soft for shaping the light onstage.

It is important to remember that your task in hand is to determine which lanterns will give the correct feel for the vision you have in mind. You may be forced to compromise later when you consider the stock available, but you should be clear, at this point, as to which lantern would be ideal.

Consider the "Letter Aria" from *Eugene Onegin*; Figure 10.1 roughs out the setting: an attic with casement windows O.P. [stg. rt.], inset doorway upstage, couch and table with a lamp low on the far P.S. [stg. lft.]. It's night; moonlight through the window and the lamp burning; as the performer moves about the stage, you want

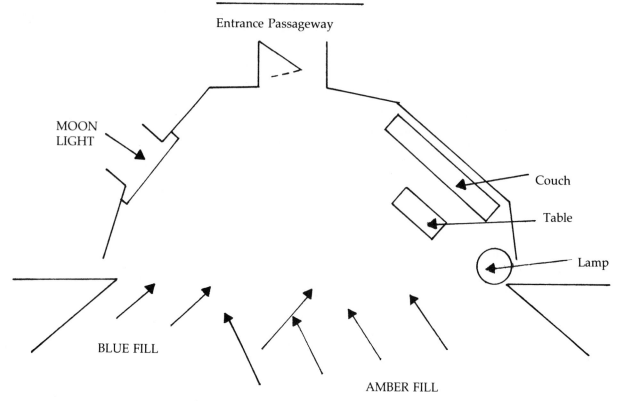

Figure 10.1
Letter Scene from Eugene Onegin.

her shadow cast across the setting. What is the feeling of the moonlight through the window? Most would feel that it should be hard, which implies the use of a profile [ellipsoidal]—or does it? The window itself will give shape and hardness to the image cast onstage; you need only ensure the lantern is sufficiently contained so that it does not spill over the top of the flats and has enough power to be perceived as the keylight to the O.P. [stg. rt.] side of the stage; any lantern type between a Fresnel and profile would be satisfactory. As keylight to P.S. [stg. lft.] you need a lantern low on the perch sufficiently wide and relatively soft, yet controllable—you don't want it spilling into the auditorium. A good solution is a single Fresnel fitted with barndoors. For both fill circuits you will need profile lanterns, since they will be front-of-house, but bifocal units will be easier to blend softly into a fill/wash.

10.7 Selecting Lanterns by Means of a Section

Assume that you have an unusual placement and that you're not sure which lantern to choose; alternatively, you must select lanterns for a space that has no stock whatsoever, and you have no information other than the proposed hanging positions.

Before we can begin any calculations, you must define the angle at which you intend to light the show. There is continual controversy as to which is the correct angle but there is general agreement that it is 35–45 degrees from the vertical (*Note*. Convention has us measuring either from the vertical or horizontal, depending on our train-

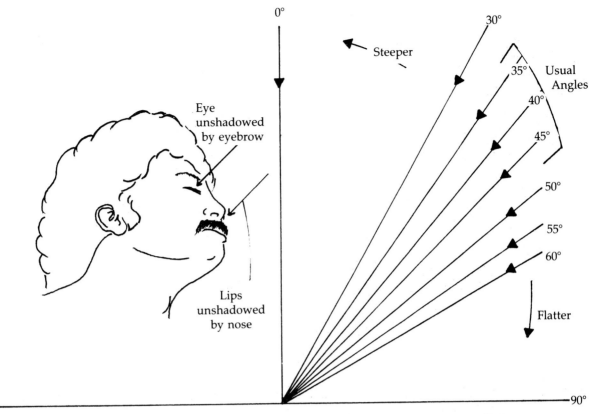

0°

Steeper

Eye
unshadowed
by eyebrow

Lips
unshadowed
by nose

30°

35° Usual
Angles

40°

45°

50°

55°

60°

Flatter

90°

Figure 10.2
Angle for Lighting Faces.

ing.) The choice of angle depends entirely upon the show; this is not taking the easy way out; on the contrary, it is the only realistic approach. Your purpose is to light the eyes and lips of performers so that the audience can see clearly these most expressive instruments of performance; if both are shadowed, the audience will not be able to read the emotion expressed within the eyes or to read lips (even those with good hearing rely somewhat on lip-reading).

Your choice of angle depends to some degree on the shape of the actors' face (if they have deep-set eyes, you need to go flatter) and also to a large degree upon the staging (See Figure 10.2.) If you're lighting kings who keep their heads up, you can afford a steeper angle; but, if the staging requires performers to be continually looking down (as from rostrum E down to stage level in Figure 10.4), then you need a flatter angle. Generally, you must keep as steep as possible to ensure maximum isolation; the flatter the angle, the more likely you are to spill onto items you don't wish to light (like the cyclorama). Having chosen the angle for the production, say 40 degrees, you should attempt to maintain it consistently (apart from when you deliberately break the convention), particularly throughout the acting areas. If the lighting angle changes drastically when performers move between areas (especially upstage and downstage), this will be perceived by the audience as a dip in light. Take the example illustrated in Figures 10.3 and 10.4 to investigate the process; look closely at the central acting area (AA), which is going to give you some unpleasant problems.

Your principal tool is the section drawing of the set; however, you are not lighting the stage but the actors. They are, on the av-

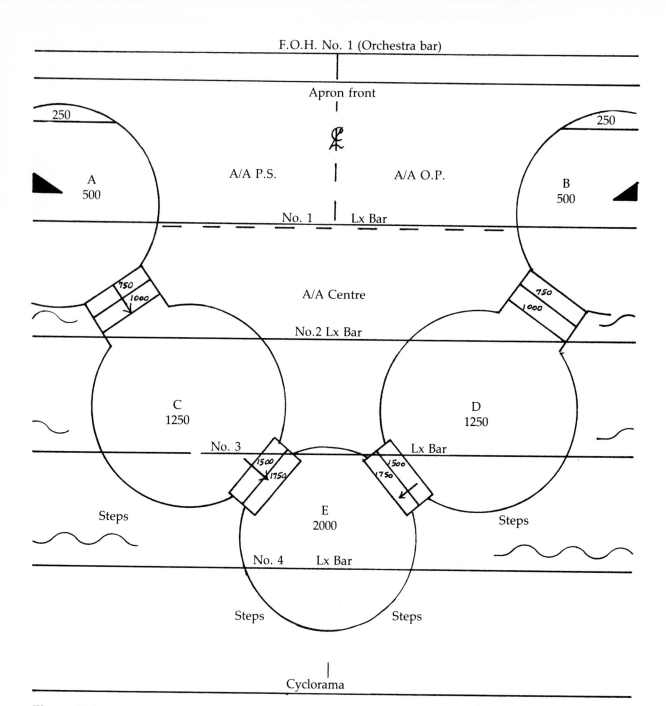

F.O.H. No. 1 (Orchestra bar)

Apron front

250

250

A
500

A/A P.S.

A/A O.P.

B
500

No. 1   Lx Bar

750

1000

A/A Centre

No.2 Lx Bar

750

1000

C
1250

D
1250

No. 3

1500

1750

Lx Bar

1500

1750

Steps

E
2000

Steps

No. 4   Lx Bar

Steps

Steps

Cyclorama

Figure 10.3
Plan of Acting Areas with Hanging Positions.

erage, about 1.8 metres [6 feet] tall; therefore, pencil in the head height, the height at which lighting must be consistent. Those who forget this maxim are referred to as foot-focussers; their stages appear beautifully lit until performers step onstage; then all the holes and dips at head height become obvious. Take the midpoint at head height of the centre acting area, and project back a line at the chosen 40 degrees to discover which position is most suitable to light this area. In Figure 10.4 you can see that this line falls between No. 1 and 2 front-of-house (FOH) bars but is far closer to the No. 1. Which is the most suitable position from which to light this area at 40 degrees? Answer: No. 1 FOH bar. Given that you use only this bar, how well will the area be lit?

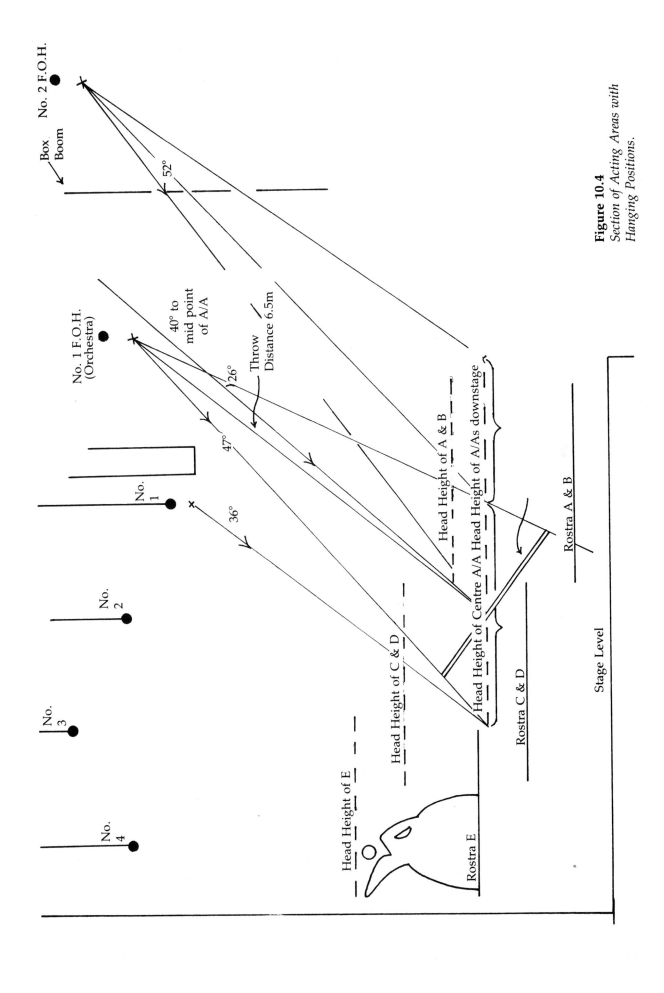

Figure 10.4
Section of Acting Areas with Hanging Positions.

Precise investigation demands that you position the lens of the lantern on the bar, generally about 300 mm [1'] below the bar itself. In a large house this is less important, but on short throws it's worth considering. The lantern dimensions given on the manufacturer's specification sheets will be the easiest source of this information. From the lens position, project lines to both the upstage and downstage extremities of the area; in this case the variation is from 26 degrees to 47 degrees, and therein lies your first problem. Assuming that you light the downstage acting areas from the No. 2 FOH bar, as an actor passes the point at which the areas join, there will be a sudden change from about 45 to 26 degrees—far too great.

Of course, you are looking at a section through the centreline and considering only one lantern; once you use a crossed pair and separate them horizontally on the bar, the angle of incidence on the faces of actors at the intersection will increase. However, these same factors will worsen the upstage extremity of the centre acting area, which is already at 47 degrees and considerably flatter than you would like. You must also consider the likelihood of casting spill onto the front of the proscenium arch from lanterns on the No. 1 FOH bar, a perfect example of why Fresnels are generally unsuitable front-of-house. These points give no answers, but all of them must be considered when you search for the best compromise solution. You can measure the throw distance and beam spread of lanterns on the No. 1 FOH covering the area from upstage to down; that is, beam spread of 2.5 metres [8 feet] over a throw of 6.5 metres [21 feet]. Now refer back to Figure 10.3; a 2.5 metre spread will cover only half the area—you need a wider beam angle.

To cover the area but not spill outside it, you would need to drastically shape your round beam, which means a considerable proportion of your light is going to be lost; it will serve no purpose other than heating the shutters (or barndoors). This is in addition to spreading the same amount of light (500 watts, say) over a far greater area. Again, you have no solution but a better appreciation of the difficulties and, perhaps, a couple of alternatives suggesting themselves.

The first solution uses four small lanterns from the No. 1 FOH bar (each of about 2.5 metres [8 feet] spread) with another pair of lanterns on the No. 1 onstage bar, which continue a consistent angle into the upstage portion. It's relatively efficient use of light, since you won't be losing much in shutters/shaping, but it will require a large lantern stock.

The second possibility uses two wide-beam lanterns well separated on the No. 1 FOH bar shaped drastically (as above); you will have difficulty getting these lanterns into the upstage portion of the acting area, and you are sure to need another lantern on the No. 1 onstage bar. This circuit has a major problem: the most dominant acting position within this area will be along the centreline, yet you are placing lanterns as far as possible from that spot and almost sidelighting. You can now see that your choice of solutions has been made.

Consider the first solution in more detail. How many lanterns do you need? You probably want a crossed pair into the left, right, and upstage sections of the area. Six lanterns on a 2 kw dimmer? As a 333 watt lamp is not made, you'll be forced to use 500 watts, which limits you to four lanterns. Figure 10.5 suggests one method of placing them.

Problems! You have managed to distribute intensity so that the centreline is brighter, but the light upstage will be two-dimensional and quite harsh. Further, at the points marked with a cross, performers will be lit by only one lantern; the onstage side of their faces will be shadowed. To improve the situation, you may choose a lantern for the centre unit on the FOH bar that is able to cover the whole area, but this will diminish the intensity of the downstage centre position. Since the units from either side will be more intense (narrower spread), the performer will appear to be pulled to either side of the stage away from the dominant position. The simple solution is to increase the dimmer power to 5 kw and revert to your original solution of six lanterns (four FOH, two onstage), even if it means changing your dimmer allocation to achieve it. Whichever solution you use, you can now detail the wattage, throw distance, and beam spread of each lantern, together with a quite precise positioning.

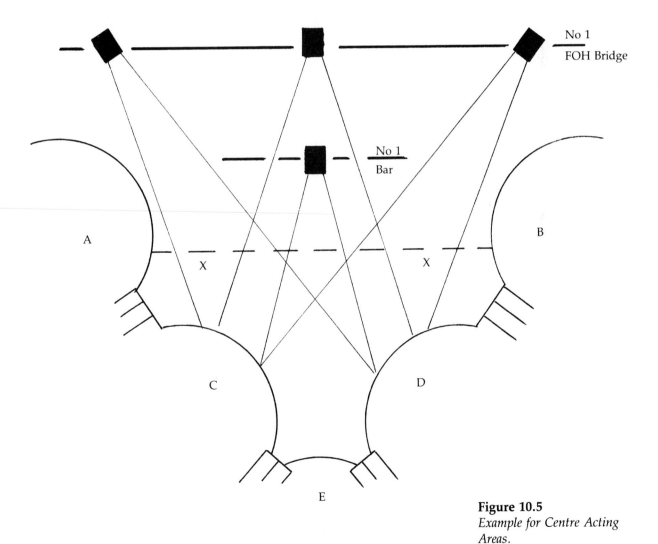

Figure 10.5
Example for Centre Acting Areas.

You now compare these details with data supplied by manufacturers specifying the capabilities of their lanterns. For this purpose you must collect data sheets, not only for ranges currently available but also for older lanterns. Unfortunately, since there is no standard format for presenting this information, you must interpret manufacturer's sheets to extract the details you require. Chapter 11 discusses the terminology used; be sure you understand what's being quoted (for example, half or tenth-peak angle, beam width or field) before you decide upon the appropriate lantern.

If information is unavailable, you must experiment to determine the capabilities of a lantern. You may record this information as illustrated in Figure 10.6; but, however you do it, keep the information on file to save time in the future. With experience this laborious process (using a section to choose lanterns) is less necessary as educated guesses become more common; however, you must understand the elements involved in making those guesses. A clear understanding of principles is far more important than filling your mind with pattern numbers and performance figures that many of your colleagues can quote. Memorising can be a waste of time; instead, using file information for a quick check of all specifications guards against silly mistakes.

10.9 Detailing Circuit Information

Now that you've selected the ideal lanterns for the centre acting area, you should return to your 1:100 [⅛":1'] sketch and record the information, as in Figure 10.7. Note that it's a sketch and not particularly sophisticated. It doesn't use lantern stencils but ensures that all information is clear—dimmer number, capacity, circuit title, lantern details, and so on. It leaves space for colour and patching, which will be taken up shortly. Also note that it differentiates between the capacity of the dimmer and the load assigned to it. A

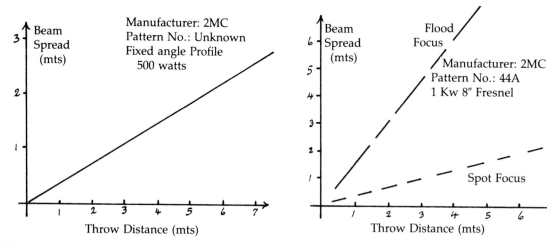

Figure 10.6
Beam Spread Graphs.

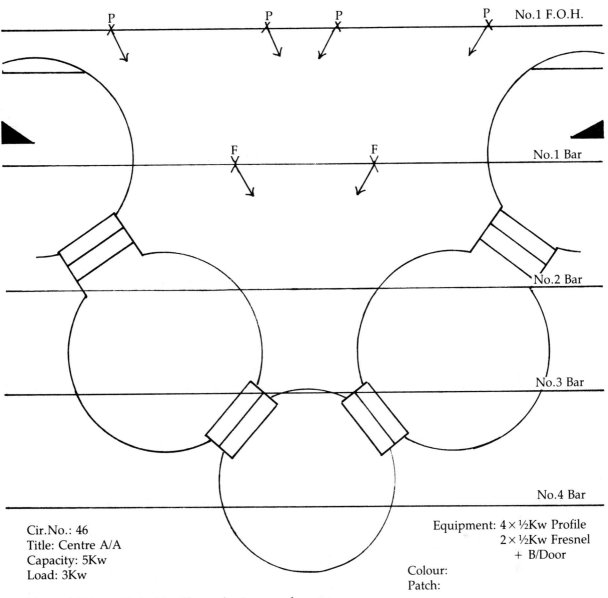

P   P   P   P   No.1 F.O.H.

No.1 Bar

F   F   No.1 Bar

No.2 Bar

No.3 Bar

No.4 Bar

Cir.No.: 46
Title: Centre A/A
Capacity: 5Kw
Load: 3Kw

Equipment: 4 × ½Kw Profile
2 × ½Kw Fresnel
+ B/Door

Colour:
Patch:

Notes: ? Colour #3 & #4 with emphasis around centre.
        ? Backlight—if possible!

Figure 10.7
*Completed 1:100 [⅛":1']
Sketch.*

difference implies inefficient use of the capacity and, as a saturation rigger, it's worrisome; however, six lanterns are all you need to do the job efficiently, and it would be pointless to add lanterns for the hell of it!

As a hypothetical example, say you have a nagging suspicion that the backlight circuits you were forced to cut will be sorely missed. If each of the acting areas had spare capacity, such as the example above, you may include a backlight in each. It's not ideal (since you won't be able to separate either component from the other), but at least you retain some vestige of the concept.

Before moving on, note that Figure 10.7 includes comments on colour gathered from experimentation, along with the query regarding the backlight covered above and a note that the Fresnel lanterns will require barndoors. All this information will be useful as you continue, but, more important, this sheet encapsulates all you need to keep in mind while creating the circuit. If you have any information you consider pertinent, note it in some way.

Fill out one of these sheets for every circuit contemplated, including those not allocated to a dimmer but powered independently from a general power outlet or batteries (such special effects circuits as lightning flashes, power to colour wheels, and mirror balls). By making out a sheet for each, you ensure allocation of space on the bar, patching, and other items that must be included on your final plan [plot].

10.10 Evolving Nonstandard Rigging Requirements

As you continue through the circuit, oddities will surface that cause concern. Perhaps there's no appropriate hanging position or no instrument in stock that would achieve the desired results. Note on the sheet what would be desirable, but complete the process for all circuits; collect all these oddity notes together and view them as a whole.

Perhaps on three or four occasions you note the need for an additional perch position; the course of action is obvious. Investigate the feasibility of the position by discussing it with the set designer, production manager, and stage manager; if they concur, include it. It is your responsibility to see that it obstructs no other department! But if, say, you require a boom to support only one lantern, efficiency demands that you consider its cost effectiveness; first, be sure there isn't another way of achieving the result with less labour.

Lack of suitable equipment is a more difficult problem. Of course, hiring/renting is the obvious solution but it could be beyond your budget; you must find a cheaper—but, almost certainly, less satisfactory—compromise. Investigate how stock equipment may be adapted to achieve the results you need (see Figure 10.8). Example: The old range of STRAND profiles [ellipsoidals] (Pat 23 and 263/4) could both be made into wide lanterns by including a lens cannibalised from another Pat 23. This increases their beam angle from about 22 to 36 degrees, but with such modifications you cannot expect perfect optical performance. Section 10.7 discussed how to adapt lanterns by varying the wattage of the lamp for which they were designed. You may reduce wattage quite happily, but to increase a Pat 23, for example, to 1 kw is dangerous. It was never designed to dissipate that amount of heat; before long, the insulation burns and the components melt. It becomes a time bomb: fire and/or electric shock result. Don't do it! Reducing lamp wattage, however, is a very useful technique. An example: Recently I did a show that required a soft dawn glow from a boom position. The most suitable lantern was a 500 watt flood, but I wanted the effect to reach well across stage and the floodlight was unable to achieve that. From an overhead bar, I added a 1 kw 8″ diameter Fresnel but fitted it with a 250 watt lamp. In this way I was able to extend the effect so

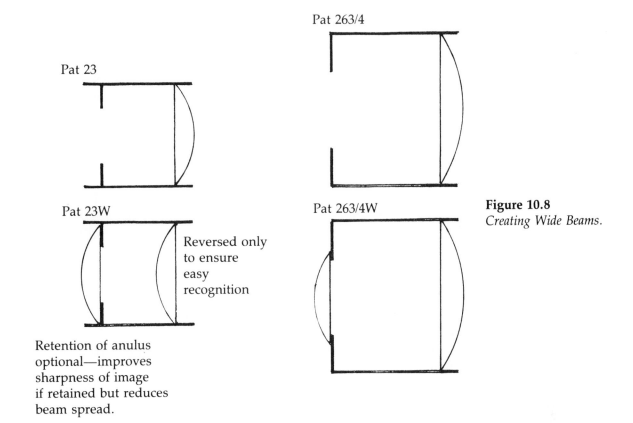

Pat 263/4

Pat 23

Pat 23W

Reversed only
to ensure
easy
recognition

Pat 263/4W

Figure 10.8
Creating Wide Beams.

Retention of anulus
optional—improves
sharpness of image
if retained but reduces
beam spread.

that performers immediately in front of the boom weren't too brightly lit, though I admit there was some discrepancy of angle.

Another dangerous practice often considered when trying to stretch our circuits further is to load a dimmer far beyond its capacity but refrain from bringing it to full (for example, 4 kw on 2 kw dimmer never raised above 50 percent). The designer is obviously attempting to cover a large area with unsuitable equipment—it may be one solution contemplated for the problem in section 10.7. But it's dangerous: accidents happen, mistakes are made, the fader will slip above 50 percent, and you'll blow the fuse—risks that are untenable during a performance. Further, the colour temperature (see chapter 11) will be low; the best you can expect from such a circuit is a low intensity *warm* wash.

In many modern installations architects are using 48 mm [2″] o.d. (standard bar size) piping for hand rails, supports, and the like, on which lighting designers can hang lanterns or, alternatively, anchor scaffolding. In one theatre I've worked, guard rails on the fly floor were aligned so that I could drop vertical bars to just above head height onstage; these replaced booms anchored into the stage. Access on and off stage was greatly improved, and accidental damage to the boom's focus was reduced; the rigging rate was also vastly improved. Other theatres include transverse bars, which are winched just outside the line of the counterweighted barrels; they are used for additional masking and to support lighting ladders. (See Fig. 10.9.) Keep tabs on any similar innovations to determine whether

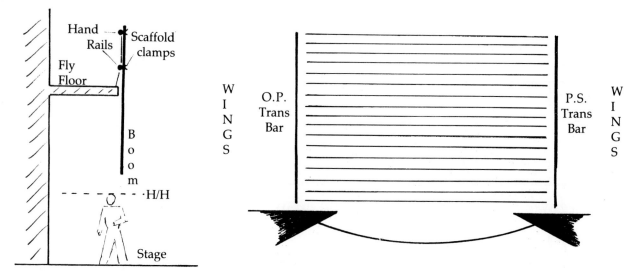

Figure 10.9
Side Lighting Positions.

they're of use as one-use or permanent additions to your usual facility.

Don't forget the unconventional solution. Figure 10.10 illustrates a scene from *The Elephant Man* produced in three-quarter-round. You wish to comment about the fitness of the Doctor to supervise the Elephant Man. In this scene the Doctor is showing slides of Merrick, who stands beside the images; you wish to cast a shadow of the Doctor to suggest that the audience make a comparison. The only possible position for the lantern—in the middle of the audience entrance—would be against regulations and common sense! But how about securing a shatterproof mirror against the wall without causing obstruction and then secrete a lantern under the seating to reflect light onstage? It's this type of uncon-

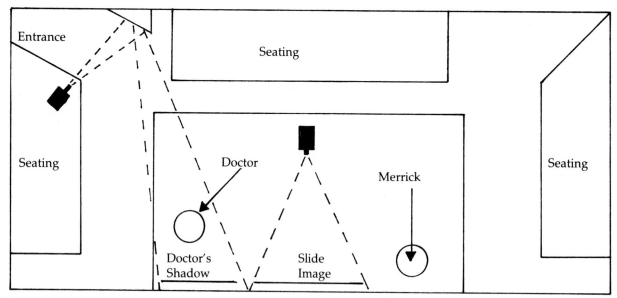

Figure 10.10
Using Mirrors to Obtain Correct Angles.

ventional solution that you'll want to investigate. Many of these solutions are born of expedience and are not entirely satisfactory— even a high budget can't ensure complete satisfaction—but they will improve your chances of obtaining exactly what you need.

Now it's time to study the stock list supplied by the head electrician. Have it alongside as you extract from your 1:100 [⅛":1'] sketches a list of the stock you would like; then compare the two. You will end up with something similar to the table shown.

Lantern	Stock	Required	Over/Under		
STRAND Pat 743 (1 kw Fresnel)	15	16	−1	)	
STRAND Pat 223 (1 kw Fresnel)	7	Nil	+7	)	−3
CCT Starlette (1 kw Fresnel)	22	31	−9	)	
STRAND Pat 123 (500 w Fresnel)	30	32	−2	)	
STRAND Pat 45 (500 w Fresnel)	8	Nil	+8	)	+4
CCT Minuette (500 w Fresnel)	15	17	−2	)	
STRAND Pat 263 (1 kw Profile)	30	34	−4	)	
STRAND Pat 264 (1 kw Bifocal)	8	10	−2	)	−6
STRAND Pat 23 MK 2 (500 w Profile)	22	26	−4	)	
STRAND Pat 23 MK 1 (500 w Profile)	17	5	+12	)	
CCT Minuette Zoom (500 w Profile)	8	6	+2	)	+8
BERKEY 30/40/50 (500 w Profile)	4	6	−2	)	
CCT Minuette Pebble-convex (500 w)	6	4	+2	)	+2

At first glance it seems that you must drastically cut your requirements; your desire to fulfill every requirement of the show, together with your studied ignorance of the stock, has brought you to the point where you must either cut or indulge in an expensive hire budget. Not true! Group the lanterns by type (such as 1 kw Fresnel, 500 watt profile [ellipsoidal]) to obtain a better guide to the difficulties involved. In the table there is a reasonable balance, but obviously a power differential between the Fresnels (down three 1 kws, up four 500 watts). There are, however, two spare 500-watt pebble-convex units that may supplement them. There is a drastic shortage in the 1 kw profiles [ellipsoidals] but a surplus in the 500 watts.

First, be sure that you know precisely the difference between the lanterns. This stock is typical of what you'd find in most theatres—some new, some middle-aged, and some quite ancient. Until you know precisely each capability, you will be unable to select and compromise with both advantages and disadvantages in mind. Take the 1 kw Fresnels: the only difference between the 223 and the 743 is the lamp base—in all other respects they are the same.

The CCT Starlette does not extend to the same beam width as the STRAND equipment but is fitted with a very efficient barndoor that makes for better control; it appears that the designer was very aware of this and overindulged on Starlettes.

You are assuming that all lamps are tungsten-halogen; if, however, the Pat 223 is fitted with the older tungsten lamp, you must add to your list of differences the colour temperature of the 223s. They will produce a far *warmer light* and are more suited to amber washes than blue.

With the Over/Under figures in mind, go through each circuit sketch to ascertain that the lanterns you selected were appropriate: do you really want a Starlette with its narrower beam, or would a 743/223 be more suitable? At the same time, find those lanterns that allow for flexibility in their choice; these lanterns will enable you to shuffle them about. Compromising a little with them will save you from that worst compromise of all—cutting elements of your vision.

Perhaps you have chosen to highlight with a Minuette Fresnel, which would be better handled by the pebble-convex; or you've used Starlettes to create a broad amber wash that might be better done by Pat 223s. Maybe you've used Pat 123s to highlight items of the set, although that could be done quite well by Pat 45s. In this way the Fresnels may balance out so that you are missing three Starlettes but have six Pat 45s in hand. This is a balance in power, though the Pat 45 is far less efficient and has a narrower beam spread than the Starlette does. You could never expect one group to replace the other. In a pinch, you could shuffle the Pat 123s and 45s to obtain four spare 123s and two 45s; these may be more useful to replace the least important purpose you intended for the Starlettes. Try shuffling around the profile [ellipsoidal] lanterns yourself; quickly summing up, you find that you may be forced to cut two lanterns. Finally, after a lot of juggling and jiggling, you shape the lantern requirements to fit within the stock (with, perhaps, a minor hire/rental budget). It's essential to include all the changes on your in-

Continuing the Breakdown: Choice and Placement of Lanterns [Instruments]

dividual circuit sketches so that they are a true record of what you intend.

Section 9.11 suggested that leftover lanterns might be used with spare dimmers to cover doubts; now that you know what stock remains, detail these circuits. If you still have lanterns available, check if any circuits might benefit from added lanterns, as was suggested in section 10.9. Don't rig lanterns regardless of their usefulness, but you do want to harness every dimension possible in the service of the show.

A circuit consisting of only one lantern increases the risks of failure in performance enormously; if it's crucial to the show, add a circuit as backup, or, at least, add a second lantern on the same circuit. If one blows, you can quickly change the fuse and restore light with the second lantern.

Keep in mind that it's advisable to keep one spare lantern of every type to cannibalise or to use as a replacement during production week, when you don't have time for maintenance. When considering the Stock List in section 10.11 I ignored this completely. A spare is ideal; but, should the show demand, you sacrifice this convenience. Assess the stock's reliability; ask the head electrician for advice on whether it's imperative to keep spares, and make a decision on the strength of that opinion.

10.13 Check Solutions against the Theatre

Before you finalise solutions, return to the theatre and compare your sketches to the real thing. . . . but don't kick yourself too hard! Such a check will bring to light mistakes and fine adjustments; you should congratulate yourself if they are relatively minor. I remember one show where I forgot how the auditorium chandelier obstructed lanterns on the front-of-house bridge if they were used across stage. It's easy for these mistakes to slip through; and, unless you check the theatre itself, you may find the focus session (see chapter 18) chaotic.

No problems with lantern placement may appear, but try to image how those lights will feel to both performers and audience. Sometimes on paper the circuit appears to work; but, once you are on the stage imagining the end results (the angles, shadows, light and shade), you can feel warnings of problems to come. It's gut reaction time again, and the theatre will tell you better than paper what is going to work.

10.14 Check of Patching and Bar Weights

Having chosen the lanterns for your circuits, you still need to check two areas before you can say the rig is feasible. For each of the flown bars [pipes] (particularly if they are counterweighted), extract a rough total weight of the lanterns and cabling to compare with maximum loads supplied by the head mechanist/flyman. If it's at all critical, you must include fine details such as fittings and accessories (such as hookclamps and barndoors). Manufacturer's specifications sheets include all necessary lantern information, but estimating cable weight is often difficult. When in doubt, overestimate to ensure you aren't forced to cut lanterns during the rig in order to lift the bar out. If you're using a winch, make sure the total weight falls within its safe working load; generally, the winches you'll be using are 0.5 tonne [½ ton], but you must be certain before you put that amount of weight over the heads of other human beings.

You must also ensure that the patching arrangements are sufficient for the rig you intend; for each position there should be at least one outlet from the patch panel for every circuit, or part thereof. Section 15.12 will discuss the process in detail, but, for the moment, consider an example. The No. 1 bridge will carry thirty-five lanterns—that's beside the point! You need to know the number of circuits those lanterns represent—let's say sixteen. Ensure there are at least sixteen outlets available; if there are more, you need less cabling between lanterns on the bridge, since the excess outlets can be used to run each lantern to the patch panel where they can be grouped/circuited as required. If, however, there are fewer, you could be in trouble. For some positions it is feasible to run extra lines direct to the patch panel or to utilise outlets from nearby (such as box boom spares run to front-of-house bridge). To run extra lines from front-of-house to the panel (assuming fire regulations permit) will be expensive in labour, and it may be more cost-effective to cut circuits or to reposition them where there are spare outlets. As was mentioned before, sometimes shows are designed with no regard for the theatre; from a lighting viewpoint, a rig requiring extensive alteration of the patching system is the equivalent. You may have no choice in a poorly designed facility, but you must be certain that what you ask is within reason. The early warning you receive from this process may enable you to install looms [cable runs] prior to the rig.

Leave the allocation of outlets to circuits until the 1:25 [½":1'] plan is complete; only then will you be sure of precise lantern positioning and be able to gauge the most effective solutions. Some, however, may be obvious and can be noted on the circuit sketch as a reminder for that later process (see section 15.12).

10.15 Colour Choice

Now consider each circuit for colour; again, use as an example the centre acting area in Figure 10.7. You've noted that, during the experimentation on the model, colours 3 (straw) and 4 (light amber) are effective and also that you are hoping to maintain an emphasis around centre. You need to have performers on the extremities of the area (that is, either side and upstage) be less dominant than a performer centrally located. Colour choice will aid this impression if you select straw for the central lanterns on the FOH bar and light amber for the remainder. Note your colour choice beside each lantern, and list total colour requirements for the circuit.

Complete the process for each circuit and extract a summary. Again, you have early warning of colour requirements (from stock or by order) and can begin the boring task of cutting colour as early as possible.

This section has considered colour only briefly, as at this time you are concerned simply with the way in which it is associated with the 1:100 [⅛":1'] sketch approach. A detailed discussion is left until chapter 13, when you will have a better appreciation of the theory and principles involved.

10.16 In Summation

You have quickly summarised the process of completing the breakdown, defining every component needed to achieve the rig. You know that everything is feasible from the viewpoint of both stock and facilities. You have early warning of colour requirements and additional fittings, but, most important, you retain a high degree of flexibility. If the need arises, you can compromise to incorporate extra demands without destroying labour-intensive scale-plans. Further, the process of creating your 1:25 plan [1:24 plot] is now merely a matter of compiling information you already hold and will be considerably faster and less traumatic. Very few people, apart from yourself, need access to this information; of course, extracts detailing hire/rental stock, colour, extra patching outlets, and bars should be passed to your staff as early as possible, but they would have difficulty deciphering your 1:100 [⅛":1'] sketches; hence, there is no need for publication in any form.

CHAPTER 11

Properties of Light: Lanterns [Instruments] and Performance

This chapter is background to the work being done during the third week before opening night; it's part of the theory behind processes covered in chapters 9 and 10. It is intended as a re-vision of light, its properties, how it is produced, and how lanterns [instruments] harness it usefully. As you will need further study for a full understanding, you may want to consult the Bibliography, in particular a delightful volume entitled *The Light Fantastic* by P. Mason.

11.2 State of the Art

Not so long ago, I had the pleasure of handling a beautifully designed touring lantern. It was relatively safe to handle, had a near-point source of light that remained in a fixed position with respect to the reflector, and possessed beam-shaping barndoors that folded away into the housing. It was well ventilated, carried its own supporting hook, was well balanced, and telescoped to a cylinder 40 mm [1½"] in diameter and 100 mm [4"] long. It was state-of-the-art engineering—though the machine was over a hundred years old. (See Fig. 11.1.)

The term *state-of-the-art* is as important now as ever. We have reached a stage in the development of both equipment and personnel where the profession is able to take time to refine its craft, to redevelop outmoded equipment, and to demand performance standards never before known. Yet the basic principles of today are little different from those used in the state-of-the-art touring candle. This chapter will concentrate on principles and leave you to investigate the ranges of lantern [instrument, luminaire] currently available. With these principles clearly understood, you should be able to comprehend lantern types quickly and to gather some appreciation of how useful they will be. Investigate each of the ranges from an ever-increasing number of manufacturers bidding for your dollar; competition between them is fierce and very healthy.

11.3 Properties of Light

The argument is always there: "What is light?" Is it corpuscular or wave form? Can it bend? The frontiers of knowledge continue to expand, but, from your viewpoint, only a basic understanding is

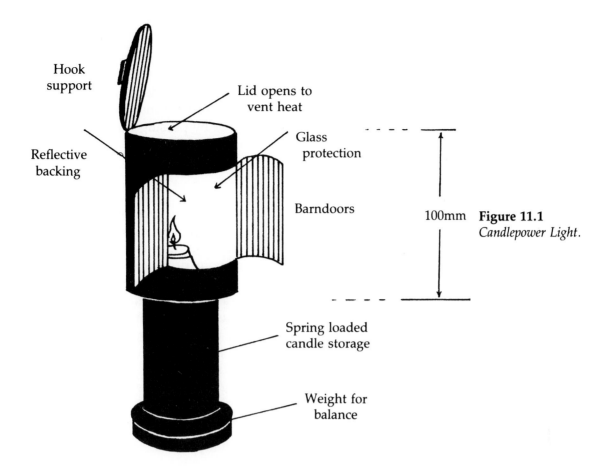

Hook
support

Lid opens to
vent heat

Reflective
backing

Glass
protection

Barndoors

100mm **Figure 11.1**
Candlepower Light.

Spring loaded
candle storage

Weight for
balance

required to carry out your responsibilities efficiently; you may leave
the frontiers to Einstein and his modern-day counterparts.

Light is that narrow element of the electromagnetic spectrum
(wavelength 730 to 380 nanometers) that is perceived by the human
eye (other animals perceive differing spectra). (See Fig. 11.2.) It
travels in straight lines at a speed near 300,000 km per second [186,000
miles per second] and does not require a medium in which to travel.
Sections 11.3.1 to 11.3.4 note some further properties that amplify
this brief definition.

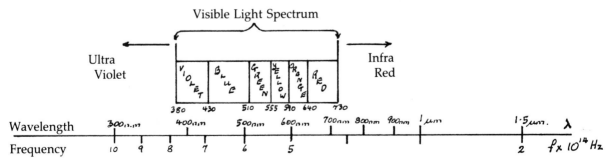

Figure 11.2
Light Spectrum.

11.3.1 Polarity

Generally, light can be considered to be bipolar; in other words, the radiation may be represented as two waves at 90 degrees to each other. (See Fig. 11.3) Rarely does the lighting department need to consider the polarity of light, though audio/visual technicians use polarisation (the removal of one vector by passing through quinine crystals) most effectively (see chapter 14).

11.3.2 Spectrum

Chapter 13 will investigate colour and how it is associated with wavelength. On the low energy end of the spectrum (730+ nanometers) is infrared radiation, which is perceived as heat; it's this unwanted heat that causes many of your problems, such as burnt fingers, burn-out colour, and melted insulation. Knowledge of how to separate heat from light is expanding (for example, dichroic reflectors), but huge amounts of heat usually go along with the light you intend to use. On the energetic end of the spectrum (380-nanometers) is ultraviolet, which is of use as special effects lighting—but remember that this is the energetic end of the spectrum. Ultraviolet light of sufficient power or lengthy exposure may be dangerous to the human eye.

11.3.3 Refraction, Reflection, and Absorption

When light hits any object, it may be reflected, refracted, or absorbed; generally, a little of each occurs. As light passes from one medium to another of different density, it will bend in a predictable fashion, depending upon the angle at which it enters and the re-

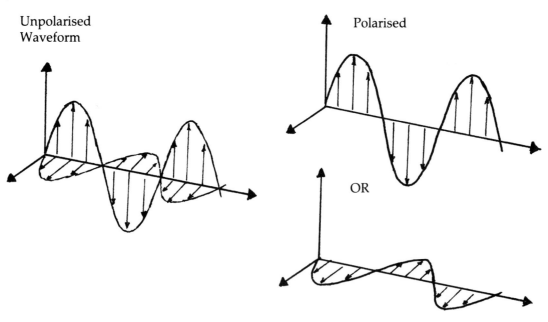

Figure 11.3
Electromagnetic Waveform.

fractive index of the medium. This is known as refraction and is the basis for all our lens systems.

Those surfaces that reflect most and absorb least are a means of changing the direction of light in a predictable way. Figure 11.4 illustrates both refracted and reflected light, together with the law of reflection: the angle of incidence (i) must always equal the angle of reflection (r). It's also interesting to note that, in the process of reflection, light is polarised. You will be studying reflectors in more detail later, but, for the time being, you should note that your lanterns [instruments] generally use spherical, parabolic, or ellipsoidal reflectors.

11.3.4 Inverse Square Law

This law states that the intensity of light on a given area varies inversely with the square of the distance from a point source of light. In other words, if you hold your palm up to an unassisted source of light (bare lamp) at one metre distant, then move your hand to three metres distant, the amount of light on your palm will reduce to one-ninth.

11.4 How Is Light Produced?

Living plants and solar power verify that light is energy; and, since energy cannot be created or destroyed (a basic law of physics), you must expend energy to create light for theatrical purposes—along with the associated heat! It's an inefficient process, a fact highlighted for me during recent consultation with air-conditioning engineers. The cooling capacity demanded for a quite small theatre was enor-

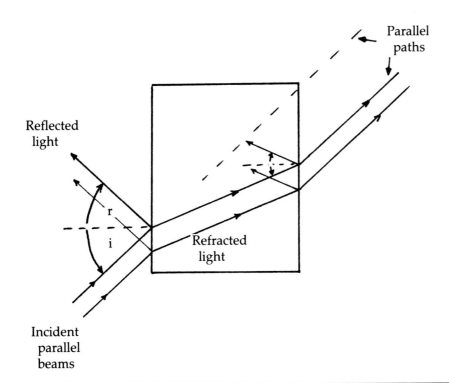

Figure 11.4
Refraction and Reflection.

mous—not because of the audience but because of the heat generated by lighting units. All of it was wasted and required more energy to remove it.

In most theatrical applications the light source is either an arc or an incandescent filament. Simply, an arc is a discharge (spark) of electrons between two electrodes; in the process a great deal of heat and light is generated. In the past (largely in follow-spots) electrodes were carbon sheathed in copper; they were consumed in the process and needed to be continually fed. More recently, discharge lamps have been developed in which the arc is struck inside a quartz envelope by a high triggering voltage and maintained without the electrodes being consumed. Arc light cannot be dimmed by electrical means and needs mechanical devices for this.

Usually, you will create light by incandescence, using a filament. This is a long piece of tungsten wire whose electrical resistance is such that the passage of current heats it sufficiently to produce light (not the full spectrum, but close enough). However, most optical systems are based upon a point source, and Figure 11.5 shows how the long piece of tungsten wire is coiled and arranged to approximate a point. Note the increased efficiency of recently developed biplane configurations, which compact the source of light even further. Even so, the device is not perfect; as you raise the temperature to produce nearer the complete spectrum, tungsten evaporates in the same way that water produces steam. This weakens the fil-

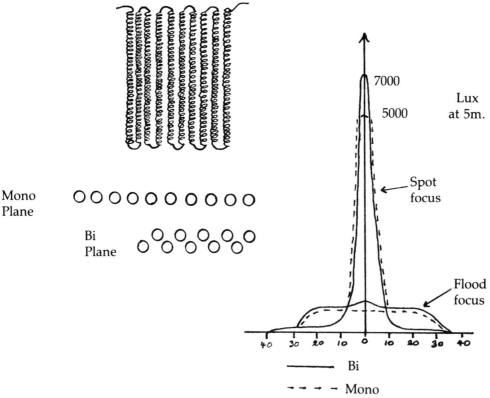

Figure 11.5
Filament Configurations.

Properties of Light: Lanterns [Instruments] and Performance

ament; and, as the vapour settles, it clouds the envelope, thus greatly reducing the light output and life of the lamp.

More recent developments have produced the tungsten-halogen lamp, which uses a quartz envelope to contain a halide gas; it does not stop filament evaporation but prevents the gaseous tungsten from settling anywhere but back on the filament. This greatly increases the life of the lamp and allows for higher temperatures; it also increases the price. You must never touch the envelope with bare hands, since oils on your fingers cause the quartz envelope to deteriorate rapidly.

There is no space here to discuss dimmers and how they operate. That, too, must be an area for your further investigation, at the end of which you should be able to differentiate between the various control systems and types (resistance, saturable reactor, auto transformer, triac, SCR, and so on) and to understand the advantages and disadvantages of each.

Some recent technology will interest you—that of low-voltage lanterns. (See *Theatre Crafts* [July and August/September 1985] in the Bibliography). A variant of Ohm's law states: watts = volts × amps. If you decide to maintain the same power (watts) but reduce the voltage (as low as 6 volts), the current (amperage) must increase. This demands shorter, more robust filaments with less heat-radiating surface; this, in turn, allows for higher temperatures or, alternatively, the same light output for less power. Some manufacturers are claiming a 1,000 watt performance from a 400 watt low-voltage source with (a) improved optics because of the closer-to-point source filament; (b) improved colour-temperature; and (c) improved lamp-life because of the more robust filament. Many lighting designers use low-voltage sources for one-use-only special effects, but the recent innovation of a reliable electronic transformer (instead of the heavy wire-wound devices) has enabled lantern manufacturers to develop a new generation of lanterns (see section 9.3).

11.5 Beam Spread Definitions

Four definitions (sections 11.5.1 to 11.5.4) will help you to define and analyze the performance of any lantern.

11.5.1 Peak

Defined as the point in a beam at which the light intensity is maximum, peak is known colloquially as the "hot-spot." Usually this coincides with the optical axis of the lantern, that is, the line joining the centre of the reflector, source, and lens system.

11.5.2 Half-peak [Beam] Angle

This is the angle subtending that area of light in which the intensity does not fall below one half of the peak. The human eye is not a good light meter; it has difficulty discerning the difference between peak and half-peak and would view that area as an even distribution.

11.5.3 Tenth-peak [Field] Angle

This angle subtends that area of light in which the intensity does not fall below one-tenth of the peak. This is an intensity differential that the human eye can certainly discern, and most perceive this as the angle at which the light appears to drop off rapidly.

11.5.4 Cut-off Angle

This is the angle beyond which intensity drops to less than 1 percent of peak.

From Figure 11.6 you can see the potential for the four definitions above to define and compare lanterns. Example: A hard-edged lantern with an even field should, by definition, have all three angles (half, tenth, and cut-off) close together, whereas in a flood they will be widely separated, the cut-off angle approaching 180 degrees. Section 10.8 showed how this information is used when selecting lanterns but noted that terminology used by various manufacturers is frequently at variance. Figure 11.6 includes a sampling: generally, half-peak, beam, and spot spread are synonymous, while tenth-peak, field, and flood spread are also interchangeable; cut-off is rarely mentioned. Don't become confused by a term such as *lux*; it measures light intensity and may occasionally be useful to compare similar units from different ranges. Keeping these definitions in mind, you are able to trace the development of lighting units.

11.6 Floodlights

To understand floodlights, think of the time when lighting units were most basic. Assume a point-size source of light in all examples, though you know that is rarely achieved. Now place a single source between the audience and stage so that light falls onto the face of the performer, as in Figure 11.7. The point source behaves according to the inverse square law and propagates light in all directions; to light the performer more brightly it should be as close as possible to her—hence the footlights—but, even so, some light will fall directly into the eyes of the audience. This is anathema; the eye tends towards the brightest object in its field, the light—not the performer. It's alarming how frequently lighting designers ignore this premise.

You need some means of containing the light falling upon the audience so that it does not interfere with their vision of the stage. In Figure 11.7 the dotted line represents a simple mask that absorbs the light falling upon it (matte black surface), converting it to heat. If you are an efficiency-minded individual, this waste of light is untenable. If your mask were changed to a reflective surface, that would improve matters; but you can go a step further and replace it with a spherical reflector positioned so that your point source is at the focal point (centre of the sphere). See Figure 11.8. You use the laws of reflection to turn the previously wasted light back onto the focal point, effectively doubling the output on the performer. You have created the most basic theatre lighting unit—the flood-

BEAM ANGLES

Generally:
    Floods—all angles widely
        distributed.
    Fresnels—Tenth and Cut-off
        angles closer.
    Profile—Half and Tenth
        angles close.

500w Halogen PROFILE.
STRAND Pat 23

Cut-off angle 30° max.
Half peak angle 17° max.

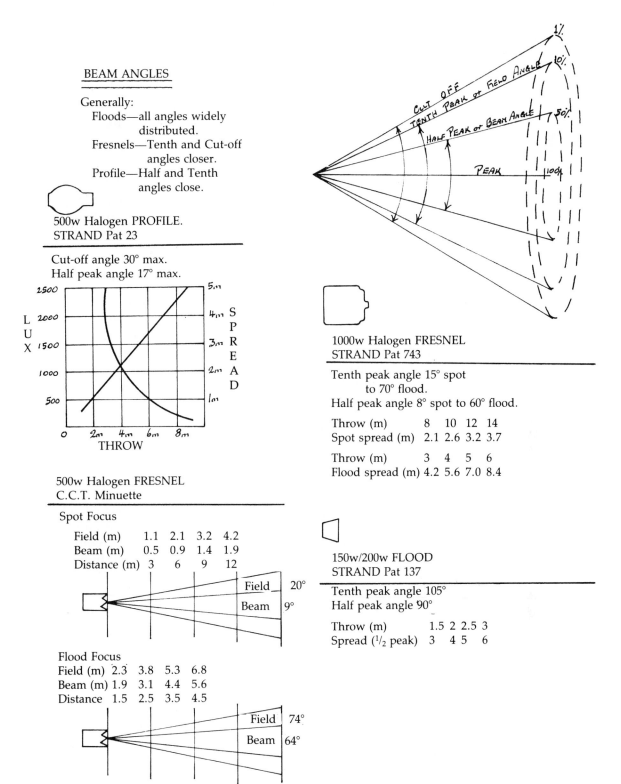

500w Halogen FRESNEL
C.C.T. Minuette

Spot Focus

Field (m)	1.1	2.1	3.2	4.2
Beam (m)	0.5	0.9	1.4	1.9
Distance (m)	3	6	9	12

Field 20°
Beam 9°

Flood Focus

Field (m)	2.3	3.8	5.3	6.8
Beam (m)	1.9	3.1	4.4	5.6
Distance	1.5	2.5	3.5	4.5

Field 74°
Beam 64°

1000w Halogen FRESNEL
STRAND Pat 743

Tenth peak angle 15° spot
    to 70° flood.
Half peak angle 8° spot to 60° flood.

| Throw (m) | 8 | 10 | 12 | 14 |
| Spot spread (m) | 2.1 | 2.6 | 3.2 | 3.7 |

| Throw (m) | 3 | 4 | 5 | 6 |
| Flood spread (m) | 4.2 | 5.6 | 7.0 | 8.4 |

150w/200w FLOOD
STRAND Pat 137

Tenth peak angle 105°
Half peak angle 90°

| Throw (m) | 1.5 | 2 | 2.5 | 3 |
| Spread (½ peak) | 3 | 4 | 5 | 6 |

Figure 11.6
Definition of Beam Angles.

light. For many centuries this has been a basic workhorse and has remained virtually unchanged.

    The precise half-peak, tenth-peak, and cut-off angles depend upon the source, the efficiency of the reflector, and unit construction. With its angles widely dispersed (the half-peak perhaps at 90 degrees and the cut-off near 180 degrees) a floodlight is difficult to control and almost impossible to shape; Figure 11.9 shows two at-

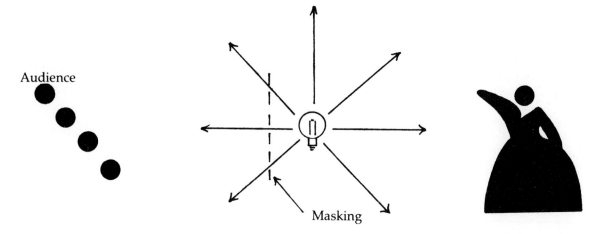

Audience

Masking

Figure 11.7
Bare Bulb Source.

tempts. The first does virtually nothing to control the beam spread and succeeds only in reducing intensity. The second is somewhat more successful, though inefficient and cumbersome; imagine the tube length required to form a head-and-shoulders spot.

Before leaving floodlights, consider their most frequent use, cyclorama lighting, and some recent developments. Figure 11.10 illustrates the way floods have been used to light a cloth or cyclorama. The inverse square law applies, and the centre of the cyclorama is sufficiently distant from both lanterns to make it the dullest point on the surface. Generally, though, you need to have the centre be more dominant. (Even if you floodlight from booms on either side of the cyclorama, you are in exactly the same situation.) Only recently have ranges included a cyclorama unit fitted with a reflector that redistributes light to produce an even field from a given distance. See Figure 11.11. These lanterns generally require an increased distance between the lantern and cyclorama (though it may be as low as 1.5m [5'] to create a 5m [16½'] even field).

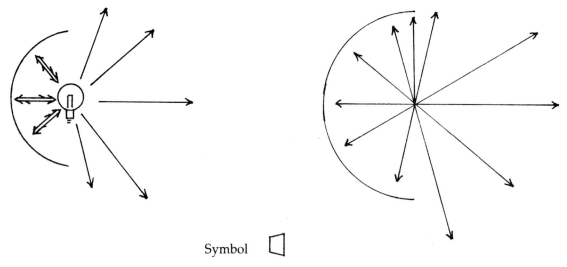

Symbol

Figure 11.8
Hemispheric Reflector.

Properties of Light: Lanterns [Instruments] and Performance

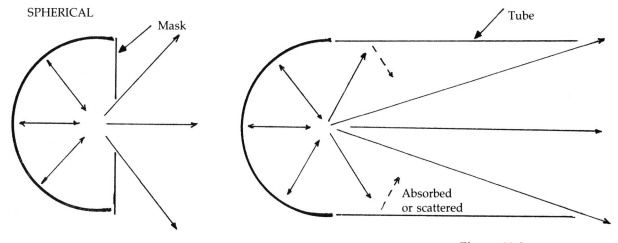

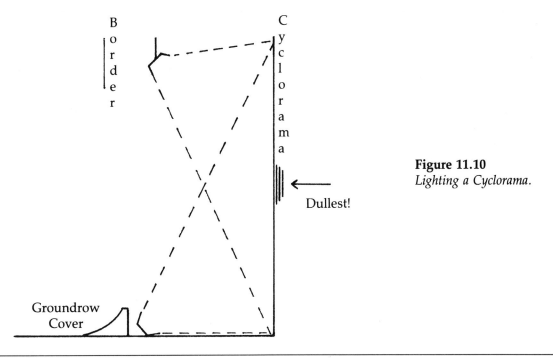

Figure 11.9
Control of a Floodlight.

11.7 Beamlights

An early method to control the spread of light used a reflector shape known in geometry as the parabola. If a point source is placed at the geometric focal point, the reflector produces a parallel beam of light no bigger than the reflector itself (for example, wartime searchlights).

In the first example (Fig. 11.12) not all the light is collected by the reflector; some escapes, creating a zone of uncontrolled light that will affect your tenth-peak and cut-off angles. The second includes a small spherical reflector designed to redirect this light back onto the point source and thus to the parabolic reflector; however, there is a dull spot at the peak of the beam, the shadow of the hemispheric reflector. Until now you have always placed your source

Figure 11.10
Lighting a Cyclorama.

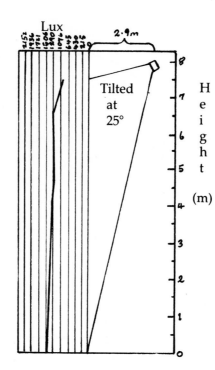

Lux

2.9m

Tilted
at
25°

Height (m)

8
7
6
5
4
3
2
1
0

Distribution of light
for 1250w units
spaced (centre to
centre) at 2.5m
intervals.

Figure 11.11
*Performance Specifications of
Cyclorama Units.*

at the focal point of the reflector; in Figure 11.13 you see what
happens when it is varied to either side. Further beam shaping can
be achieved with barndoors (see Figure 11.16).

The variable beamlight has greatly improved control over the
floodlight and, particularly in European theatre, it's very popular.
In the form of sealed-unit fixed-beam PAR lanterns, the rock concert
lighting industry use them almost exclusively; they are relatively

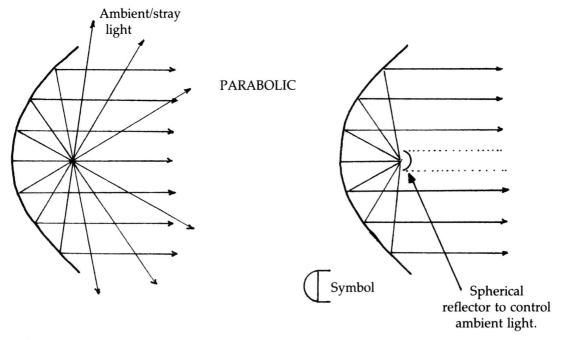

Ambient/stray
light

PARABOLIC

Symbol

Spherical
reflector to control
ambient light.

Figure 11.12
Parabolic Reflector.

Properties of Light: Lanterns [Instruments] and Performance

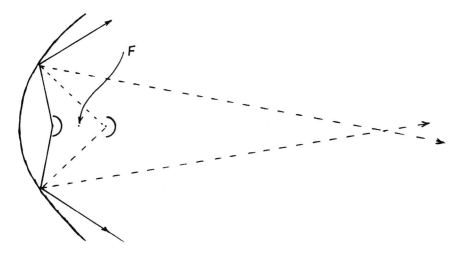

Figure 11.13
Shifting Source from Focus of Parabolic Reflector.

cheap, light, and very robust, which makes them suitable for touring. The fixed, slightly oval-shaped beam of PAR lanterns reduces their usefulness for many theatrical productions; however, there is nothing to prevent you from using them, if they suit your purpose.

11.8 Spotlights—Plano-convex, Pebble-convex, and Fresnel

The poor shaping capabilities and unevenness of field in a beamlight caused our forefathers to look further. Return to the tubed version of the floodlight illustrated in Figure 11.9 and introduce a plano-convex lens as a means of concentrating the light, as in Figure 11.14. If the point source is at the focal point of both the reflector and the lens, this instrument will produce a parallel beam of light similar to a beamlight. There are other similarities: shift *both* the reflector and

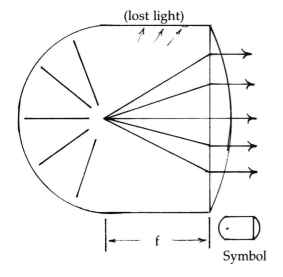

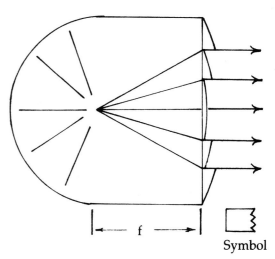

Figure 11.14
Plano-convex and Fresnel Spotlights.

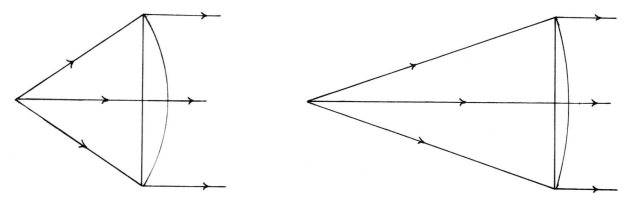

Figure 11.15
Differing Focal Length Lenses.

the source of light (keeping their relationship constant) outside the focal point of the lens, and the beam is brought to focus; shorten the distance, and you spread the beam. Looking good! But examine the two lenses illustrated in Figure 11.15.

To shorten the lantern you need a very thick plano-convex lens, but the result of enormous heat on flaws in thick glass is, frequently, shattered lenses. All lanterns should be fitted with a safety grill; if not, be sure to fit a crossed-wire colour-frame even if you don't intend using colour. This damage is more likely to occur when the lantern is focused near-vertical, the atmospheric temperature is cold, the lantern has not been warmed through, and the intensity of the lamp is high. Our forefathers opted for thinner lenses and a longer housing, which made the lanterns clumsy and inefficient; they quickly lost popularity after about 1920.

The 1980s, however, are seeing a resurgence of plano-convex lanterns, since modern materials enable us to cool the lanterns better and to manufacture heat-tempered lenses. The lanterns currently available are a little longer than an equivalently powered Fresnel lantern with similar beam spread performance but with half-peak, tenth-peak, and cut-off figures very close to a profile [ellipsoidal]. The shaping difficulty remains, but with these performance figures a barndoor produces clean lines almost as defined as that produced by a shutter in an ellipsoidal. Figure 11.16 illustrates a further innovation, a barndoor on which the individual doors rotate in addition to the whole housing.

Our forefathers tried to solve the lens thickness problems by using two variations—the stepped lens and the Fresnel lens. See Figure 11.17. It's not the amount of glass in a lens that bends light, but the angle between the surfaces. Stepped and Fresnel lenses maintain these angles but remove the bulk of glass to reduce weight and thickness. Unfortunately, both variants introduce reflecting surfaces that distort the optical performance of the lens, and its cut-off angle, in particular, is increased. This was most apparent in the stepped lens, and it was quickly discarded. A solution was sought with the Fresnel by painting the return surfaces matte black, which did little more than reduce light output. To hell with it, said our forefathers; since we have spill, let's make a feature of it, stipple the plane surface of the lens, and create a soft spot with wide beam variation. This is the form taken by most Fresnel lanterns in use

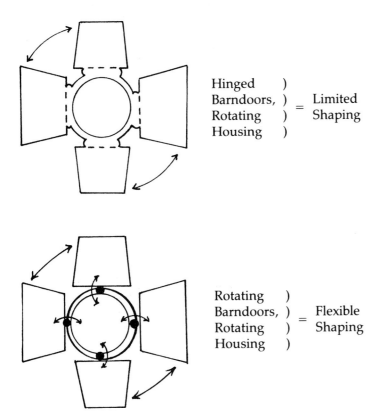

Hinged)
Barndoors,) _ Limited
Rotating) ‾ Shaping
Housing)

Rotating)
Barndoors,) _ Flexible
Rotating) ‾ Shaping
Housing)

Figure 11.16
Types of Barndoors.

today. Shaping is still a problem; barndoors have only a limited effect with performance figures so widely spread. Hence, these lanterns are extensively used onstage where the spill is contained within the proscenium and often form acting areas and washes of colour. Recently, there has been a resurgence of the pebble- or prism-convex lens. It's nothing more than a plano-convex with a stippled plano surface (see Figure 11.17) and is halfway between the Fresnel and the plano-convex lanterns both in performance and difficulties. It has wide beam variation but retains a closer relationship between

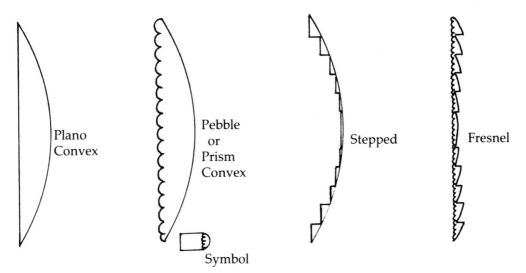

Plano Convex

Pebble or Prism Convex

Symbol

Stepped

Fresnel

Figure 11.17
Lens Types.

half-peak and tenth-peak angles than the Fresnel does; because of the stipple, the cut-off angle is still wide and a barndoor may be fitted to control spill. Barndoors also shape the beam effectively, but the lantern is often used as a highlight where shaping is less important.

This segment has covered three important lanterns, two of which have only recently returned to the range. In the past they would have been recommended for onstage use only, but particularly the plano-convex is useful front-of-house, where a wide beam variation is needed; for example, short-throw orchestra bar positions. Investigate these lanterns fully before you allocate your new-equipment budget for next year.

11.9 Profile [Ellipsoidal] Spots

Up to this point you still have not solved your shaping problems. The device required is yet another type of reflector—the ellipsoidal. See Figure 11.18. This reflector has two focal points; given a point source at the first, you can form an image of that source at the second. If you introduce a lens at a distance equal to its focal length from f_2, you can project any image formed at f_2. Herein lies the enormous potential of this lantern; you are able to shape an image within the lantern. If you introduce light-shaping equipment at any point other than f_2 (known as the gate), you will be out of the focal plane and will produce a soft image; that's a feature used in bifocal lanterns. (See Figure 11.19.)

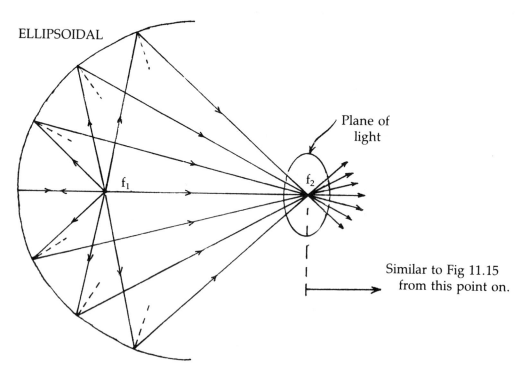

Figure 11.18
Ellipsoidal Reflector.

Properties of Light: Lanterns [Instruments] and Performance

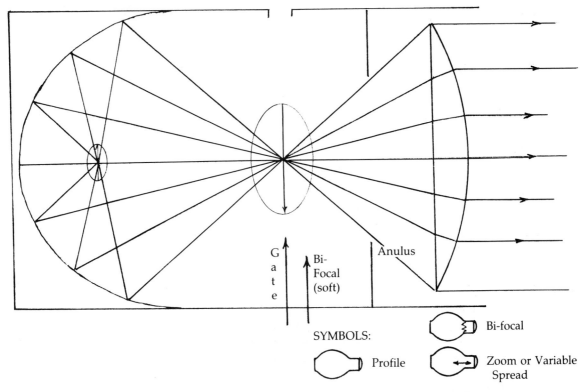

SYMBOLS:

Profile

Bi-focal

Zoom or Variable Spread

Figure 11.19
Profile Lantern.

The single lens may be replaced with a system of lenses that further increases the flexibility of lanterns. In Figure 10.8 you saw how wide lanterns were created by introducing a second lens; a lens system makes a design feature of this. A variable system has two lenses free to move in a track (zoom lanterns), while others adjust to certain fixed positions (multiple-angle lanterns). To allow a beam variation similar to a Fresnel lantern's, the system would be quite complex—and expensive. Manufacturers have either created a range of lanterns of different beam ranges or produced a single housing with a choice of lens system; that is, 22–40 degrees, 15–32 degrees, 11–23 degrees, and 9–20 degrees. (Note that performance figures are quoted for *clean* lenses and reflectors. Each speck of dirt on a lens acts as a point source of light radiating equally in all directions, and a dirty lantern will create a beam so soft it could be produced by a Fresnel.)

Before you read about beam-shaping equipment, study the list of temperatures below.

92°C [198°F] Envelope wall temperature 100 w B.C. lamp

130°C [266°F] Acetate filters melt.

140°C [284°F] Polyester filters melt.

160°C [320°F] Polycarbonate filters melt.

590°C [1094°F] Usual exterior wall temperature 1 kw tungsten-halogen lamp.

720°C [1328°F] Gate temperature 1 kw tungsten-halogen lamp.

860°C [1580°F] Gate temperature 2 kw tungsten-halogen lamp.

2550°C [4622°F] Filament temperature 750 w tungsten-halogen lamp.

Note: All temperatures are approximations and are intended only for use as a guide.

The temperature at the gate of a 1 kw is far above the melting point of all colour filters and is sufficiently high to melt pure aluminium (M.P. 660°C/1220°F).

These figures are intended to emphasise the care you must take when introducing devices into the gate—you must know beforehand that it will not melt or burn. Now look at a few devices (11.9.1 to 11.9.7) that may be introduced into the gate successfully:

11.9.1 Hard-Edged Shutters

Fitted to most profiles [ellipsoidals] (though some old units are without), shutters are used to trim the beam's edge from top or bottom, left or right. However, since the lantern's optics invert the image, select the reverse shutter to the image adjustment you require. Though most are made of stainless steel, older units used tempered steel, which, of course, rusts. Because of the heat, you are unable to lubricate with anything other than graphite powder—not grease—and it's imperative that shutters receive regular maintenance.

A recent innovation introduced rotatable shutter housings. (In the past they were fixed, thus preventing the lighting designer from creating odd angles.) This innovation allows you to roughly adjust the entire housing to a new alignment, placing the individual shutters in their optimum position. There are varying opinions about the cost effectiveness of this, and it will be interesting to see the degree of acceptance by users. (See Fig. 11.20.)

11.9.2 Soft-Edged Shutters

The soft image is largely achieved by placing the device outside the focal plane, but in most bifocal lanterns this is improved by using shutters with a saw-tooth edge. However, saw-tooth images can be seen around the stage when both the designer and focusser are remiss and focus the lantern so that the image of the soft-edge shutter is projected. (See Fig. 11.20.)

11.9.3 Iris

By means of multiple leaves controlled externally, the iris can be adjusted to vary the size of a circular aperture at the gate. It's an integral part of a follow-spot but is available—at a price—as add-on equipment for the gate of most profiles. (See Fig. 11.20.)

11.9.4 Masks/Gobos

From this point on, the terminology becomes fuzzy; what is a gobo in one house will be recognised as a mask, cookie, or plate in another. They all refer to precut shapes in metal that are inserted into the gate as required. The aperture can be a circle, square, rectangle, or ellipse—any shape desired. (See Fig. 11.20.)

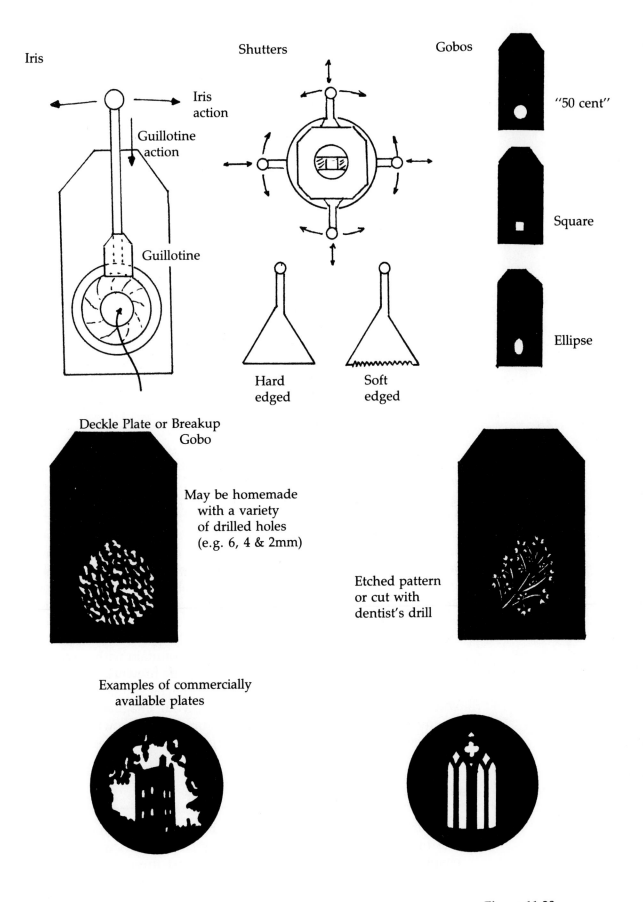

Iris

Iris action

Guillotine action

Guillotine

Shutters

Hard edged

Soft edged

Gobos

"50 cent"

Square

Ellipse

Deckle Plate or Breakup Gobo

May be homemade with a variety of drilled holes (e.g. 6, 4 & 2mm)

Etched pattern or cut with dentist's drill

Examples of commercially available plates

Figure 11.20
Gate Accessories.

11.9.5 Deckle Plates

In most houses this refers to a metal plate in which random holes or shapes vaguely reminiscent of leaves have been cut. They are frequently used for "leafy glade" scenes and may be used just as effectively, if pulled out of focus, to establish a texture. Stainless-steel plates can be purchased or you can etch them yourself (see *Theatre Crafts* September 1978), but ensure that the metal you use is capable of withstanding the temperature at the gate (the more open the design, the more likely it is to survive). For very detailed plates (see Fig. 11.20) I use the equivalent of a dentist's drill; it's very time-consuming, but I find the effects satisfying.

11.9.6 Texture

During experiments my students discovered that glass fibres (not resin-bound fibreglass sheet!) could withstand the temperature at the gate and, if used sparingly, created an interesting texture. Similarly, mica can be used. They both joined the usual list of mesh and grills suitable for creating texture—which is nothing more than varying the quality of light by the mechanical addition of light and shade.

11.9.7 Others

There still exist examples of mica slides our forefathers used very effectively. Two sheets of mica were held in a frame that fits the gate; an image (often storm clouds) was painted in black on the inner surface. I still find them useful but have been unable to discover a heat-resistant ink in the modern range that would enable me to use this method again. Like so many old techniques, the craft has died of neglect. There are now many commercially available images that are cut by laser in stainless steel; the range is enormous and getting bigger, but the price is still high. One recent addition is a group of plates designed to be used with a chaser (most computer desks include a feature which automatically activates circuits in a set sequence) to create the impression of a fountain with cascading water; another sequence creates quite realistic fireworks.

This brief summary of gate-formed images should indicate to you that the potential is limited only by your imagination. Given ingenuity, common sense, and an adventurous spirit, you may greatly enhance your design by the tasteful application of projections.

11.10 Behaviour of Colour in Each Lantern Type

What happens when you introduce a half-colour (say, half red and half open-white) in front of each of the lanterns discussed in this chapter? Figure 11.21 shows that in the first three—flood, beam, and plano-convex—the half-colour will be clearly defined in the image produced by the lanterns, since the rays of light from the lamp cross at no point. In both the pebble-convex and Fresnel,

Properties of Light: Lanterns [Instruments] and Performance

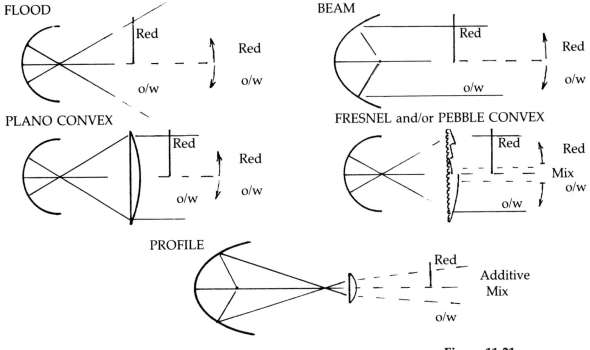

Figure 11.21
Colour Performance in Various Lanterns.

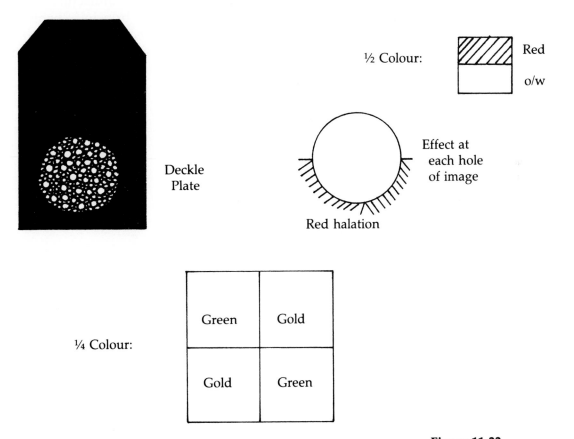

Figure 11.22
Colour Performance with Deckle Plate.

the stippling will cause a degree of mixing between the colours. In the profile, however, you lose all sense of definition; you have an additive mixture of red/white, though you may find a bias on one side. *Note:* These comments assume optical performance that is recognised as an ideal but is not often achieved.

Consider the special example illustrated in Figure 11.22. When you introduce a deckle plate into a profile lantern—particularly if you do not focus too sharply—each hole of the image will have the additive mixture in the centre, but on each edge an inverted image of the colour frame can be detected. Remember, this occurs for each hole in the deckle plate. Imagine the effect of the green and gold quarter-colour (also illustrated in Figure 11.22). That's the way to manufacture leafy glades.

11.11 General Comments

From this brief re-vision of lantern types, two points are obvious. First, there is a great deal more to be learned by handling each lantern type in a performance situation. Second, the range available to you has mushroomed of late with equipment being introduced by many more manufacturers than in the past. There is no way you can keep abreast of all this information without frequently referring to the specification sheets supplied by the manufacturers. It is far more important that you comprehend the principles behind each lantern and intelligently interpret their specifications than to memorise a confusing amount of pattern numbers and performance figures.

CHAPTER 12

Lighting Angles with Some Common Placement Problems

This chapter, the background to work being done during the third week before opening, also refers to processes covered in chapters 9 and 10. Section 10.2 listed the equipment with which you create lighting circuits; this chapter discusses the second variable—angle, both vertical and horizontal. Lighting angle and colour are the most powerful variables available; too often, however, angle is chosen with a view to what is conventional rather than what is suited to the show.

The pressures forcing lighting designers towards conventional solutions are strong. Equipment in the stage-house is largely designed to lift the lanterns overhead, generally the best position from which to light naturalistically. The layout of theatres frequently prevents the use of all the angles available. You may well envy film lighters, who may place lanterns anywhere so long as they're not in shot (view of the camera). Some in the profession use these restrictions as justifying the same solution to every problem. Example: Backlight is often rigged but the lighting designer is unable to explain why; it seems that backlight is part of a standard approach and is included in every rig, whether or not it has purpose.

This chapter will summarise conventional angles, plus other angles available, what they are likely to achieve, and their disadvantages. In this way you will have a broad spectrum from which to select appropriate solutions. The conventional answers are for the guidance of the inexperienced but may be disregarded by the adventuresome as they seek to command the variety of solutions Barry Landy hints at in Figure 12.1.

12.2 Vertical Angle

Section 10.7 discussed the conventional 35–45 degrees (measured from the vertical) that not only lights eyes and lips but also achieves maximum isolation. However, since you have 180 degrees from which to choose, toplight to footlights, you must ascertain what is most appropriate for each moment in the production. Recently an opera director made these comments, which illustrate the point:

> I want the scenes late in act 2 to be very harsh, with lots of shadows and black sockets for eyes and mouths. That late in the piece everyone knows the characters—they're recognised by their voices—so we don't

B. LANDY

Figure 12.1
Effect of Various Angles on Faces.

need to see their faces clearly and can afford to risk clarity for the sake of an emotional statement.

Similarly, footlights are a unique statement that many find synonymous with a particular period of theatre history. They may, therefore, be used to establish that era in the minds of the audience, who suffer the poorly lit faces and weird shadows for the sake of the melodramatic atmosphere.

12.3 Horizontal Angle

As if there weren't enough choice from vertical angle, horizontal placement gives you a further 360 degrees to complicate matters. Assume a single lantern with which to illuminate an actor; your choice of horizontal angle is remarkably limited. It should be on the line between the performer and the centre of mass (the point around which the audience is evenly distributed) at a position giving the desired vertical angle. See Figure 12.2. With a single source some patrons perceive a partial or, perhaps, distorted view, but they are generally in seats for which they have paid a lesser amount. They are not to be ignored, but you must consider this problem from the viewpoint of the majority.

The spatial relationship between the audience and the performer also prohibits other choices. Many angles, particularly from upstage, result in excess light continuing on into the auditorium and causing aggravation. Patrons accept the convention that anything lit is included in the action onstage. When working in-the-round I've had a lantern move (poor rigging!) so that it included a member of the audience; it's interesting to watch the reaction. If the play is light, they'll generally survive, though they are uncomfortable; the heavier the content, the more likely they are to sleep, shift

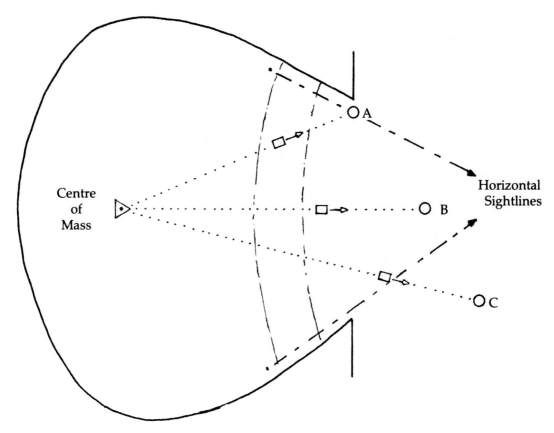

Figure 12.2
Positioning a Single Lantern
Spot.

seats or leave, since they do not wish to be included in the subject matter onstage. The same principle applies whatever the style of presentation: proscenium, thrust, or in-the-round.

Between these extremes there are a myriad of choices which, singly or in combination with other lanterns, give potential for enormous variety of shape and mood.

12.4 Combining Vertical and Horizontal Angles

Throughout the following discussion, assume that the source of light is masked from the audience in some way. A trend away from this convention is introducing a problem that many lighting designers seem to be ignoring, particularly when using back and side lighting. The human eye is drawn to the brightest spot onstage, which in an exposed rig is the lantern itself; this pulls attention away from the object of our lighting—the performer. The influence of the source can be lessened by ensuring that lenses are immaculately clean and by using barndoors; however, you should thoroughly justify an exposed rig in terms of the production concept before considering its use.

12.4.1 Top Lighting—0 Degrees from the Vertical

This is generally achieved from an overhead bar [pipe] using a narrow beam lantern, as in Figure 12.3. Toplight has the advantage of

Lighting Angles with Some Common Placement Problems

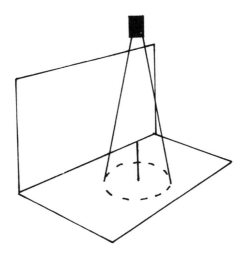

Figure 12.3
Toplight.

giving maximum isolation; it lights only the object intended to the exclusion of all else. It's not good for faces, as Figure 12.4 illustrates, but it's useful for highlighting. Isolation has other potential; given two or three top-lit characters dotted about the stage, audiences will accept that they are removed from each other in time and/or space.

The shadows created by the toplight can be filled with colour, texture, and so on for a further dimension to the character. Take

Figure 12.4
Effect of Toplight.

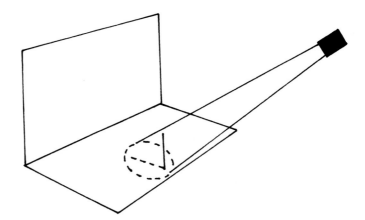

Figure 12.5
35 Degree Frontlight.

Figure 12.4 and imagine the shadows filled with warm textured light or a green wash. You now have two entirely different characters; one may be quite attractive, while the majority of us would avoid the second.

12.4.2 Conventional Angles—40 Degrees from the Vertical

This is the angle considered suitable for "naturalistic" lighting and is generally achieved from overhead or front-of-house positions, as illustrated in Figure 12.5. From front-of-house you achieve reasonable illumination without creating shadows that compete with the artist.

This will depend largely on where you sit; those in the circle [balcony] will be more aware of the shadows than those in the stalls [orchestra seating], but 40 degrees seems the best compromise when all variables are considered. Figure 12.6 illustrates what happens when you shift the source through 90 degrees to a position known as highside; you may use overhead bars, ladders, or booms to achieve this angle. Again, the shadows and quality of illumination are satisfactory but the change in angle adds potential for modeling figures, which is not obvious when the same vertical angle is used from front-of-house. Figure 12.7 illustrates what is meant by modeling. Accentuating the profile and body shape, highside is useful in all styles of theatre—drama, opera, and dance. Highside may also help

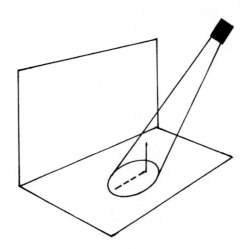

Figure 12.6
35 Degree Sidelight.

B. LANDY.

Figure 12.7
Effect of Highside Light.

solve the problems inherent in flat sidelight (see section 12.4.3). Despite the efficiency of modern lanterns, the inverse square law dictates that objects closer to the source are more dominant than those farther away; that is, flat sidelight tends to pull focus from centre stage. Highside can minimise the difficulties but can't solve them entirely, and Figure 12.8 suggests a further improvement involving lantern power. This solution maintains the dominance of the centre-stage performer by means of intensity while maintaining a consistent angle either side. It's usual to circuit lanterns to retain control over direction rather than area; that is, the 1 kw units are separate with the P.S. [stg. lft.] and O.P. [stg. rt.] pairs patched together.

A choice of 40 degrees or less for most backlight is a good one, since you achieve a reasonable coverage without having light fall into the eyes of the audience (see Figure 12.9). Bounce-light off the stage, however, must enter the auditorium and can make it difficult to discern little beyond the gross outline of the actor. But backlight has a major potential! Most people perceive a backlit character to be

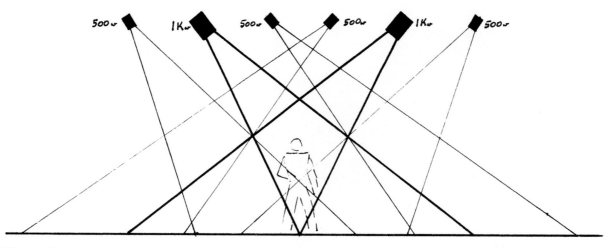

Figure 12.8
High Side Focussed to Centre.

more dominant than those without backlight; it seems to thrust a performer forward, and he or she appears farther downstage. This is useful to ensure the superiority of a character without recourse to rostra and the like.

When assessing the potential for backlight, be aware of the actor's head-covering and also the material forming the shoulders of the costume; both will dominate under backlight.

12.4.3 Flat Lighting—90 Degrees from the Vertical

Flat lighting from front-of-house can generally be achieved only from low on a box boom or a circle front [balcony rail] position. See Figure 12.10. Not only are shadows obvious on scenery upstage but also they may obscure other performers upstage.

Those of us cursed with facial structure resembling a moon find low front-of-house lighting unflattering. It flattens the features by removing all shading created by the eyebrows, cheekbones, nose, and so on—it's a very bland, sterile feeling. But this angle may equally well engender youth or illness! It's difficult, even for the best actor, to look sick on cue. Lighting may assist by adding green light from the circle front to fill the shadows created by conventional 40 degree keylight.

Figure 12.9
35 Degree Backlight.

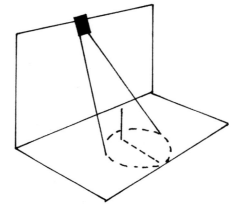

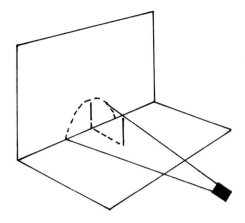

Figure 12.10
90 Degree Frontlight.

Conversely, you can assist those aging performers who are cast in more youthful roles by filling all the tiny shadows formed by wrinkles from circle front using no-colour pink or another colour chosen to complement the make-up. In this way you flatten out the complexion, then overlight from more conventional angles to contour the face in the normal way.

Flat sidelighting, illustrated in Figure 12.11, is the major offender in creating the problems raised in 12.4.2. But let's not forget the major advantage of this angle—the modeling and strength of profile suggested in 12.4.2—which makes it well suited to performers who use their body as a means of communication. Note that, for the first time, most of the performer's shadow is out of view of the audience; it disappears into the wings on the opposite side.

Flat backlight is rarely used, since light must fall into the auditorium; and, even if you swing the lantern to ensure that the excess light falls within the stage-house, the source is almost impossible to mask.

On occasions you may choose to light the auditorium using blinders. Blinders are flat-focussed floodlights along the edge of the stage that blast into the audience to blind them temporarily while fast scene changes occur. I don't favour this technique, but the show may arise which demands such drastic action.

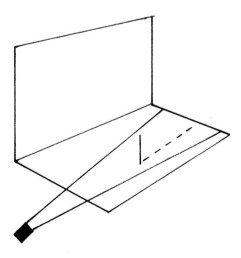

Figure 12.11
90 Degree Sidelight.

You've all seen film effects, such as in *Cabaret*, where a flat backlight is used, but the camera lens is protected from its direct glare by the artist's shadow. Since in theatre you do not have the advantage of viewing through a single eye, such effects are impossible without causing discomfort to the majority of the audience—but I have seen that attempted!

12.4.4 Underlight—120 Degrees or More from the Vertical

Footlights (underlight from front-of-house) were the earliest lighting position, chosen because the minimal light available could be used to maximum effect; but the inherent problems were also disguised by the lack of brilliance.

Your first problem with footlights is to prevent the lantern from obstructing the sightlines. Often, the orchestra pit has lanterns on stands or secured to the structure. Because members of the orchestra find these difficult to cope with, you must work very closely with the musical director if you intend using them. However, from such positions you can create an interesting illusion; performers lit from under seem taller than they are. This may be due to the shadow size and also to the distortion of naturalistic shadows and contours.

With side underlight from "shin-busters" (low on stands or booms), it's difficult to improve upon flat sidelight, as illustrated in Figure 12.11, with perhaps two minor exceptions. Shin-busters allow you to avoid the stage floor entirely; and, if costume and stage colouring are carefully selected, you can "float" performers above darkness. As they also emphasise feet, shin-busters may be useful in dance pieces such as *The Red Shoes* ballet. Back underlight is not difficult, especially where you have multiple levels, ground-row covers, and the like to hide the lanterns. Careful positioning and choice of lantern will ensure that excess light falls within the stage-house, and some quite remarkable distortion effects can be created.

This brief summary was intended to refresh your appreciation of the full range of angles available. By now you are probably convinced that they must be chosen by first analysing the effect you want. Important: Never forget that light continues beyond the subject; it causes shadows and lights items other than those for which it was chosen. Since you can't get rid of this light, you must design not only the subject but also the shadows.

Figure 12.12
Footlights.

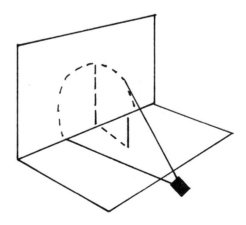

Lighting Angles with Some Common Placement Problems

Figure 12.13 details positions within proscenium arch theatres. It shows the more conventional positions that may take various forms depending on the age and style of structure. You must not feel limited to these alone, but anything further must be considered in terms of cost/labour effectiveness and how other departments and performers would be affected. In Figure 12.13 note that the circle front position and stalls are also known as the balcony rail and orchestra seating respectively; the front-of-house (FOH) bridges/bars may be known as beams or coves; and a loom is the bundled cabling from a position to the patching system. The convention when numbering lighting (Lx is the abbreviation) bars, booms, and the like requires you to start at the proscenium or setting line (a benchmark for stage measurement, usually just downstage of house curtain and parallel to it) and number upwards as you proceed upstage or front-of-house.

12.6 Horizontal Separation

Consideration of single lantern effects, as in section 12.4, will be beneficial as you determine specials, highlights, and spots; but you need to broaden your analysis to include the acting area. Figure 12.14 illustrates the minimum number of lights to light a performer evenly through 360 degrees. For every position on an in-the-round stage, you need at least three lanterns separated by 120 degrees for the performer to be visible to all members of the audience. Note that the increased number of lanterns introduces a potential for overlighting. As you withdraw performers behind a proscenium arch, you can dispense with the third lantern or convert it to backlight. Even in the intermediate format—thrust staging—the need for 360 degrees lighting extends well upstage until the performer is beyond the extreme upstage sightlines (see Fig. 12.14); in other words, the requirement for the third lantern is not removed until there are no patrons able to view them from behind. Frequently, thrust lighting follows proscenium techniques, whereas it should depend far more on in-the-round!

It's often stated that in proscenium lighting you need only two lanterns to light from one ear to the other (90–120 degrees horizontal separation); but this is often impossible and frequently undesirable. Take an interim example—end staging (Fig. 12.15). The general rule regarding separation needs to be modified to include lanterns on either extremity, which can be only at the sightline position; fortunately, nothing more is needed to light faces effectively. This modified rule can be extended to proscenium and thrust—see Figures 12.2 and 12.14.

Figure 12.16 illustrates the spill from a 90 degree crossed pair. With *any* horizontal separation you lose isolation. Light must spill to either side of the subject which may distract the audience. The need to contain spill over the edge of acting areas will vary from show to show. In some it will not matter, as areas are rarely used

Figure 12.13
Lighting Positions in a Proscenium Theatre.

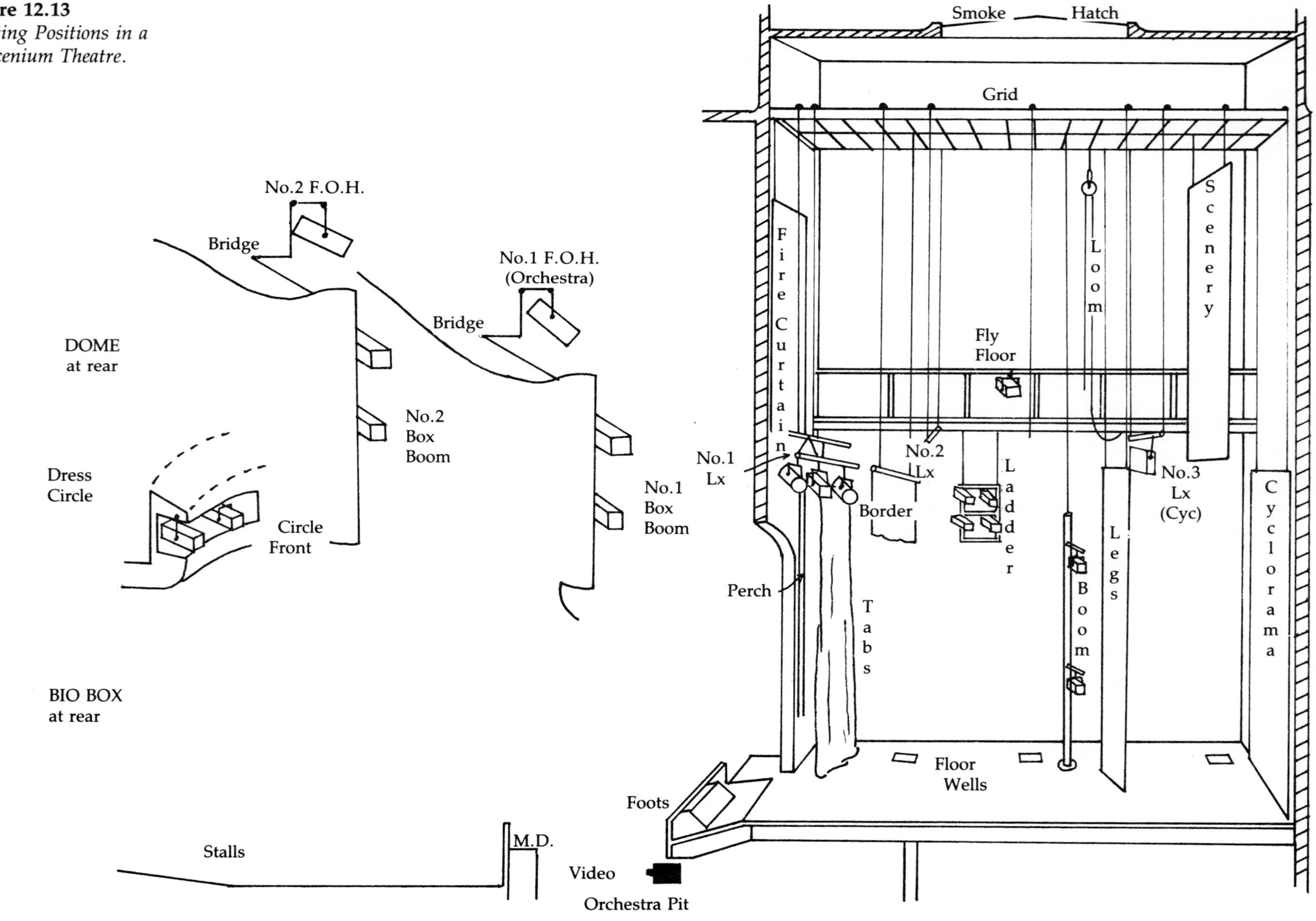

Smoke — Hatch

Grid

Scenery

Loom

Fly Floor

No.2 Lx

Border

No.1 Lx

Fire Curtain

Perch

No.1 Box Boom

No.1 F.O.H. (Orchestra)

Bridge

No.2 F.O.H.

Bridge

DOME at rear

Cyclorama

No.3 Lx (Cyc)

Legs

Boom

Ladder

Tabs

Floor Wells

Foots

Video

Orchestra Pit

M.D.

No.2 Box Boom

Circle Front

Dress Circle

BIO BOX at rear

Stalls

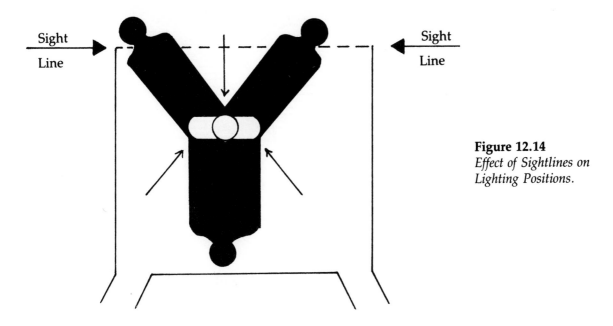

Figure 12.14
Effect of Sightlines on Lighting Positions.

in isolation; but others demand that each acting area be sharply defined—very nearly a spot. This can be achieved only by reducing the lantern separation to little more than the width of the area; however, the more isolation, the greater your problems when trying to blend areas into an even wash of light.

As with so many lighting difficulties, there is no clear rule as to how widely you should separate lanterns. It's a balance between isolation and blending, and even within these criteria there are other considerations: the size of the area to be covered, the throw distance available, and the evenness of the field required.

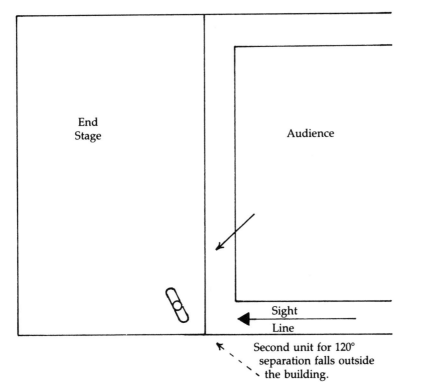

Figure 12.15
End Stage Lighting.

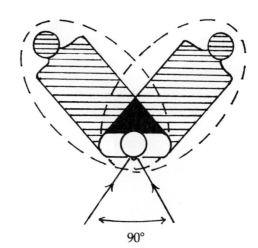

Figure 12.16
Horizontal Separation of Lighting Units.

90°

If you opt for an easy blending of acting areas in a theatre with a short throw, you will find that the problems illustrated in Figure 12.17 frequently develop. Because of beam spread limitations over a short throw, you may be unable to cover the entire area; this creates a dull wedge centre, while on either side faces are only half-lit. You may swing the lanterns downstage, but then the upstage portion of the acting area becomes dull; you may reduce the separation, but that makes blending more difficult. The simple answer is to add a third lantern or to use lanterns with a wider beam spread—assuming that they exist.

There is a difficulty I have found among those who have studied the McCandless method (see Bibliography). They focus a pair of lanterns (separate dimmers) into the same area, one with a cool tint

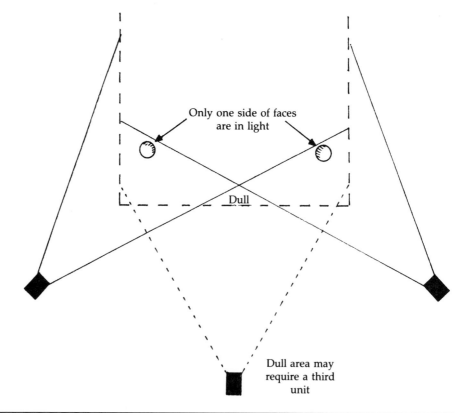

Figure 12.17
Lighting a Wide Acting Area.

Only one side of faces
are in light

Dull

Dull area may
require a third
unit

and the other warm, to mix a range of cool-to-warm atmospheres for that area. But a short throw and wide separation result in the performer's face being divided evenly into a cool and warm side. These lighting designers forget that McCandless stipulates less than 60 degrees separation and advises against excessive contrasts in colour; further, he suggests "double McCandless"—four lanterns paired into the same area (two dimmers).

12.7 Blending Acting Areas across Stage

Consider three evenly spaced acting areas across the forestage lit from the front-of-house (FOH) bridge. Figure 12.18 illustrates a frequent but unsatisfactory solution to the problem. Because of an overzealous desire for isolation, the lanterns are placed to coincide with the extremities of the acting areas. With precise focussing, this solution may give the impression of a reasonable coverage if you check by holding the palm of your hand slightly above head height, facing the audience, and move across stage. However, if you rotate your palm to face the wings, you will see the real problems. At points 2, 5, and 8 your hand will be evenly lit on both sides; but at 1, 4, and 7 it will be lit only from O.P. [stg. rt.], while at 3, 6, and 9 the picture is reversed. At the point where areas join, there is likely to be a brief darkness. Figure 12.19, though a more successful solution, loses isolation, as there will be spill from one area into another. You broaden the horizontal separation between paired lanterns and overlap pairs to ensure that each point onstage is covered by at least one lantern from either side—but you may introduce a problem! At the intersection between acting areas, there may be four lanterns servicing one point, resulting in a sudden increase in intensity. Use the outer edge of each field (between half and tenth peak) so that the four lanterns match the intensity of two lanterns at their peak.

How should these six lanterns be circuited? In the ideal situation each would be allocated its own dimmer to ensure complete flexibility, but you are sure to have less than ideal numbers available.

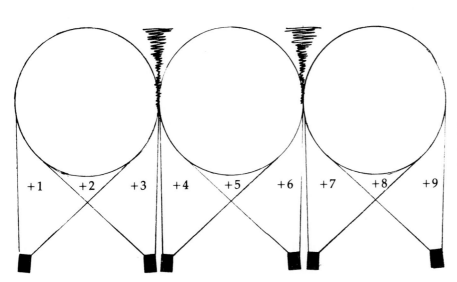

Figure 12.18
Isolation versus Blending of Acting Areas.

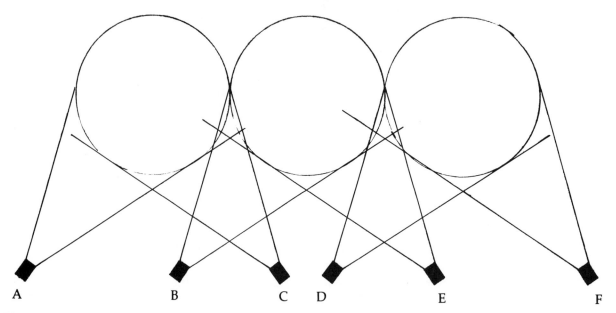

Figure 12.19
Blending Acting Areas.

A   B   C   D   E   F

If you require isolation, group into three circuits of matched pairs (A and C, B and E, D and F). If you're more concerned with a directional wash from either side of the stage, you may group A, B, and D against C, E, and F (assuming ample dimmer capacity).

Thus, your six lanterns can be usefully controlled by anything from six to two dimmers. You may choose any combination. Example 1 would be A and D, C and F as partial directional washes with isolation centre by pairing B and E. Example 2 would be A and C, D and F paired for isolation, with both B and E separately controlled for flexibility centre. You must precisely itemise the purpose for each grouping before you reach the compromise that best serves the show.

12.8 Blending Acting Areas Upstage and Downstage

Section 10.7 discussed the importance of maintaining a consistent angle up and down stage and noted that additional lanterns can be added to maintain this angle. The added unit in Figure 12.17 is similar; whether you add downstage or upstage depends on your assessment of where the lanterns will best smooth the transition between acting areas as illustrated in Figure 12.20. (Note that H/H indicates head height.) The addition of extra lanterns must increase the size of areas and may work against a need for isolation. If dimmers are available, you should allocate these units to separate dimmers. It doesn't matter that they're perhaps two-dimensional; they'll never be used in isolation.

Section 9.5.1 hinted at something else that may make upstage and downstage blending difficult: that is the smooth blending of light where areas overlap. Wherever possible, minimise the number of acting areas that join at one spot. As you saw in section 12.7, it's difficult enough to join two, and with every additional circuit you increase the dangers of overlighting. Figure 12.21 illustrates an al-

Lighting Angles with Some Common Placement Problems

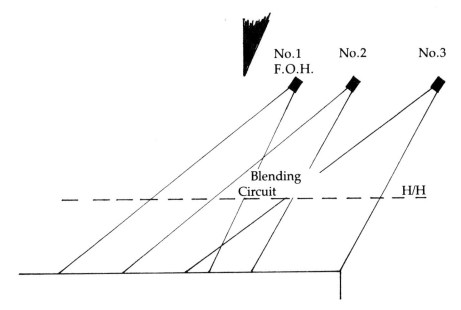

No.1   No.2   No.3
F.O.H.

Blending
Circuit   H/H

Figure 12.20
*Blending Acting Areas Up-
and-Down Stage.*

ternative. The dotted area may form a new circuit created to fill a
hole deliberately left between the other areas; you effectively reduce
the number of overlapping areas to three at any point.

If all the above considerations have influenced your lighting,
your layout of acting areas will have a similarity from show to show.
The layout in Figure 12.22 achieves a good coverage of the stage,
echoes the effective wedge (that area of stage included by both
horizontal and vertical sightlines), and minimises the number of
areas joining at one point. To allocate fourteen dimmers (twenty-
eight if you cover each area in both cool and warm tints) seems
excessive, even for a large stage; but it's the price to pay for isolation
and blending.

Even after a painstaking focus you may find, when you bring
all the acting areas to full, that there is an uneven quality about the
coverage. Look again at Figure 12.22. Areas 2, 3, and 6 generally
appear less intense than the remainder—assuming that each area
is of similar size, is powered equally, and is on a bare stage. Exactly
why this appears so, I've not been able to discover; it could merely
be an optical illusion—but it's still a problem to solve! As a matter
of course, I arbitrarily increase the power of these circuits; if the
other areas are lit with three 500 watt lanterns, I light areas 2, 3,
and 6 with three 650 watt units or increase the number of lanterns
to four.

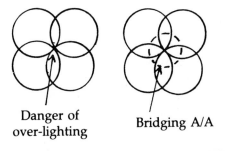

Danger of
over-lighting

Bridging A/A

Figure 12.21
Joining Four Acting Areas.

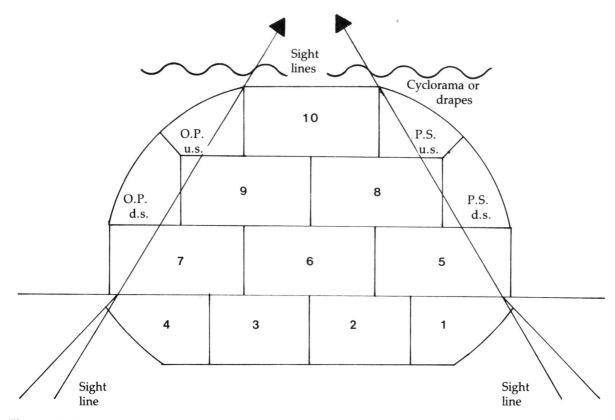

Figure 12.22
Common Arrangement of Acting Areas.

Another method of correcting this illusion is to range colour to reverse the effect and create a stage balanced around centre. Example: The centre areas could be straw tint; areas 1, 4, 5, 7, 8, and 9 could be straw and the remainder light amber. This can also add a sense of perspective to the stage. On a smaller stage, dimmer intensity alone may be sufficient to correct the illusion.

While the foregoing may have seemed to place undue emphasis on a minor difficulty, the discussion was also intended to illustrate the range of variables (colour, intensity, and so on) available when you tackle the problems that you will confront. The following paragraphs will discuss a number of problems from the narrow point of departure of lantern placement and angle, but you will see how the range of variables may also assist these solutions.

12.9 Maintaining Consistent Angles Approaching a Cyclorama

Assume that a cyclorama is required immediately upstage of area 10 in Figure 12.22. Figure 12.23 illustrates one approach to avoid stage lighting spilling onto the cyclorama which allows control of distracting shadows and ensures that cyclorama lighting is not washed out by bounced light. Acting areas 1 to 7 will cause few problems. Even areas 8 and 9 can be lit without direct light falling onto the cyclorama; however, bounce off the stage will form a halo of diffuse light along the bottom of the cloth. As you continue upstage, it becomes impossible to maintain a consistent angle and still avoid shadows.

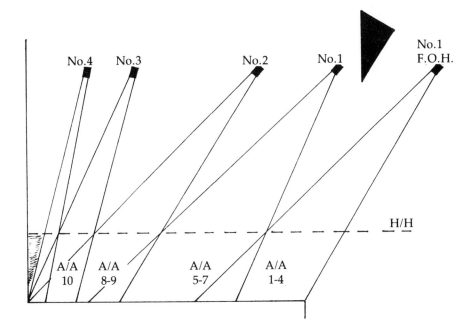

Figure 12.23
Acting Areas Approaching a Cyclorama.

The obvious answer is to increase the separation between it and the cyclorama or not to use acting area 10. Every effort should be made during production concept discussions to point out the difficulties, but a designer confronted with a shallow, crowded stage may be forced to inflict this problem on you. There is no solution; at best you can only minimise the damage.

One approach is to shift the lanterns so as to convert them effectively from frontlight to highside. The bounce is directed into the wings, and any shadows on the cyclorama also disappear in that direction. Bifocal profiles [ellipsoidals] will give better control of spill, but you must make the change in stages (for example, Fresnels on bars 1 and 2, pebble-convex on 3, and bifocal on 4). To maintain Fresnels throughout is to ignore the property that makes them so easy to blend; the cut-off angle is wide and will spill badly onto the cyclorama—even the best barndoors cannot contain it. If you are forced to use Fresnels, avoid the problem illustrated in Figure 12.24. With both barndoors closed to produce a slot of light, you will see no decrease in halation (light spill due to the large tenth peak and cut-off angles from a Fresnel) on the cyclorama, since the downstage barndoor is bouncing light directly onto it. Remember: no matte-black equipment is a perfect absorber; light will be reflected! You will improve the situation by pulling out the downstage barndoor and allow the light to spill uncontrolled; it may cause troubles else-where, but at least it won't damage the cyclorama.

12.10 Blending Acting Areas to the Set

A daunting sight for the lighting designer in rehearsal is an actor staged hard against a piece of set (for example, flat line); it will be impossible to light the performer without drawing undue attention to the background. The problem is similar to that discussed in section

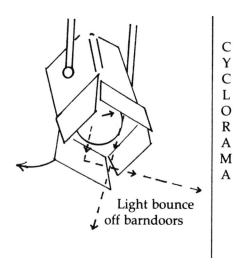

Figure 12.24
Effect of Barndoors Near a Cyclorama.

Light bounce
off barndoors

C
Y
C
L
O
R
A
M
A

12.9, but the difficulties are reduced if the set runs upstage or even diagonally. (See Fig. 12.25.) The O.P. [stg. rt.] lantern has few difficulties; a barndoor will trim excess light, and the closer the lantern is hung to the line of the wall (dotted in Figure 12.25), the better your chances are of avoiding the wall altogether. However, the onstage lantern required to fill the features of the performer is going to cause a very distinct outline on the wall behind the artist. The solution illustrated in Figure 12.23 is unlikely to be successful, since you need to maintain 35 degrees for clear vision of the eyes and lips. The set designer should be asked to include a picture rail (an architectural feature from which, in some periods, all the room's decorations were hung) or, perhaps, an increase in shading to disguise the upper edge of the light. (See Fig. 12.26.) Edges upstage and downstage can be gently graded off, using additional units or, perhaps, diffusing medium, colour, and texture to blend the acting area and the circuits lighting the set.

12.11 Problems of Isolation

Say a carpet needs to be isolated completely from the remainder of the stage; you must define the edges precisely, since performers will be staged right up to the edge. See Figure 12.27, where lanterns A, B, and C nearly fulfill the requirements. You would use bifocal

Figure 12.25
Lighting Actors Against the Set.

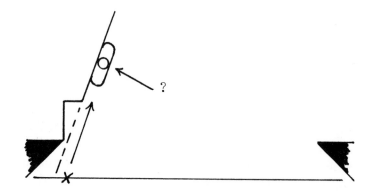

ellipsoidals for both A and C and a pebble-convex with barndoor for lantern B. Bifocal is required, since the upper edge of each beam should be softer to avoid hard lines as the performer moves through it; the pebble-convex will assist in this but may not wash out the edges entirely. However, on both edges the face of the actor is not lit from the centre of the carpet. A compromise uses lanterns precisely positioned to coincide with the edge of the carpet (points x and y). This places light down each edge without spilling off the carpet; faces now have some light—though it must be two-dimensional. A similar group of lights may be required upstage to extend the light to that edge without spilling off.

Although this problem is considered from a proscenium viewpoint, it is exactly the same faced by in-the-round lighting designers for each edge of that kind of stage. They must contain the light onstage, yet faces of performers along the edge must be clearly illuminated for those patrons opposite. The precision required for a small in-the-round theatre is far greater than for a major proscenium stage.

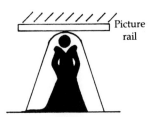

Figure 12.26
Hiding Light Edge in a Picture Rail.

12.12 Varying Levels

The problems of maintaining a consistent angle discussed in sections 12.8 and 12.9 are apparent once again in Figure 12.28, but in a different form. The solution used in this case involves a large number of hanging positions that match the changes in level; alternatively, another is illustrated in Figure 12.29. This demands a variety of lanterns on a gallery system, more usually found in European theatres, or you may be able to manufacture the equivalent using a number of bars underslung one from the other to form a gigantic ladder—a very weighty affair.

12.13 Puzzles and Solutions

The problems taken up in the latter half of this chapter will broaden your perception of the range of solutions available to you. Experience

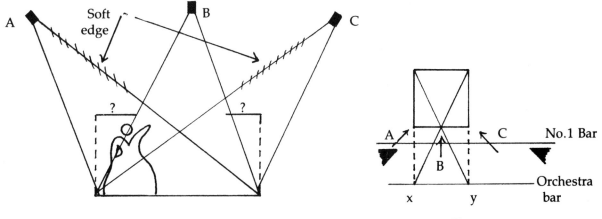

Figure 12.27
Lighting an Isolated Area.

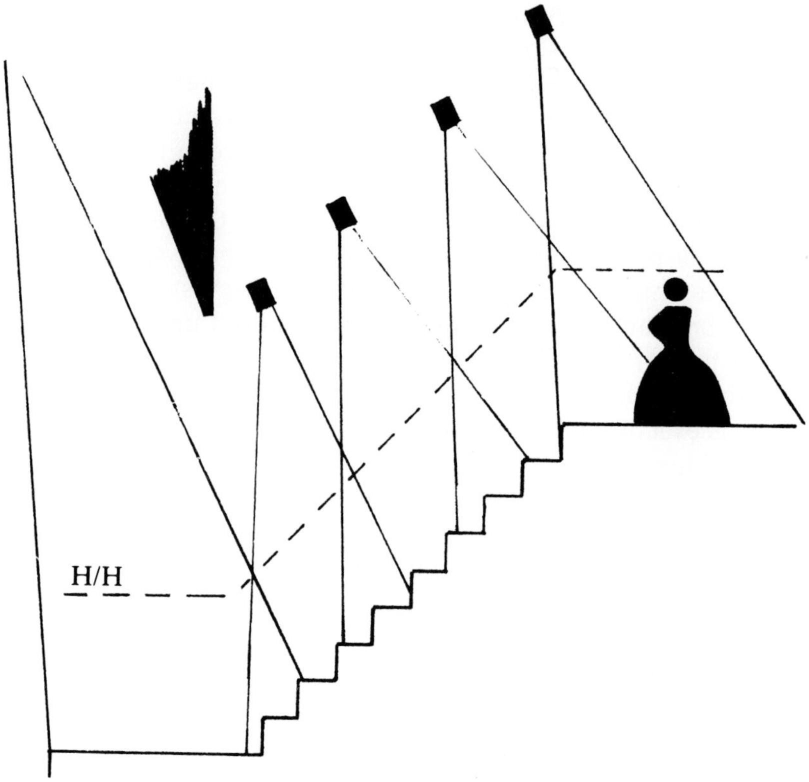

Figure 12.28
Lighting a Stairway.

H/H

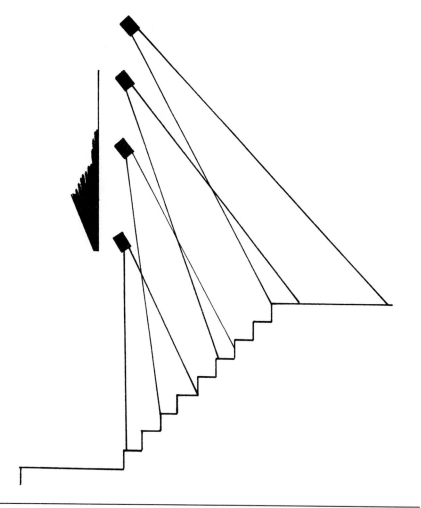

Figure 12.29
Lighting a Stairway—
Alternate Method.

Lighting Angles with Some Common Placement Problems

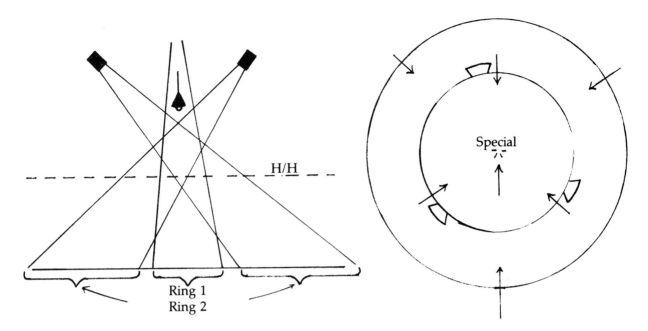

H/H

Ring 1
Ring 2

Special

Figure 12.30
Representing a Point Source.

will help you to appreciate that many of the solutions and problems are associated, and you must be able to recognise and analyse them from documentation (such as designer's plans and theatre layouts) before being confronted with "unforeseen circumstances" in the theatre.

The chapter will end with two problems often met in practice but rarely solved satisfactorily. The first is how to create the impression of sunlight or moonlight; the second is how to create a point source of light (for example, a single shaded lamp) without using a powerful source in the practical lantern (an item of stage scenery from which light will emanate) that would draw the attention of the audience to it. My own solutions are below, but seek your own before reading on.

* * * * * *

Light from any distant source (that is, sunlight and moonlight) is parallel, which creates in nature a perfectly even wash of light. Yet all your lanterns, with the exception of a tight beamlight, create an expanding cone of light; the angle on faces passing through it varies from one side of the beam to the other. To reduce this variation you may increase the length of throw, but you are limited by the stage-house size; and, further, the greater throw creates problems of supplying sufficient power. A more realistic solution uses many lower-power sources evenly distributed over the stage. Again, there will be problems supplying sufficient power, but the smoother wash will compensate.

Re-creating a point source also requires using many small sources; each will require very precise focussing and positioning.

Consider the light from the point source as a series of concentric rings—at least three, depending on the area to be covered. The first is immediately under the apparent source.

Provide a hot-spot (perhaps 500 watts) from a position giving the impression that the light is vertical *without* allowing *any* light to fall on the *top* of the lampshade. The next ring comes from at least three lanterns separated by 120 degrees focussed to pass under the lampshade, yet to light a figure only on the opposite side. This ensures that all light appears to be coming from the apparent source. The next ring will require more lanterns focussed under the lampshade, but at a far flatter angle, so that they light a more distant ring beyond the two already established.

Choose positions between lanterns creating the second ring (see Figure 12.30) to help even out the bumps. You may use deeper colours to give the impression that this light is farther from the source and, therefore, less intense. Should you need to extend the light beyond three rings, abandon the under-the-lampshade approach and use soft lights positioned near the first three lanterns but pointed in the opposite direction.

CHAPTER 13

Colour: Theory and the Process of Selection

You are still in the third week before opening and still considering the background material to chapters 9 and 10. This chapter takes up the theory of colour and how to select colour for best serving a production. Consult the book *Colour* (see Bibliography), a superb compilation of articles on the subject. Though intended mostly for artists who work in pigments and referring only indirectly to lighting, it contains much detailed knowledge, none of which is unimportant. Those who find *Colour* a little daunting, may turn to *The Light Fantastic*, also in the Bibliography and referred to previously.

13.2 What Is Colour and Who Discovered It?

> Nature and Nature's laws lay hid in night:
> God said, Let Newton be! and all was light.

This was a worthy tribute by Alexander Pope to Sir Isaac Newton (1642–1727), a towering genius who not only dispelled the clouds of ignorance surrounding the movement of the universe but also formulated the body of knowledge known as optics. Some say that Newton's inspiration was a hole in his window blind that allowed a beam of light to enter the darkened room; it struck a prism on his workbench and a chord in his intellect. The thin beam of white light from the sun was bent to create the rainbow (see Fig. 11.2). Newton reasoned that nothing new had been formed, but that the component parts of the white light had been spread so that they were apparent to the human eye. As proof he used a second prism to reverse the process, recombining the rainbow to form white light again.

What is happening in the prism? The degree of refraction (bending) depends on the wavelength of the light; a shorter wavelength (blue) is refracted or bent less than the longer wavelengths (red). (In Figure 11.2 you saw that light comprises a spectrum of wavelengths.) When you repeat Newton's experiment, be sure you use white daylight. If you use light from a street lamp or if you leave your experiment until near sunset, you will gain the mistaken impression that Newton was wrong. Many street lamps (for example, yellow sodium vapour) create light by discharging electricity through a particular gas that produces monochromatic light. Instead of creating a rainbow, this forms a single band of light with, perhaps,

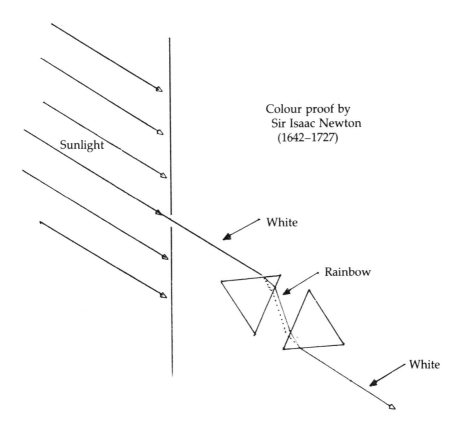

Colour proof by
Sir Isaac Newton
(1642–1727)

Sunlight

White

Rainbow

White

Figure 13.1
Newton's Experiment with Colour.

a couple of lesser bands nearby. Near sunset you would be attempting to spread light that has already been diffused by the earth's atmosphere. Air molecules diffuse blue light up to seven times more than the longer red wavelengths, and at sunset light has passed through a great deal more air to reach us; the shorter wavelengths have been diffused, leaving only orange/reds, which are caught by the bigger particles closer to ground level—hence red sunsets and blue skies.

A spectrometer uses a diffraction grating to split light into component parts; it's a more convenient method of proving Newton right, though you are unable to recombine the elements to form white light.

13.3 Using Filters to Create Colour—Subtractive

Over the years we have used a variety of mediums (such as silk, glass, gelatine, acetate, vinyl, polyester, and polycarbonate) that subtract elements not required from light to create colour. Figure 13.2 illustrates a typical absorption graph for a blue-green filter. Notice that the scale extends beyond the visible spectrum (730 to 830 nanometers). Between 730 and 800 is infrared (heat), and the manufacturer has designed the filter to allow this heat through; it continues onto the stage, together with the colour generated. If the manufacturer constructed the filter to absorb this heat, it would have a very short life, needing to be continually replaced. Recently, heat shields have become available. They're expensive; but, when in-

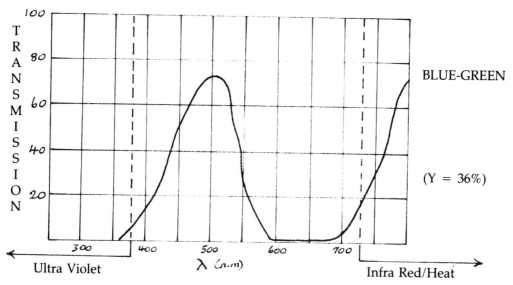

BLUE-GREEN

(Y = 36%)

Ultra Violet λ (n.m)   Infra Red/Heat

Figure 13.2
*Transmission Curve for
Blue-Green.*

serted before the colour filter, they absorb the infrared and protect
both the filter and performer from excessive heat. (See Fig. 13.3.)

In Figure 13.2 the graph assumes that the lanterns generate
white light (equal amounts of the whole spectrum). The pigment in
the filter allows through only those colours that are common with
itself; those at variance are absorbed and converted into heat. The
area above the graph represents the energy lost to us; and the Y
factor, given in parentheses on one side, details the percentage of
light allowed to continue on to the stage as useful light—in this case
only 36 percent. In dense filters the Y factor will be low, which
implies that the filter will need to withstand considerable heat. Until
the introduction of polyester and polycarbonate, which have far
higher heat tolerance, lighting designers would have had to replace
dense filters continually. Many chose to avoid them because the
expense was too high. Supergels (the trade name for these new
filters) are also expensive compared to the acetate variety, so you
need to be sure of their effectiveness for the show.

Figure 13.4 gives the absorption graph for a light blue. If you
place this filter into a lantern in addition to the blue-green illustrated
in Figure 13.2, you impose a double subtraction. Only the light that
is common to both filters will be allowed onstage (that is, in the
second part of Figure 13.4 only that area under *both* graphs). You
can imagine how inefficient such a filter combination can be, but it
clearly demonstrates the process of subtractive mixing. It is important to appreciate what this term implies, since it is the basis of
pigment mixing (such as paint and dyes) and the process that enables
us to perceive colour (see section 13.5). If you chose three disparate
colours and placed them together in the same lantern, little or no
light would emerge. It is exactly the same for paint and dye; if you
mix together primary red, blue, and yellow (assuming pure colours),
you create something very near black—complete absorption as there
is no colour in common. Remember that the three primary colours
mentioned above—red, blue, and yellow—apply only to subtractive
mixing of pigments!

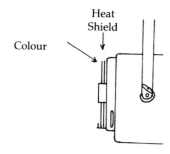

Heat
Shield

Colour

Figure 13.3
*Heat Shield in Colour
Frames.*

Colour: Theory and the Process of Selection

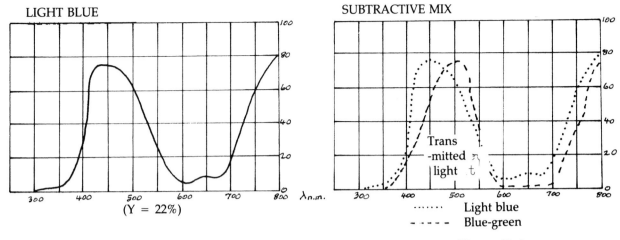

LIGHT BLUE
(Y = 22%)

SUBTRACTIVE MIX

Trans
-mitted
light

········· Light blue
- - - - Blue-green

Figure 13.4
Subtractive Mixing.

13.4 Colour Temperature

Do you assume that light from a lantern is white? Not the case! Tungsten filaments produce light biased towards the lower end of the spectrum (less blue), since the filament is not sufficiently hot: the hotter the filament, the whiter the light. The scale used to measure colour temperature is degrees Kelvin (K); tungsten produces light around about 3,200 degrees K, daylight is about 5,500 degrees K, and tungsten-halogen lamps are about 3,600 degrees K. To create the impression of light with a high colour-temperature, most ranges of filters include correction media, which are designed to reduce the low energy portion of the lamp output yet allow maximum blue through. The transmission curves in Figure 13.5 illustrate how this is achieved. Correction filters are available up to daylight (5,500 degrees K), but a full-stage wash with the quality of daylight would require tremendous power to compensate for that lost within the filter. The film industry uses other correction filters, which reverse the process and convert daylight to tungsten; they are useful to create interior scenes or period atmosphere. They are rarely used in

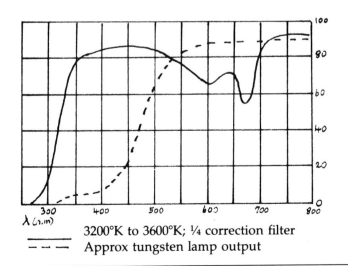

3200°K to 3600°K; ¼ correction filter
- - - Approx tungsten lamp output

Figure 13.5
Transmission Curve for 3,600 K Correction Filter.

theatre except, perhaps, as a means of creating a variety of chocolate tints.

13.5 How the Human Eye Perceives Colour

Assume that white light falls on a red costume; it is *subtractive* mixing that enables you to see red. All the colours of the spectrum impinge on the red costume, but only those that are common with the fabric pigment are reflected back to the eye; all other colours are absorbed and converted to heat. That's why people in hot climates use light colours to reflect most light and heat, whereas those in colder areas tend to dark colours.

What happens if you use the blue-green from Figure 13.2 on the red costume? (Remember, only those colours that are common to both light and pigment are reflected; others are absorbed.) If you put blue-green light on a red costume—nothing in common—that costume will appear near-black. Neither the pigment in the costume nor the filters are pure; that is why the result is *near*-black. Also, certain surfaces in the fabric reflect the blue-green, since they are polished and act as a mirror. Hence, the lighting designer is interested not only in colour but also in texture—a term used to describe the quality of the surface. You must haunt the cutting room of wardrobe to obtain swatches of every material being used in the costumes; an impression of colour alone is not enough.

Colour is being reflected from all over the stage to enter the eyes of your audience. You need an appreciation of the physiology of the eye to construct your colour choices so that you don't contradict natural law. Figure 13.6 illustrates that marvelous instrument so often taken for granted—the human eye. There are two receptors: rods and cones. Rods are for night vision; they are more plentiful and are evenly distributed over the retina; they require very little light (5–10 photons) to excite them. Although they cannot differentiate well between colours, rods have a particular sensitivity to light of 505 nanometers (about blue-green). Cones are less numerous and distributed more centrally on the retina. There are three variant forms, each designed to detect particular colours (cyanolabe for blue, chlorolabe for green, and erythrolabe for red), and together have a bias towards light of 550 nanometers (yellow). Cones are much less sensitive, requiring about 250 photons to trigger them.

From this brief summary a number of phenomena can be explained. For instance, what colour is moonlight? Since it's white sunlight reflected from the moon, it must be near-white but at low levels; it's the bias of rods to 505 nanometers that gives us the impression of bluish moonlight. This justifies the theatrical convention of using blue to represent moonlight, but at an intensity sufficient to trigger cones. If you produced naturalistic moonlight of less than 250 photons, the effort required by your audience, using their rod receptors to see detail, would force them to leave. Since cones are more sensitive to 550 nanometers, yellow light is "easy" to perceive, and humans feel comfortable in this range. A bee, bird,

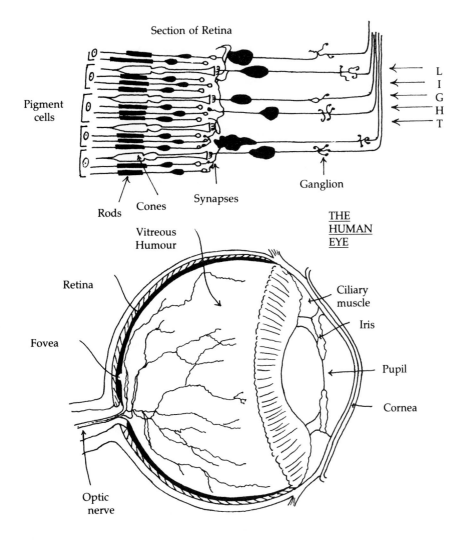

Section of Retina

Pigment cells

Rods Cones Synapses

Ganglion

L
I
G
H
T

Vitreous Humour

THE
HUMAN
EYE

Retina

Fovea

Ciliary muscle

Iris

Pupil

Cornea

Optic nerve

Figure 13.6
Anatomy of the Human Eye.

or predatory cat will bias to different colours; perhaps this is the origin of the saying "a red rag to a bull."

Rods have poor sensitivity to colour, whereas cones have three chemical variants that, in simple terms, are sensitive to red, blue, and green. As the chemicals absorb color, the molecules straighten and bleach; this triggers an electrical stimulus to the brain, where the coded messages are unscrambled and the results recognised by name—red, blue, green, yellow, and so on.

13.6 Additive Mixing

You are now in a position to mix light in the same way that pigments are mixed to form various shades. Try experimenting with three profile [ellipsoidal] lanterns that are independently controlled and focused to overlap on a white screen in the manner that Figure 13.7 illustrates. Fit one lantern with a 650 watt lamp, but leave the others at 500 watts. Into the more powerful lantern fit a primary blue filter (or fractionally lighter); into another fit a primary red. So far you're following the primary colours for subtractive mixing, but you will not find a primary yellow among the range of filters. Instead, there's

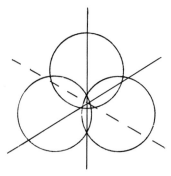

Figure 13.7
Colour Wheel for Additive Mixing.

a primary green; use it in the third lantern. Balance out the lanterns (generally, blue at full, green near-full, and red about 60 percent) until the area covered by all three lanterns is white. Three additive primary colours (red, blue, green) mix in air to form white light; however, once that light falls onto an object, the rules of subtractive mixing apply once again. Vary the intensity of each of the primary colours to create a range of tones far in excess of the three colours used to manufacture them.

To recap: near-white light is produced in the lantern, and you subtract elements from it by means of filters to form coloured light; you then use other lanterns for additive mixing of new shades in air, which behave subtractively with the pigments in costumes. It is central to the craft of lighting design to understand the difference between additive and subtractive mixing of colour and to be able to identify which process is applicable at any point.

Colour Plate 1 illustrates three lanterns focussed to a slightly raised white disc against a white background. In addition to red, blue, green, and white, three other colours are formed at the intersection of any *two* lanterns; these are the secondary colours. Red and blue coincide to form magenta; red and green form yellow; and blue and green form cyan. Also note that you can create white by mixing a primary colour with its associated secondary (that is, red and cyan, blue and yellow, green and magenta).

Taking a collection of coloured cards or a swatch of materials from wardrobe, try to identify them all under each of the primary colours. It's very difficult to identify colour under these unnatural shadings, and you'll be surprised at the amount of "impurities" that form everyday colours. For example, most reds will react under both blue and red, while many greens are, in fact, blue-green.

Also test what skin tones do under each of the primary and secondary colours. If possible try different skin tonings (Oriental, Caucasian, Negroid, Mediterranean, and so on), and note the different reactions they have to colour. It's interesting to try mixing a colour that creates Caucasian tones on Oriental skin, and so on. Given a show that demands the whole cast change skin tone, you may be able to assist with lighting—a far cheaper solution than nightly applications of full-body make-up.

13.7 Why Not Use Open-White?

You can now mix white using three different lanterns—that's nine lanterns and three dimmers for every point on an in-the-round stage. This is exorbitantly expensive, so why not ignore this silliness with mixing and use open-white lanterns onstage? Remember that lighting designers are trying to control every aspect of light, selecting for each moment what is appropriate for the show. Open-white gives no flexibility whatsoever, whereas a mix gives you the opportunity to select and vary at will. This is not to say that open-white should never be used; many shows need nothing more. If you are concerned with the power available to light actors, it may be better to ignore flexibility in order to provide sufficient illumination. (After all, that is your first responsibility.) Again, there are no fixed rules; you must select those colour combinations that are most suitable for the production and use them in the most flexible manner.

13.8 Mixing Secondary Colours and Tints

Often, economies must be made (as in space, dimmers, and stock) without losing colour flexibility. How? Remember that mixing secondary and primary colours also creates white, and this is more common in practice than a three-colour mix—particularly the blue and yellow combination for naturalistic productions. This enables us to create white (midday), warmer shades (morning and evening), and blue (moonlight). Amber and a greener blue are more useful, since they create a better basis for sunsets and moonlight. This colour shift involves rotating the axis in Figure 13.7 through a few degrees. You must not "bend" the axis if you are to ensure that the colours chosen are complementary (that is, mix to form white).

You will find the absorption graphs [transmission curves] useful when selecting complementary colours. Figure 13.8 illustrates an *additive* mix of two tints (less dense forms of the colour), which sum to a near-flat curve with a blue bias to compensate for the lack of blue from your filaments; this should enable them to be used as a complementary pair. When selecting pairs, you need to be aware

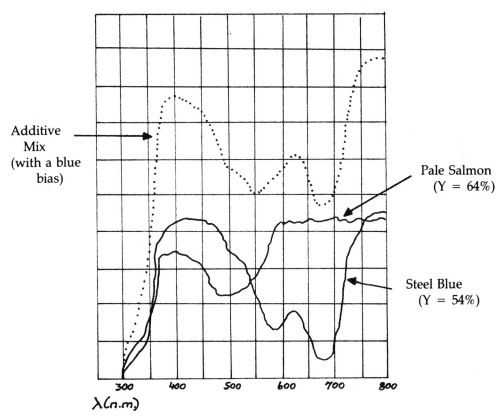

Figure 13.8
Transmission Curves for Additive Mixing.

of the Y factor for each if you hope to strike a balance. The salmon is 64 percent, but the blue only 54 percent; you may need to increase the power in the blue lantern if the bias in the resulting mix is insufficient. You could reduce the intensity of the salmon, but this would reduce the colour-temperature of the lamp, forming a redder source. By using tints, you make far more efficient use of the power in your lanterns. There's more light onstage; and, since you are converting less light to heat, they last longer and you retain the flexibility to cool or warm each area. What you reduce is the *degree* of shading available.

What about the less naturalistic combinations: magenta and green, cyan and red? These combinations and their tints are just as useful onstage but somewhat more stylised. Remember the multi-coloured shadows as you passed your hand through the arrangement of lanterns in Figure 13.8? A similar effect is useful in cabaret simply for spectacle and variety, using a three-colour mix of primaries *or* secondaries. Imagine a production of *Dracula* or, perhaps, *Sweeney Todd* using a magenta and green combination; the unusual shadowings created would form an ambience well suited to the mood of the material. Or you may be required to give the impression of a stage within our stage; for instance, within the reality of the show onstage, you create the impression of another performance space, such as a girlie show in a saloon bar. You could use a naturalistic amber and blue mix for the saloon itself and a red and cyan combination for the girlie show. This would accentuate the costuming besides forming a different ambience to the saloon.

13.9 Further Examples of Subtractive Mixing

Confusion is common when considering cycloramas in terms of additive and subtractive mixing; many are unsure which rules apply. This is one lighting question that can be clearly answered: subtractive! But if you use additive primary colours (red, blue, and green) as the three basic cyclorama washes, how can this be subtractive? Since you rely upon reflected light from the cyclorama into the eyes of the audience, the answer must remain subtractive. If a cyclorama is white (from which all colours are reflected), under these circumstances the rules of subtractive mixing echo additive mixing; however, most cycloramas aren't white. Age reduces cotton cloth to an off-white cream, though most plastic cycloramas maintain their whiteness. You must be particularly careful when selecting colour for grey and light-blue cycloramas. A blue cyc emphasises the blue end of the spectrum, making it easier to create sky and related effects. Grey is used—though it's difficult to find a good grey cloth—to give a hazy impression, which might be better achieved by inserting a black gauze downstage of both the cyclorama and cyclorama lighting.

Often, I've been accosted by set designers convinced that, by means of lighting, I can radically change the mood of a painted cloth or highlight particular elements to the exclusion of all else. Wrong! Colour Plate 2(a) notes the choice of colour Barry Landy uses in the

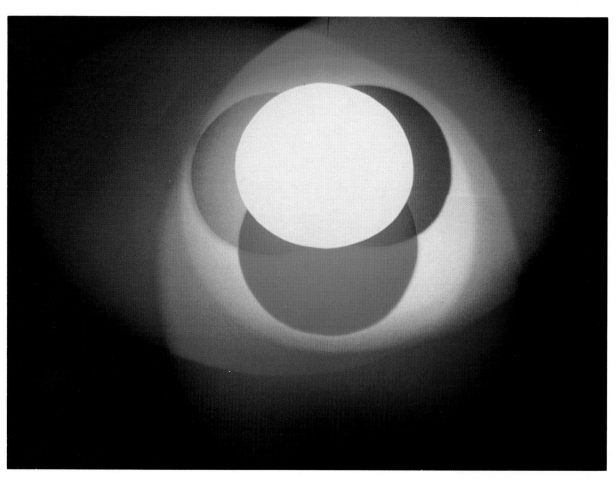

Colour Plate 1
*Additive Mixing. (Photo by
Peter Holderness.)*

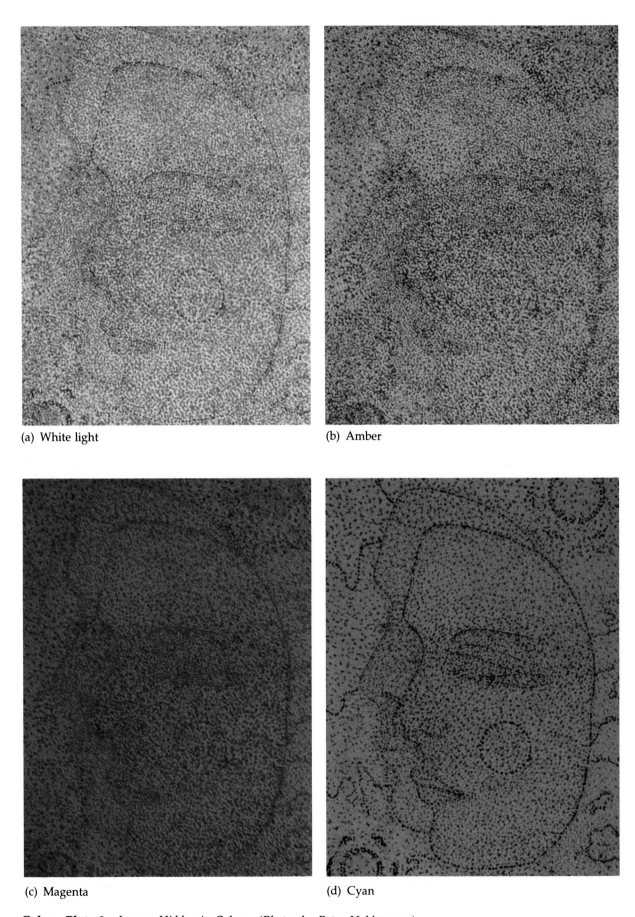

(a) White light

(b) Amber

(c) Magenta

(d) Cyan

Colour Plate 2 *Images Hidden in Colour. (Photos by Peter Holderness.)*

original to form an indistinct image; but, however hard he might try, the presence of the masks cannot be disguised under white light. Colour Plate 2(b) is the same image photographed under amber light; the masks merge into a dark background created as the blue and green react subtractively with amber. Under magenta light in Colour Plate 2(c) a similar reaction occurs. However, under cyan light in (d), subtractive mixing occurs with the red-based pigment of the masks, sending them into bold relief against the blue-green background. Note the useful colour choice in the lighting—the three secondary colours that will mix to form white.

If you attempt to use colour to reveal images in this fashion, both set and lighting designers must work closely. Colours and pigments need to be chosen with tremendous care. The best way the scenic artist can work is under a full cyclorama rig on the paint frame at the angle and intensity expected in the theatre; otherwise, false impressions will be created and time and effort wasted.

I discovered an associated technique by accident while lighting a surface that had been frequently spray-painted. The surface was lightly sprayed with thick blue paint and, buried deep within the pits, was the prior painted surface (figures on white background); the overcoat formed little more than a mist of colour that raised the surface but still enabled vision into the pits—if the angle of light was suitable. Figure 13.9 gives an impression of that surface magnified. If flat-lit from the front, this surface accepted most colours and revealed the figures. If lit at an angle, however, it behaved more like a blue scrim, reflecting only blue light and hiding the figures. As I said, this was an accident, and I've found difficulty reproducing exactly the same results, though I had sufficient success to make the effort worthwhile.

13.10 Experimenting with Colour

You need to consider in more detail experimentation with colour on a 1:25 [½":1'] model (see Fig. 7.4). Up to this point, you have been assuming the lanterns supplying colour to be at or near 100 percent. Your first experiment on the model should find out how your colour choice performs as the intensity of the lamps varies. The red/orange/yellow range remains reasonably true to pigment with only a deepening of tone as you fade down. With colours of shorter wavelengths (greens and blues) you find that, with low intensity, the result on the model is anything but true colour rendition.

The reasons for this have already been discussed. As the colour temperature of the filaments reduces, they produce less blue and

White Undercoat

Blue Overcoat

Figure 13.9
Images Hidden in Texture.

green; without these colours being manufactured in the lantern, there is no hope of their being transmitted to stage. Even open-white becomes a warm red at low intensity. Thus, before you can choose colour for any scene, you must picture in your mind's eye the intensity at which those washes will be used in performance. Example: To establish a strong wash of dark-blue moonlight, choose a dense colour (low Y factor) in powerful lanterns run at near 100 percent. A low intensity wash of the same blue will need a circuit of less powerful lanterns spread to a wide beam angle; that means running the lanterns at near 100 percent to maintain true colour rendition at relatively low intensity. That's the secret: you must run lanterns at nearly full! Colour selection is, therefore, closely linked with the coverage and intensity of each circuit. Like most "problems" in lighting, this phenomenon can get you out of trouble under some circumstances. Say that you're desperate to save dimmers yet have designed both a light and dark amber wash; you may be able to use the amber tint at low levels to form the dark-amber atmosphere you want.

With this model set up, briefly assess the effects of underlighting (low intensity) for prolonged periods. Using yourself as a guinea pig, take the level down until you are able to discern only gross detail, and maintain it there while you try to take an interest in fine detail (for example, performances). It won't be long before your attention wanders. That is the way it is with patrons, too. For short periods they make the effort to attend; but, as that effort becomes greater, their annoyance grows and they eventually give up entirely. The interesting thing is that most patrons will not blame the lighting designer; they blame the performers for being "lacklustre." If the scene requires prolonged low-level atmospheric lighting, by all means use it; but include a gradual build of intensity to aid the audience as the scene progresses.

Many of your colleagues will seem to spend most of the rehearsal process with one or another colour filter held to the eye as they observe everything from scene-change rehearsals to the building of the set. Try it yourself on the model. View the effect under open-white light with the filter held to the eye and then with the same filter in the lantern. The filter-to-the-eye approach gives only an indication; experience improves your ability to judge truly, but only the lantern method gives you an indication of what the results will be onstage. This is particularly the case where a colour mix is involved (for example, cyclorama).

The number of manufacturers producing colour filters has recently expanded. As many ranges are similar, the only way to determine the performance of an individual filter is to experiment. Stay abreast of additions to the range. For example, cosmetic filters were recently introduced; they are pastel tints that also incorporate a light diffusion and are suitable for toning and filling shadows on skin. Directional diffusion medium is also a recent introduction; Figure 13.10 illustrates its capabilities. It is particularly useful when forming slots of light where diffusion either side is undesirable (for example, highside) or when attempting to light a cyclorama evenly when using older-style floodlighting. You must collect swatches of colour

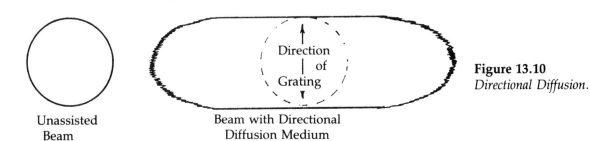

Unassisted
Beam

Beam with Directional
Diffusion Medium

Figure 13.10
Directional Diffusion.

medium in the same way you collect lantern specification sheets. There is no other way of keeping in touch with rapidly expanding ranges or of being familiar with the colour used in the house where you'll be working next week.

13.11 Evocative Use of Colour

In today's world technicolour is the norm, and natural shadings are losing their impact, largely because of the advertising industry. Colour is used less for subtle influence and more for effect. In the same way that I can no longer listen to a particular Tchaikovsky symphony without visualizing a brand of cigarettes. (I'll never forgive them for that; the symphony is my favourite), many of the colours in the range available to you have impact upon your audience above and beyond what you would have expected in the past. You cannot ignore the fact that a certain shade of blue-green is now "menthol-fresh," while another green is associated with Nordic forests and blonde hair; similarly, a healthy skin tone is now considered to be one that has been toasted and oiled in a most unnatural manner. You live in a world of fashion, and to ignore its influence is to fly in the face of your audience.

In most cases the advertising industry chooses colours with extreme care, with a particular attention to subconscious responses to colour stimulation. Red is a hot, dangerous colour that is instantly lethal to insects, whereas blue is a cooler, more remote colour used to identify surface sprays that kill insects less obviously. Blue is cool—red is hot. Green is on the cooler end of the spectrum; it may be sick, but it can also be country-fresh when associated with the yellows and ambers in earth tones. Magenta is warm-to-hot and passionate, but purples are royal. Cyan is sea-green and cool. Red is healthy meat, and blue is fresh fish; and, if the colours are chosen successfully, suspicious odours associated with them can be ignored.

You need to add this range of seemingly trivial information to your battery of knowledge not only to capitalise upon what is trendy but also to avoid associations in the minds of your audience that are not appropriate to your production. You should also be aware of how each of us is affected by colour. I attend shows and, without looking at the programme, work out who designed the lighting by the arrangement of lanterns and choice of colours. All designers have a distinct signature, particularly biases that may be at variance with most in the audience; compensate for that bias when choosing colours for a production. For instance, I tend toward the deeper tones of blue that have an ultraviolet feel, and I use green in very unlikely places to add depth and texture. They both appeal to my taste, but the green frequently meets opposition from directors and set designers alike, and the blues are inefficient.

13.12 Colour Saturation

You need to investigate one further aspect of colour perception. In many ways I find it the most useful application of colour theory, yet least understood. Given a particular sample of colour, do you perceive it to be the same today and tomorrow, assuming that lighting conditions remain constant? Try this experiment. You need a white screen about 1.5 m[5'] square against a matte-black background. In the centre of the screen place a small black dot. Focus two profile [ellipsoidal] lanterns so that they each cover the screen with an even field of similar intensities without spilling onto the background. They should be on individual dimmers or switches and need to be fitted with complementary colours, say, blue and amber.

Ask your subjects to cover one eye with a hand so that it is completely blacked out, yet not pressured or restricted in any way; at the end of the experiment this eye will be used for comparison, since it will be "at rest." Black out the environs and flood the screen with either colour, say blue. Ask the subjects to focus on the black dot; they should try not to blink too much, and the eye must not be allowed to stray from the dot (both will become more difficult as the experiment continues). Expose the eye to blue for 60 to 90 seconds, then switch to amber and compare one eye with the other. *They do not see the same amber*, which proves that colour perception is a dynamic process; that is, what they perceive now depends upon what they've been doing immediately beforehand and for how long. Most people have little difficulty during the first 30 seconds of the experiment keeping the blink rate low and the eye on the spot. Between 45 and 60 seconds both these tasks become more difficult; as the eye strains, the blink rate increases, and it becomes hard to resist the urge to shift focus. After 60 seconds most people find it impossible to keep their focus on the dot, and their eye wanders. As it does, around the perimeter of the blue screen, amber afterimages are formed. You know there is no amber in the stimulus; therefore, it must be formed within the eye. (Some people report afterimages other than amber; medical advice is that this indicates a slight deficiency in vitamin A to which the eye's chemicals are closely related—nothing to worry about!) Between 45 and 60 seconds into the experiment the blue appears to wash out; to some it looks grey, but all report a diminishing blueness—again not based in fact. After 90 seconds all effects should be marked in all individuals. With the change to amber, the eye that has been exposed to blue perceives a dynamic amber, whereas the eye that has been at rest sees a mundane variation of the same colour. After 10 to 15 seconds this will start to even out, but, in some individuals, the effect may continue for up to 20 minutes. There is no possible damage to the eye from this experiment, and the subjects should be assured that all effects will wear off quickly.

There is an analogy—a ball-bearing in a parabolic cup—that should simplify the explanation of this phenomenon, yet not deviate too far from the physiological facts. (See Fig. 13.11.) A shift of the bearing to one side indicates a perception of blue, while the other indicates the complementary colour—remember that there are three chemicals in the eye, one for each complementary pair. Note that there is a finite amount of chemical available for change and that perception depends upon the rate of change of chemical, not merely the amount changed. In the unstimulated eye the bearing stays at rest at the bottom of the cup (marked A). Similarly, an eye perceiving white light will be close to rest, since there are equal amounts of blue and amber. The eye exposed to blue commences movement from point A to B. Initially, the rate of change is relatively fast, which ensures a clear perception of blue; however, as the gradient rises, the rate of change decreases and the perception of blue is diminished, causing the greying out mentioned above. Near point B the ball-bearing will have a natural tendency to run "downhill." When the eye shifts away from the black spot in those receptors on the retina that are released from the blue stimulus, the ball-bearing starts to drop, causing amber afterimages around the edge of the screen. When you switch to amber light, your eyes are respectively at A and B. When perception commences from A, the amber perceived is "normal." In the saturated eye, however, the ball-bearing commences a rapid run downhill, producing a high rate of change, and your perception of amber is elevated.

How can you use this phenomenon constructively, or can you ignore the principles involved? Some years ago a dance company created a piece that, in rehearsal room, appeared to have enormous potential, but in the theatre it died. It was conceived as a red ballet; the costumes, stage, and lighting were all various tones of red. Even the best choreography and performers could not survive this abuse of colour theory. The audience's eyes became saturated, and, in the same way that they would have had difficulty watching your black spot, they had difficulty watching the performance.

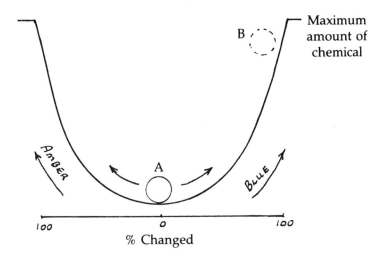

Figure 13.11
Analogy of Colour Saturation.

Solution? Blue-green (complementary) had to be introduced to the picture (for example, in the cyclorama) to allow the audience's eyes to rest. Because the eye will linger on the minority colour to balance off the majority stimulus, you locate those items you intend the audience to watch within the minor field.

Take the moonlit smuggler's scene from *Carmen*: Carmen is in the foreground telling her own fortune—death. The scene works best when the performer underplays the emotion, yet the background is vast and may upstage such a performance. The lighting designer can assist by keeping the focus firmly on Carmen. In addition to isolation, intensity, and so on, you could use colour. Include Carmen in an amber pool in the midst of the moonlight flood with perhaps a hurricane lamp as the apparent source. As the eyes of the audience become saturated in blue, they look for the complementary, and there they find the performance you intend to be their centre of focus.

Let's go a step further: Don José, Carmen's lover who will eventually murder her in a jealous rage, is upstage in the moonlight wash without any lyrics to sing and is therefore generally unnoticed by the audience. If, every time Carmen turns up the Ace of Spades— death—we arrange for Don José to walk through the amber light from a small campfire hidden deep in the setting, we will establish in the minds of our audience the tragic associations that will be realised in the closing moments of the opera.

Another example: Suppose the leading lady must appear in the midst of a scene as if from nowhere, yet the appearance needs to be spectacular and dynamic. The scene is set on the terrace of a candlelit cafe against a night sky, and the leading lady is costumed in blues and aquamarines. Immediately prior to her appearance the chorus has a dance break, which she must interrupt. How can you use saturation? During the dance break, saturate the stage with amber (justified by candlelight), reduce the night sky to remove the complementary colour, and maintain this state for 60 seconds or more—but make the fades very subtle. At her appearance from behind a column, swing the balance of colour to blue. You have used your experiment in reverse. You saturated the audience with amber, which will also depress her costume and enable her to sneak on unseen. At the swing back, her appearance should have a dynamic as big as the sky.

These examples illustrate the enormous potential of this phenomenon. It's a subtle and evocative method of directing the audience's attention without their realising they are being manipulated.

13.13 *Factors Influencing Colour Choice*

You now have a sufficient grasp of colour theory to select colours for a production, but remember that in a practical situation you cannot normally isolate your colour choice from shape, angle, movement, intensity, and the like. Refresh your cue synopsis notes, plus those notes taken during production concept discussions and after experiments upon the model. Use this information as a basis from which to work. The production will choose many colours for you, but you need to control and balance each element so that they form a colourful unity.

What style had you decided upon for the production? Is it a deep tragedy or a light, bright comedy? Is it naturalistic, or does the concept demand some interpretation? The answers to these and similar questions will quickly define choice for acting areas, washes, and so on. Start thinking in terms of open-white, and use these questions to work out how much variation you require (such as cool or warm), the depth to which this variation must extend (such as tint or dense colour), and the breadth of variety to encompass the whole show (such as three- or two-colour mix).

Use your cue synopsis to define the apparent source and/or the keylight; then look to nature or your imagination to give it a colour, keeping in mind any subliminal impressions you wish to infiltrate into the minds of the audience. Example: Daylight in the tropics (*South Pacific*) will demand different colours for acting areas and washes than an Ibsen piece would, set high in the northern hemisphere; but the corners of the tropical daylight need an air of mystery to evoke Bali Ha'i, whereas Ibsen's needs a brittle, unemotional quality. Is the circuit to create ambience, to decorate the set, or to highlight an actor? Ambience is more likely to complement the colour of acting areas, whereas set decorations are chosen to emphasize pigments (paint or fabrics). Are the highlights an extension of the naturalistic setting (for example, a beam picking out the performer in the same colour as the sunset wash), or are you making a subliminal statement about the character? In this case you need to select shades that trigger the required response in your audience and react with pigments in the make-up.

You may grade, shape, and texture circuits using colour (see section 12.8). Acting areas may be biased with colour to give directionality, to emphasise depth and perspective, or to highlight performers within the effective wedge. Sidelight may use complementary colours from left and right to emphasise the shape of bodies further. Backlights may be a lighter tint of the acting areas to make them more useful as highlights, or you may choose dense colour as an emotional statement.

As each colour choice forms in your mind, return to the scale model to ensure that the impression in your mind is supported in fact. Place a sample of the costume material you intend to highlight on the model, and ascertain that the colour you chose not only highlights the costume but also suppresses the background. If both setting and costume are emphasized, you need a localized spot and not a wash to create the effect; in the plotting [dry tech.] you can then juggle colour, isolation, and intensity.

13.14 Example of Colour Analysis

Return to the *Oklahoma* ballet sequence, for which a cue synopsis was discussed in section 8.11, and allow me to explain my colour choice. Two major factors influenced the reasoning. The script demands that Laurey, the singer, remain in view throughout the ballet—it is her dream, and the dancer is merely a device that enables Laurey to see herself within the dream. I further reasoned that the ballet splits into two major portions. The first extends to the end of the wedding sequence and is seen through Laurey's eyes; the second, set in the saloon, is what Laurey believes Jud's fantasy to be.

The basis for Laurey's fantasy is the green-gold deckle used during the opening of the show, when the audience and Laurey first see Curly, the object of her dreams. This initial effect was achieved using green-gold quarter colours and deckle plate projections overlaid on straw-coloured acting areas against a naturalistic blue cyclorama with white clouds that had a warm dawn glow. In my interpretation of the ballet, the spot in which the singer Laurey was held throughout contained three elements: straw head-and-shoulders shot from front-of-house, cold light from back and side light for emotional variations, and green-gold deckle texture from side. The cold and deckled washes were angled to emphasize the seated singer's face, while the dancer standing behind was in outline only. These three circuits gave opportunity to cool and to warm; to isolate performers, with a strong bias to the singer (it's always her dream); and to echo the opening happy moments of the show. The initial sequence of the ballet had used considerable green-gold texture, though highside circuits were used to model dancers better.

The naturalism of the sky was heightened to achieve the extra clarity and vibrancy one would expect of a dream. Then, when the entrance of dancer Curly required a virile feel, I used a variation on the dawn flood from Act 1, Scene 1 to create a strong path of untextured light that emanated from the direction of singer Laurey; the dream was still hers, and I used direction to emphasise that fact.

As the fantasy marriage continued, the green-gold texture was increased with the intention of saturating the eyes of the audience. To enhance this effect, the halo created behind the dancers Laurey and Curly was also gold, the intention being to wash out the complementary naturalistic sky. When Jud interrupts the wedding, the snap cross to cold emphasized the emotional impact of the moment. At the same time I adjusted the cool/warm balance of the singer Laurey spot to echo the onstage mood.

Jud's fantasy was based upon the costume colours, red and green. We wanted the barroom girls to be garish and to have the white wedding dress and Curly's costume seem distorted so that they looked weird and out of place. We also distorted the sky, using magenta and purple to give the green in the foreground added strength and to distort skin tones. Magenta and green were also used in Jud's earlier smokehouse scene to form subtle shadows; the ballet sequence would therefore pay off this early impression of Jud.

To summarize, colours were chosen for these reasons:

1. Their emotional influence with particular emphasis on interpretation.
2. The manner in which those colours had been introduced prior to the ballet.
3. Costume interaction.

4. Balance of the overall picture so that the keylight included the central performers while the background supplied the complementary colour.

Colour choice involves analyzing not only each scene but also the entire show. There must be a linking of character, moment, mood, and time so that the audience receives a series of impressions flowing from one to another—not merely a jumble of individual moments.

13.15 Recording Your Colour Choice

Return to your 1:100 [⅛":1'] circuit sketches and pencil in colours that you believe will suit the production. If you can't define what is needed for the occasional lantern, leave it; you'll come back to it shortly. You might, however, give a range within which the colour should fall, and you may be able to specify certain circuits once you choose the colour of another. Example: Until you choose the acting area, you cannot define the colour for the highlight that must blend with it.

If you studiously apply yourself to this task and keep finding answers to all the questions you know to be pertinent, you will define at least 80 percent of the rig's colour. The remaining 20 percent will be bridging circuits that need to be defined with reference to others. Example: You have the blue selected for both the cyclorama and the acting areas, but you are undecided what to use in the blue sides. Ask more pertinent questions to define how these circuits link. Will the sidelight assist in blending from downstage to up? Is it to add directionality, or do you need it for modeling? Blending will best be achieved by choosing a number of colours that grade the jump from front-of-house to cyclorama. Directionality is achieved by selecting two tones lighter than the acting areas for the directional side and two tones darker for the other. To model two tones lighter on both sides adds contrast. There's a device that makes choosing graded colour simpler. Taking thumbnail-sized samples, rearrange them to create a tone spectrum for each basic colour (such as blue, amber, lavender, green, and so on). It's far easier than trying to leaf back and forth through a swatch. In this way you achieve a rig of colour in which every element is linked in some way (emotionally, naturalistically, subliminally, and so on) to at least one other in the rig. That is a hallmark of a well-designed show.

13.16 Boldness and Flexibility

Remember that colour is the easiest detail of the rig to change; if it's not right, you can quickly replace it with something better. It is also one of the strongest variables available to you, particularly in terms of emotional statements. You must be adventurous if you wish to achieve maximum effect, yet flexible enough to change when your boldness has led you astray.

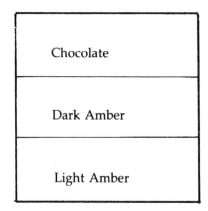
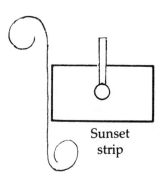

Figure 13.12
Unusually Cut Colours.

Figure 13.12 illustrates some of the odd colours you'd find in a show I've done. The "poached egg" and graded colour could both be used in the example in Figure 12.30 where we were attempting to repeat onstage the light from a point source pendant. The "poached egg" provides the hot-spot immediately below the apparent source and begins the grading into outer rings. It's formed by inserting a complete sheet of tint into the frame with a second colour that has its centre removed. The graded colour is used in lanterns of the second and third rings to grade colour as you become more distant from the point source. *Note:* Check Figure 11.21 before assuming that these will work in any lantern.

The last example in Figure 13.12 shows a lantern rigged where a floor lighting person could manipulate a strip of colour that graded through the tones of sunset. I have also experimented with a fixed strip of colour and a moving lantern so that I could vary both colour and direction. Anything is worth a try if it fits the style of the production. Boldness and flexibility are attributes that contribute to making an evening in the theatre memorable for the patrons.

CHAPTER 14

Movement and Special Effects

This is the last background information chapter associated with chapters 9 and 10; at its end you will return to the end of the third week before opening.

Theatre can and should be as attractive to "fantasy freaks" as the cinema is. While you cannot use blue-screen techniques and do not have huge budgets, you do have a malleable audience that grants you their suspension of disbelief on condition that you don't abuse it. This forms the subject matter of the chapter: how not to abuse your audience with ill-chosen, badly conceived special effects.

14.2 Suspension of Disbelief

The most powerful tool available to the special effects designer—and to the whole Production Team—costs nothing. Your patrons freely surrender their powers of disbelief for the duration of the performance so long as you respect that privilege. This means that you will astutely apply new and old techniques that you have chosen, adapted, and shaped to serve the production. You will not haphazardly apply anything new and wonderful. Too often, special effects do little more than insult the intelligence of the audience; instead, you must invite them to join with you as you use your skills to trigger their imagination and to feed their powers of invention.

This chapter discusses the more frequently used effects and progresses to some general pointers to assist you in their selection. Again, this is intended only as a summary. Like all other aspects of lighting design, studying special effects will engage you for the remainder of your career.

14.3 Follow-spots

A follow-spot is a manually operated long-throw profile lantern used to highlight a moving object/performer and is included in this chapter because we are concerned with light that involves movement. Given that a basic principle of lighting is to draw attention to performers and not to the mechanics, the first task for a lighting designer contemplating using a follow-spot is to justify it completely within the production concept. From the evidence in some shows

Movement and Special Effects

it seems that only after plotting [dry tech.] commenced did the lighting designer attempt to find suitable tasks for the spot to perform; it feels added on, a somewhat useless convention. Alternatively, the follow-spot is sometimes used to supplement the front-of-house rig, yet there is equipment idle in the bridges.

Both examples are contrary to the principles of design. The second is an expensive solution to inadequate design; it would be more cost-effective to design and execute a more comprehensive rig than to involve management in paying a follow-spot operator for the run. Like it or not, wages are the largest proportion of running costs, and you need to ensure value for money. Example: Figure 10.3 is based on a production of Michael Tippett's *Midsummer Marriage*, which contrasts the ethereal heights of purity with earthy depths of knowledge. In act 1 Jennifer takes the stairway to purity; she leaves the earthy stage and travels via rostra A, C, and E to meld with a disc that flies and illuminates as it travels heavenwards. To many, such an extended travel is justification for a follow-spot, but a solution of multiple cues, sensitively operated, was more suitable and reduced the difficulties involved in using a spot from a fixed position.

A follow-spot from the dome (see spot position in Fig. 12.13) had major problems with angle, particularly as the performer reached rostra C and E (see Fig. 10.4). The angle became flatter as she moved higher; "damage" to the cyclorama and scenery (such as shadows) was more obvious; and it was difficult to make a smooth transition between the follow-spot and the special effects flying disc.

As Jennifer removes herself further from sordid earth, a quality change is required both for her and for those remaining onstage. We chose to extend this cue into a sequence (using a computer board) that incorporated her movement. As she moved, those acting areas through which she had already travelled faded to earth tones and lower intensity, while those ahead increased in intensity and purity. Near the conclusion, rostrum E was brightest and matched the disc about to fly, while rostrum A and the onstage acting areas were very earthy; acting area C was in an interim state, heading towards earth. It required the board operator to be sensitive to the performer so that Jennifer was always in light that grew in intensity but faded immediately as she left it.

Don't assume from the above that I have a horror of follow-spots and try to make employment for operators scarce—not so! Follow-spots have particular qualities, and operators need special skills; both must be matched to the show. You cannot take any floor electrician, give a brief introduction to the machine, and expect him or her to cover up deficiencies in the design. Follow-spot operators need careful training, extensive rehearsal, and a complete understanding of their part in the production in the same way that a board operator does.

As you contemplate each dome cue, ask yourself whether it could be achieved as well or better by another lantern in the rig or if an addition would remove the necessity for the dome cue. If the follow-spot alone is capable of the cue, then its use is thoroughly justified. Consider this example from a Russian ballet presentation of Ravel's *Bolero*. In the midst of a completely blacked out stage, the follow-spot picked up the hand of a female dancer held high above her head as she stood on a table centre stage; the hand came down, caressed her body, and continued on to caress and cajole the surrounding male dancers into a frenzy. No other light available could make that pickup, then stay with her throughout the ballet. No other light can be altered from hard focus to soft or subtly change colours on cue.

Despite the expense of operators, there is still no device available that has the range of skills at such reasonable rates. Fine operators feel their light as an extension of themselves—not just a blob on the end of their arm; they rarely draw attention to themselves but sensitively meld into the action onstage. They are sufficiently aware of the staging to anticipate each movement and to adjust their light so that the performer has light to move into. They are able to adjust all controls smoothly so as to light only the performer—not the scenery. It's as though the actor/dancer controls the light; the follow-spot operator is merely an intermediary. It's a shame that they are among the lowest-paid and least-prepared members of the team.

When choosing a follow-spot, you will be using the same processes of selection discussed in sections 10.7 and 10.8; and you need the same attention to detail. There will be a position and specific type of lantern most suited to the task. To some degree the operator will be able to adjust faults but cannot be expected to compensate for gross misapplication of equipment. Often the range of effects required of a follow-spot throughout a performance demands that you make enormous compromises to find a single lantern in a fixed position to serve them all. Perhaps you need one spot in the bridge and another in the dome, with one operator travelling between?

14.4 Long-Throw Effects Projectors

How often during a soft and delicate snowfall effect have you noticed what looks like a log of wood slowly descending with the snow? Or how often have you been distracted from what's happening onstage by clouds jerking across the cyclorama? For years lighting designers have been crying out for new effects projectors that are more reliable, have greater power, and give a better choice of effects, but it is only recently (here in Australia, at least) that their cries were heard. The old range relied almost entirely upon disc effects with a variable diameter friction drive to control speed. Then a very expensive range of Italian machines, whose origin was a cinema projector, introduced an alternative method of producing effects based on film passing in opposite directions in close proximity. The different techniques are sketched out in Figure 14.1. Only recently has a Japanese company combined these systems with a choice of light output and a range of objective lenses to give both long- and short-throw effects at a reasonable price. Their range of effects is infinite, since they also supply blank discs that enable designers to etch their own artwork.

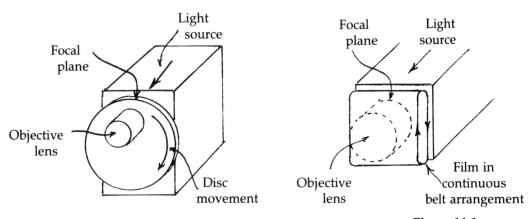

Figure 14.1
Types of Special Effects Mechanisms.

Whatever system you use, you can rarely justify its purchase in terms of the use it will receive in the average theatre. Hiring/rental is the usual answer, but that means you must decide upon the effects required early, making sure they are available for the length of run you expect. When selecting suitable equipment (that is, throw and beam spread), compare your calculations from the section with the manufacturer's specifications, especially in regard to a suitable objective lens (see sections 10.7 and 10.8). Selection of the precise effect required is less easy. First, clearly visualise the lighting concept in your mind's eye and define its components; only then can you define the element to be supplied by the projector and commence your search. Hiring houses are happy to demonstrate equipment and advise on how it may be adapted to form the precise movement and image you require. You may need to combine effects (for example, slow fleecy clouds with fast storm clouds) or shape them via the control desk, since you will be very lucky if the product of someone else's imagination matches yours.

The improved availability of equipment causes me a slight twinge of regret when I recall hours spent in research and development and with a pop-riveter creating my own instruments (see Figure 14.2). At the time no fire effect was available to give sufficient beam spread over a short throw. My idea came from some bad-taste lounge-room lamps that relied on convection to rotate the drum. I enlarged and motorised the effect, and for some years it served very effectively as water ripple, fire, and so on. That degree of ingenuity is still required frequently for adapting commercially available effects to suit your show, and that's the secret of special effects selection. Make the effect do what you require; don't be pushed into gross compromises by accepting what's available.

14.5 Short-Throw Effects Projectors

Figure 14.3 illustrates a machine designed to create, at a very short throw, water ripple. For my taste this effect is unsatisfactory, since it is mechanical and does not represent the fluid movement of water. Such machines for fire, water, or a train flashing past at night are difficult to obtain commercially, and you will need to find your own

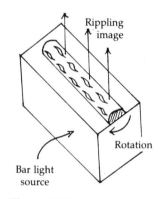

Figure 14.2
Homemade Special Effects Mechanism.

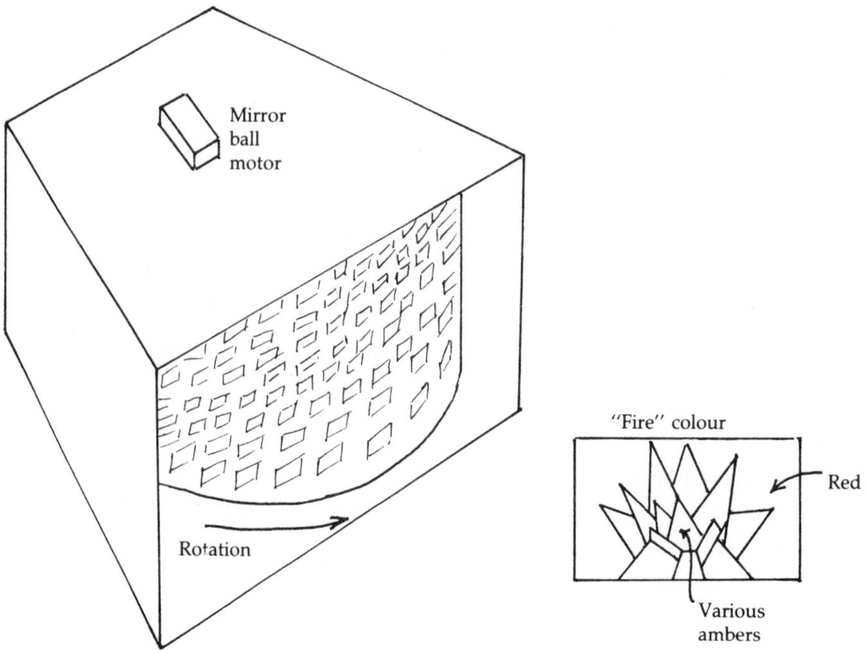

Figure 14.3
Ripple Machine.

solution. In the magazine *Theatre Crafts* (see Bibliography) ideas are frequently contributed. They attest to the need for such devices and illustrate the range of solutions and associated skills your colleagues have brought to bear on problems.

Take the example of water-ripple: Commercially available ripples (see Figure 14.3) are relatively expensive, are in short supply, are designed for a very short throw, and have a distracting mechanical feel—but they are not to be dismissed. They have served the profession well, but you need to investigate alternatives that may suit certain shows better. Logically, the most effective way to achieve a naturalistic effect is to use light reflected off moving water. (See Fig. 14.4.) The water need not be deep. In a tray with a reflective bottom, to improve the efficiency of the effect, it is agitated by a paddle or a small fan. I have also seen speakers suspended over the water and contact made via a plastic paddle to form ripples compatible with taped music.

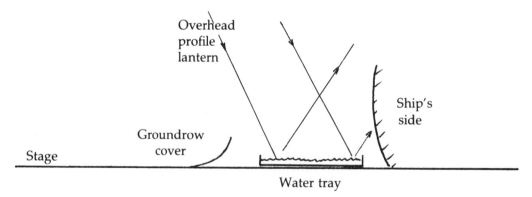

Figure 14.4
Water Ripple.

You must not neglect the fact, however, that water and electricity form a lethal combination. If there is any danger to cast or crew, you must reconsider the use of real water. Reflective sheets of plastic can replace the water if it is loosely supported and rippled by a fan, but there is some noise associated with this solution. Another device uses a single profile [ellipsoidal] through a glass dish of agitated water onto the outside of a spherical mirror that spreads the light. It's not efficient, but it covers a large area and is relatively compact. Two lanterns rigged, as in Figure 14.5, to use the same colour wheel will result in a waxing and waning of a variety of blue colours. This may be varied by replacing the colour wheel with a distortion wheel. This is a Perspex disc to which has been randomly applied clear acrylic glue (from zero to 5 mm[¼"] thick). When colour is also added, the continually fluctuating refractions vary the light interestingly; for instance, a sea-gull gobo projected through it appears to flap its wings.

There can be no "correct" answers in special effects; the range of demands and possible solutions is enormous. The limitations are created not so much by your imagination but by the setting, equipment, and style of presentation. Remain open to all suggestions wherever they originate, and study the potential of every new light source and material. You may even have the satisfaction of adding to your craft's body of knowledge, but always keep safety in mind.

14.6 Scenic Projection

In Figure 14.6 imagine the screen forming one wall of a box set with the source situated in the wings, and you have the oldest projector known in the theatre; it's called a Linnebach projector, originally powered with an electric arc. The technique fell into disuse as light levels onstage increased, washing out such effects. Modern projectors also have the same enemy—ambient light levels. The Linnebach projector could find new application with improved screen materials and high-powered light sources available today, since it has the advantage over current devices of a wide beam spread over a short throw.

Projectors may be considered like other ellipsoidal lanterns, but there are additional difficulties that must be recognised—or, to be precise, these problems are more obvious with projectors, but they are inherent in all lanterns. They include power ratio between image and ambient light, keystoning (see section 14.7), and, particularly

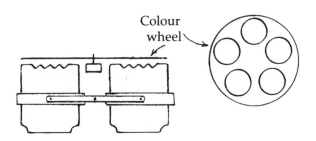

Figure 14.5
Colour Wheel Ripple.

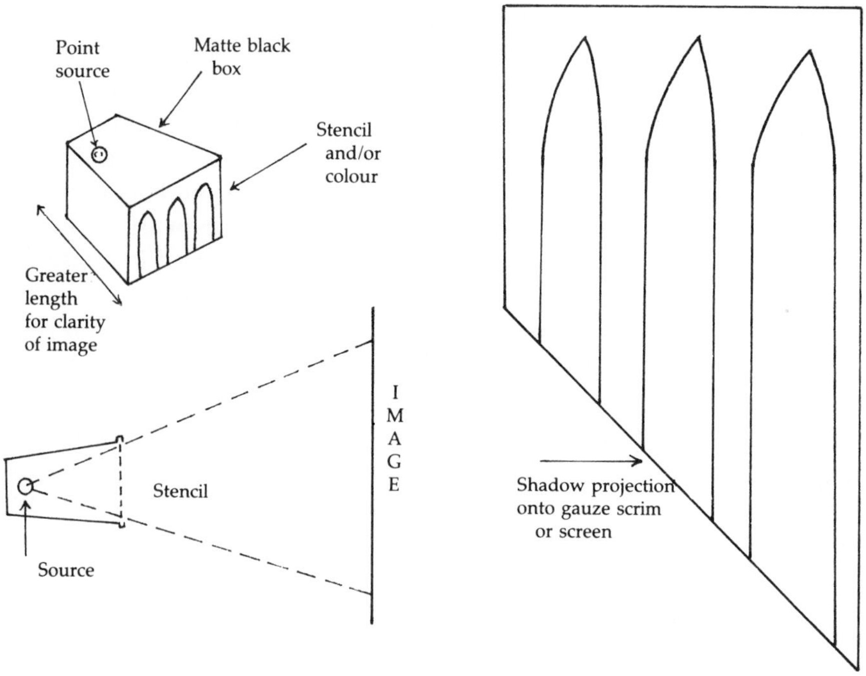

Figure 14.6
Linnebach Projector.

Point source · Matte black box · Stencil and/or colour · Greater length for clarity of image · Stencil · Source · IMAGE · Shadow projection onto gauze scrim or screen

for back projection, short-throw beam spreads. Unless you solve each difficulty, you may find it impossible to blend projected scenery with the remainder of the stage.

When selecting an objective lens, you go through the same process of calculating throw and spread that you do with any other lantern; unless you are very precise, you lose image power. Further, you must use every trick in section 12.9 to keep ambient levels on your screen to a minimum. Past methods used light-coloured screens and as little colour as possible in the projected image to ensure high screen intensity. The situation has improved with the introduction of back-projection screens that range from white, through grey to black. A *black* screen: how can it possibly work? It is actually very effective; the front surface remains matte-black, which allows for higher ambient light levels, yet images (whatever their colour) appear bright and clear.

There are some technicians on the periphery of the entertainment industry, audio/visual creators, who have been spawned by the advertising and promotional industry. Armed with specialized skills and sophisticated computer equipment, they are experts at blending sound with image. The results can be marvelous.

Using techniques of sequencing and crossfading that closely approximate cartooning and adding such devices as Polaroid waxing and waning, they form images that appear to move, blend, and meld in a manner that rivals cinematography. Such expertise is not obtained cheaply, but, like all scenic projection, it's relatively cost-effective when compared to manufacturing scenery. It is particularly suited to shows that require rapid and extensive scene changes with a touch of magic. You need to foster cooperation and an exchange of ideas with audio/visual personnel.

In every lantern there is a phenomenon referred to as "keystoning," as demonstrated in Figure 14.7. Given a square image, the only way you can create a square projection is to ensure that the light incident on the screen's centre is at 90 degrees; that is, to avoid keystoning the only possible angle is flat lighting (see section 12.4.3). If you shift the projector vertically (or horizontally), the length of throw to the top of the projection is shorter than that to the bottom; hence, distortions of intensity, shape, and focus occur.

You can correct this in two ways: Adjust the screen to a compromise angle that allows clear vision, yet returns the incident light angle to near 90 degrees. Alternatively, form the original image with reverse keystoning incorporated; when projected at a specific angle, this results in a square projection again. The problems of intensity, however, are not solved—merely disguised.

14.8 Pyrotechnics

In Bowman's *Shop Cook Book* (see Bibliography) there are recipes for various pyrotechnics that use the skull and crossbones symbol to give warning of health hazards. Recipes without a warning are the exception! Use pyrotechnics only when there is no alternative, and never forget that they are potentially dangerous in terms of fire, physical injury, and chemical poisoning to yourself, performers, crew, and audience alike. Stories abound of accidents and injuries resulting from ignorance or disregard of the dangers: death, deafness, theatres destroyed by fire. Only recently a T.V. personality killed himself by placing a blank loaded pistol to his head and pulling the trigger. I know of actors with damaged hearing resulting from

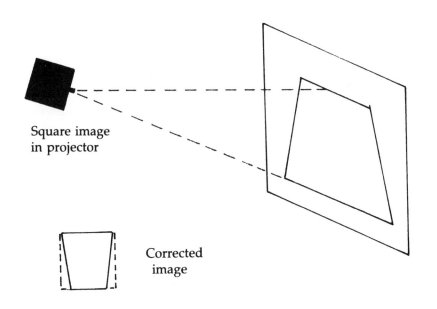

Square image
in projector

Corrected
image

Figure 14.7
Keystoning.

"safe" explosions; actor and technician alike forgot that repeated exposure magnifies damage and demands added protection.

It frightens me how little is known about the chemicals used in glues, dyes, explosives, or process residues (see *Theatre Crafts*, April 1985). Example: Actors become sick after inhaling the fumes from a "witches' cauldron" during a long-running show. Quite justifiably, governments through fire departments or departments of labour and industry regulate our industry for the safety of workers and patrons. I cannot understand the attitude of some theatre people who consider these officers as enemies bent upon destroying their artistic endeavours.

Before you use any pyrotechnic, you must know the regulations governing its use and the precise dangers involved; for example, hazards and conditions for safe storage. If you are unsure, you must seek expert advice well before the show's opening. I have found regulating officers sympathetic to the results I was trying to achieve, but they tend to assume that they will be hoodwinked. They obviously find it refreshing to be approached for advice and guidance— but those who ignore their regulations risk closure.

The fire department is sympathetic to your problems, and you must reciprocate. You share the awesome responsibility for your patrons' safety; yet, frequently, exits are obstructed, fire extinguishers are hidden, and crews have no idea where the nearest fire extinguisher is or how to use it! The ultimate responsibility for fire safety during performance rests with stage management, but the lighting and/or special effects department must cooperate fully.

Sections 14.8.1 to 14.8.10 are intended as a brief guide to what you need to consider when contemplating special effects.

14.8.1 Are You Licenced?

Before you can purchase items such as guns (even those that have been spiked) or explosives, you generally need to obtain a licence. An individual—usually the stage manager—assumes this responsibility and you must be guided by him or her, the person who would be charged with negligence.

14.8.2 Storage

Dangerous materials need to be stored with particular emphasis on fire and security. A key-safe should be available, with only sufficient stocks held; stockpiles are dangerous. And be very strict with regulations for smokers.

14.8.3 Always Read the Label

Every substance you are likely to use must carry warnings regarding its contents and handling precautions. Read them carefully. If any substance is unlabelled, get rid of it. Flushing down a toilet is generally safe; don't burn it.

Movement and Special Effects

14.8.4 Fire Retardants

Be aware of how flammable some materials used in theatre are. In the same way that certain ones are banned from children's garments, some could be dangerous to your performers and should be avoided. If you're not sure, hold a match to a sample and judge for yourself. In any case, fire-retard everything that is at risk.

14.8.5 Wet Blankets

A "wet blanket" or similar device should be at hand wherever there is fire danger for an individual. It is a blanket impregnated with a smothering chemical that also rapidly cools the subject. You and your crew must all be aware of each item of safety equipment supplied within the theatre. Study any new techniques; the fire department will be happy to advise.

14.8.6 Clear Instructions

Ignorance is the greatest danger. It is criminal negligence to design and supply equipment to your crew unless you also spend time to ensure safe operation and a clear appreciation of the precautions that must be taken.

14.8.7 Involving Performers

You have an obligation not only to inform your crews but also to involve performers. Example: Actors who will have a pistol fired at them should be invited to attend a demonstration firing and be given the opportunity to attend every loading of that weapon.

14.8.8 Double Checks

Arming and firing of devices should be attended by at least two individuals to ensure that, even if one is off duty, the second is fully aware of the details, dangers, and checks involved; for example, triggering devices fitted with "armed/safe" switches in addition to the firing mechanism.

14.8.9 Safety Meshes

Ensure all devices (such as explosions and flashpots) are completely contained in material suitable for preventing fire and physical injury. Experiment: Place a charge in a sturdy container and establish what gauge mesh is required to contain all residue from the explosion—then double it.

14.8.10 Warnings to Audience

Warnings need to be posted in the foyer and also the programme if you intend to startle the audiences by using explosives or if you use strobe lighting (see section 14.10.6).

Recently I attended a dress rehearsal for Frisch's *Fire Raisers;* at the finale smoke bombs ignited and the auditorium filled with smoke, but we never saw the end of the play. The smoke detectors had not been isolated, alarms went off, and the fire brigade evacuated the auditorium. The hilarity apparent among crew and management quickly changed when they received the bill from the brigade; ignorance can be costly in more ways than one!

When talking later with those associated, I discovered that the effect was not what the director wanted. He imagined smoke close to the ground, drifting across the stage insidiously. This points out the necessity of defining exactly what is contemplated with smoke effects: is it smoke or fog?

Fog is formed by dropping dry ice (CO_2) pellets (not chunks; they often explode!) into warm water that must be maintained at about 75°C [167°F]. Some devices use a fan to assist the gas along ducting (100 mm [4″] air-conditioning ducts are good), while others rely only on pressure built up in the container. The effect is relatively short-lived as the fog warms in the atmosphere and releases CO_2, which allows water to precipitate on the stage. Wet stages can be dangerous, and the rapid increase in humidity will untune stringed instruments in the orchestra pit. Another danger is that of mixing water with electricity; also, the extremely low temperature of the ice will frostbite unprotected hands.

Smoke is popular at the moment, probably because of the introduction of safer high-capacity devices (the oil-based machines of the past tended to catch fire). A successful method of distributing smoke around the stage quickly is illustrated in Figure 14.8. A smoke haze allows light to be seen as it passes through the air, and it's useful for dawns and other moody locations. But fashion dictates a more indiscriminate application whose purpose seems to be to pull the audience's attention to the lighting effects and away from what is happening onstage.

A number of machines using water-based mixtures are available, but they require careful cleaning after prolonged use. Also note the warnings (as, for instance, danger to asthmatics) on the bottles of mixtures. The same effect can be created cheaply with a pressure-pack water-based device or a bee-keeper's fogger. Both effects need careful technical rehearsal with auditorium and stage air-condition-

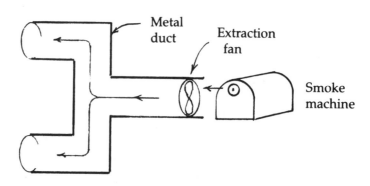

Figure 14.8
Smoke Distribution.

ing fully operational so that you see the results under the air-flow conditions you expect during performance.

The amount of special effects equipment kept in stock need be only small and basic—it's more cost-effective to hire. However, a number of simple but frequently used devices can be manufactured in the workshop or purchased quite cheaply. Sections 14.10.1 to 14.10.8 briefly describe them.

14.10.1 Microswitches

These are simple switching devices wired to 10 amperes capacity and able to control three channels. In addition to a microswitch for each channel there is a three-position control (off; flashing off, normally on; flashing on, normally off). It has many uses from lightning to momentary dips onstage and may be inserted after the dimmer or powered direct.

14.10.2 Lightning Flash

Theatre Crafts magazine (see Bibliography) detailed a device to trigger flash cubes to represent sheet lightning effectively; it has quick transience and high colour temperature. For forked lightning use the same device in a moon box (see Fig. 7.3) or profile [ellipsoidal] lanterns with appropriate gobos.

14.10.3 Manual Chaser

I happened upon a four-channel flasher/sequencer that used a cam arrangement to operate four microswitches. When it includes on/off alternatives similar to those mentioned in section 14.10.1 and the choice of manual or mechanical operation, it is very useful for many effects from a discotheque to sheeting rain across a cyclorama.

14.10.4 Mirror-ball Motors

This chapter has already mentioned a number of uses for these small motors beyond that for which they were intended (see Fig. 14.2 and section 14.5). They are available in a variety of speeds.

14.10.5 Colour/Wheels

These machines are available for a variety of lantern types and are relatively inexpensive. Although designed as automatic colour changers, they lend themselves to adaptation (see Fig. 14.5 and section 14.5).

14.10.6 Strobe

These devices, available made up or in kit form, supply a regulated flash of high-intensity, high-transient light. Warning: People affected by epilepsy may be triggered into a fit by these devices. Place a warning in the foyer and programme when you intend using them (see section 14.8.10).

Strobes are often used indiscriminately, but they do have a place in areas other than discotheques; for example, the transition between children and adult performers in *Gypsy*.

14.10.7 Colour Organ

Available commercially or in kit form, colour organ is useful for creating an association between sound and light. Basically, it comprises three dimmer channels; sound is split into base, mid-range, and treble, then is used to control each channel. Its usefulness extends beyond the usual throbbing light; for example, in *The Magic Flute*, the voices from within the temples may cause the light from the doorways to fluctuate.

14.10.8 Ultraviolet Light Source

Keep in stock a source of ultraviolet light; it can be useful from puppetry to fluorescent signs (see section 14.11).

With this stock, plus an ability with sheet-metal and pop-riveter, you can successfully service most shows.

All the effects mentioned above may be cheap, but do not disregard the cost in human resources; to rely upon enormous work-hours for results need not be economy—merely disguising the figures.

14.11 Recognising Potential in Materials

As you move about your professional and private life, keep your eye open for new materials and anticipate how you could adapt them for stage use. You will be flooded with new designer materials, colour filters, fabrics, light sources, and the like; they all have potential for special effects, even though the show they are perfectly suited to may not yet be written. Always file away information and ideas that may be useful in the future. Example: You know that neon lights are dangerous and fragile when used in stage effects; then you hear about a product recently designed for the advertising industry that may replace neon onstage cheaply and safely. It comprises variously shaped ultraviolet-sensitive plastic strips in a range of colours that can be cut and shaped to form neonlike displays.

The only limits are your imagination and the ability to recognise potential in materials. Also learn to recognise potential in individuals, for you cannot expect to be a know-it-all; it may be that your garage mechanic, university professor, research institute, or a member of your own staff may be able to advise. Individuals asked to supply expertise are generally flattered and fascinated to see their knowledge put to theatrical use. I remember the pleasure on my mechanic's face when he saw onstage a device he had made—and when he saw his name in the programme "with thanks."

14.12 New Techniques

Many will wonder why this summary of theatrical special effects has made no mention, so far, of lasers. Avoiding the subject was deliberate so that it could be used here to illustrate a point.

Not long ago I toured the C.S.I.R.O. (Commonwealth Scientific and Industrial Research Organisation) Physics Laboratory here in Sydney, Australia, to gain some insight into techniques that might be adapted for theatrical purposes. I was particularly interested to see what the optics department could demonstrate in the field of lasers, since I am of a generation that believed lasers were the future of theatrical special effects and scenery projection.

The evidence available from the C.S.I.R.O. suggests that holographic projection of scenery sufficient to satisfy an audience is well in the future. Since the Industrial Revolution it seems we have been brainwashed into believing that everything new is "right" and that everything old should be discarded. The more I compare modern technology (such as lasers) with skills commonplace in theatre a hundred years ago, the more I am urged to dispute this premise. Hence, I advise you to approach special effects in terms of what is best for the production, regardless of how old the technique may be. In the process you may reduce your budget, yet still create appropriate special effects lighting that has unity with the production.

14.13 Where Lies the Future?

Besides audio/visual techniques (see section 14.6) there is another area of expertise ripe for theatrical exploitation. I found it at the Sydney cricket ground in the huge video scoreboard/replay screen. If such a device were installed instead of cycloramas and used computers to generate appropriate signals, lighting designers would have a device with enormous flexibility. It could be used for scenic projection, spectacle, and subliminal triggering in a manner far beyond us now. It will be a very expensive device and will never displace the cyclorama, but I see it as having application in certain dance, musical comedy, and opera productions.

14.14 Self-Imposed Isolation

Before you leave this discussion of special effects, consider one final point: you are not alone. The chapter was from the viewpoint of the lighting and special effects designer and may have falsely given the impression that you alone are in a position to save the show from disaster. That is not, and must never be, the case. Every device discussed above needs to be introduced and discussed fully with the remainder of the production team. There is no point creating a marvelous spectacle when the effect might be better achieved—and more cheaply—by a subtle blending of sound and light with performances, settings, and costume. When each department believes that it alone is responsible for carrying a theatrical moment, the danger of overproduction exists. Your department may be required only to support—and that's often more difficult to do well than is going-it-alone.

14.15 In Summation

Don't let the dire warnings and prohibitions of this chapter smother the flames of your enthusiasm for special effects. After all, they allow the inventor and the child within us to blossom—just remember that enthusiasm alone is not enough to achieve safe and efficient results that are reliable night after night.

14.16 Reverting to a Real Time Frame

When this book arrived at section 10.16, you were somewhere in the middle of the third week before opening; everything between that point and this has been in parenthesis; now you must revert to your production schedule. You must now accelerate the pace in keeping with the pressures of the next ten days. Say that it's Wednesday or Thursday of the third week before opening. You've been scratching on your 1:100 [⅛":1'] sketches for the last day or so—that's all you can afford for the process (despite the fact that four or five chapters were needed to say it). At the same time you need to be assured that all orders have been placed, received, and confirmed, using the early warning gathered from your sketches. You must visit each of the other departments to see the progress in the paintshop and view the latest achievements of both wardrobe and sets. Then there are the notes to assimilate that have come to you from rehearsals, production manager, or directly from the production meetings. You need to assure yourself that the staff is on schedule with special effects manufacturing, wiring of practical lanterns in the props shop, and the like.

14.17 Final Check on Rehearsals

Finally—and this is very important—you must attend a run in the rehearsal room, rough though it may be. If possible, the board operator should accompany you with the script and follow the action with emphasis on cue positions.

Your tasks are many. You need to check the shape and location of each special and areas. A stopwatch will help time sequences, and results can be noted in the cue synopsis. Attend carefully to the tempo-rhythms that have grown during the rehearsal process, and follow carefully notes given by the director, which may give you a better idea of how what you see now differs from what the director intends for the final product. You need to be, during this final visit to the rehearsal room, a sponge that can absorb every hint, intimation, fact, and feeling; check these impressions against your documentation and allow it to guide you in the week to follow. It's time to resolve on a course of action based on the information at hand so that you can deal authoritatively with the mass of work yet to be completed. Of course, there will still be changes, and you must maintain communications with both director and deputy stage manager; but you need to base your work upon something. The rehearsal room, as you judge it on this relatively early run, is the only available indication of the final product in the theatre. It will be another week before you get back to catch a last run before production week; by then all your paperwork will be printed and distributed. Your assumptions from this viewing had better be right.

CHAPTER 15

Lighting Design
Documentation

There are two weeks before opening—only one before you enter the theatre and put your ideas to the test. You will need to work overtime to complete all that is required during these final preparations. Unfortunately, uninterrupted time is an unrealistic dream, and you must remain available for consultation with the production team. The likelihood that changes will come from the rehearsal room is high, and it's important that you keep abreast of them. After viewing the run at the end of the previous week, you need to revise and finalise your breakdown of the show's lighting: lanterns [instruments], colours, positions, and fittings. Sufficient detailed information is available, and the clock is ticking relentlessly!

Now begins the task of rebuilding your original vision from the components you have selected to form complex tools that serve the production. The process will not be complete until just before opening, even though many of your colleagues maintain that the process you are about to embark on is, in fact, *the design*. But neat paperwork and pretty plans mean nothing to your audience; until you convert that paper into well-rehearsed sequences that blend with all other departments, until each individual involved can face the pressure of the opening and the run with confidence, your documentation is not worth the paper it's written on.

During this week you must commit sufficient details of your intentions to paper in suitable formats so that the individuals who will work from them can do their tasks within the given time. The documents to be prepared include the following (sections 15.1.1 to 15.1.3).

15.1.1 Lighting Plan [Plot]

The 1:25 [½":1'] scale plan includes full details of equipment, patching, and rigging; a copy must go to the head electrician by Wednesday afternoon of this week, together with a lantern schedule and patch list.

15.1.2 Cue Synopsis

The cue synopsis must be brought up to date and copies delivered to the director and deputy stage manager, plus the stage manager/production manager/technical director, by Friday. You should also supply up-to-date copies of your alphabetic and numeric lists of circuits in sufficient time for all concerned to be familiar with them before the plotting [dry tech.] session. Include 1:100 [⅛":1'] sketches if necessary.

15.1.3 State-of-the-Board and Cue Sheets

Again by Friday preliminary state-of-the-board and cue sheets need to be available so that the board operator can become familiar with the show at the final rehearsal.

Besides preparing the above documents, you need to ensure that your crew is completing all necessary preparations (cutting and framing colour, maintenance, patching aids, and so on) and that all deliveries of materials necessary for the show are made—not just promised.

15.2 Bump-in [Load-in] Schedule

About this time the stage manager/production manager will publish the bump-in schedule (see chapter 16), which details day-by-day and hour-by-hour activities in the theatre and, therefore, the time available to the lighting designer for various processes. During the document's preparation each departmental head will be consulted to answer such questions as these:

Do we rig onstage lighting before or after the stagecloth is laid?
When can trim-painting occur?
Can sound department plot while lighting is focussing, or will we be too noisy?

The production manager will juggle and compromise to distribute available time between departments fairly but you must be sure what you envisage for the lighting is feasible within the time allocated. Once in the theatre, an hour of overtime can mean thousands of dollars. This could be the difference between a production's breaking even or going over budget. A clever production manager may be able to build latitude into the schedule, but you cannot rely upon that. You must use your time efficiently, ensuring that each task (rig, focus, plotting [dry tech.]) takes no longer than predicted in the bump-in schedule. You may need to cut elements or, at least, to create an order of priority. Rates of achievement in rigging, focussing, and, to a lesser extent, plotting [dry tech.] are variable and depend on a number of factors (as sections 15.2.1 to 15.2.4 show).

15.2.1 The Crew

More bodies with greater experience will achieve results quicker, but they cost more. You will have to juggle between the design requirements and the budget—with the budget having ultimate priority.

15.2.2 The Theatre

Depending on the type of house and accessibility of hanging positions, you will need more or less time to rig the same number of lanterns. If the bars [barrels, pipes] are counterweighted, the onstage rig will be quite fast. Winched bars are almost as fast; but on a fixed grid, where all access is by ladder, achievement rates will plummet. Front-of-house bridges are often difficult to work, dirty, and hot; achievement rates can be slow.

15.2.3 The Set

The complexity of settings and changes needs consideration. Will you have easy access to the lanterns during the focus, or must you juggle a variety of ladders up and down rostra or, perhaps, to either side of a line of flats or scenery? Is it a single setting, or must you continually change during both focus and plotting [dry tech.]? The budget will skyrocket if you need a full crew of mechanists.

15.2.4 Type and Condition of Equipment

If you must strip the previous rig before commencing your rig, add one or two hours. If the equipment is aged and failure is likely, even more time again will be required. Electronics record far faster than pencil on paper, a major advantage of computer boards over manual during the plotting [dry tech.].

15.2.5 Supervision and Guidance

During rigging the amount of supervision needed from the lighting designer and head electrician will be far less if the crew is experienced, and time-consuming mistakes will be less likely. However, during the focus your ability to control two, three, or more focussers is the major consideration.

15.2.6 Unpredictable Factors

Every space and group of individuals will have certain problems and needs that vary achievement rates. You can only make yourself aware and listen to advice from wherever it comes.

15.3 Predicting Achievement Rates

Calculating rates will always be guess-timation, but you may find the following useful when working in a reasonable facility with an experienced crew:

5–6 minutes per lantern to rig and patch
5–6 minutes per lantern to focus (includes ladder shifting)
8–12 minutes per cue state to plot

Remember that crew members work in teams of two or three. Further adjust these times for the variables listed in 15.2; but, unfortunately, only experience will guide in estimating variations for shows of various genres: opera, drama, and so on.

The best of crews handled badly and poorly prepared will not deliver on time, a group of enthusiastic and well-prepared beginners may. Similarly, a large crew may not increase achievement rates proportional to the increase in numbers. I prefer to work with a smaller crew—about six—for longer periods. You get to know them as individuals by the time the rig is completed, and this improves communication during the focus.

15.4 Lighting Plan [Plot]: What Is Its Purpose?

This most important document needs to be prepared first. By Thursday of this week it must be delivered to the head electrician, who needs it for colour and maintenance preparations, in addition to investigating patching and rigging difficulties. Late delivery will not give the two of you time to sort out discrepancies and to consider alternatives.

This document is a blueprint for the efficient rigging of the show. In principle, the lighting designer need not attend the rig if the plan is properly prepared and includes every essential detail. (This is not to suggest that you don't attend.) The hallmarks of a good plan are clarity, precision, and a reasonable standard of draftmanship; it should not show signs of alteration and addition, as this is not the place to work out details but is the final presentation. It needs to be sufficiently clear for copies to be read easily under difficult circumstances.

The plan is the only document that completely summarises the rig, including every detail from position, dimmer, and lantern down to fittings, accessories, and colour. It will continually be used as a reference and needs to be kept for company records, particularly if the show is intended for the repertoire or revival. Many designers prefer to use pencil rather than ink; it makes updating (see section 21.14) far easier. Be certain that your pencil draftmanship and copying equipment are of sufficient quality to produce good working copies.

The complete plan contains information not necessary for the riggers; thus, there is an argument for creating two plans: a less complete one for rig, while the other would be the entire document. As the riggers do not require lantern numbers or some dimmer details, omitting these makes the plan less confusing, particularly for an inexperienced crew. It's relatively simple to interrupt the drafting to put out one format before completing the other. Wait until you've read this chapter fully before you make your judgment; but, if you decide to have two versions, the riggers' copies should be recalled immediately after the rig and destroyed.

The basic tools of a lighting designer are a colour swatch, a set of pens and pencils, and stencils. These are the bare essentials, but, of course, a draftsman's desk, a swivel chair, and a good desk light make life easier. (Just the same, many excellent designs have been drawn up on the kitchen table.) Sections 15.5.1 to 15.5.3 list other requirements that you can add to as your work load and budget allow.

15.5.1 Drafting Medium

This medium is semitransparent and suitable for copying by photostat, Daizo, or ammonia methods. It's available in sheets (standard size 840 x 600 mm [36"x24"]) or in rolls. A plastic-based variety is not affected by humidity, whereas the cheaper fibre can be.

15.5.2 Stencils and Straight-Edge

Though generally in short supply and expensive, there exist stencils of symbols in both plan and elevation to represent lighting instruments (scale 1:25 or ½":1'), which allow for quick representation of lanterns and fittings. However, they are generally biased to one or another manufacturer's range, and none covers all lantern types. Use an appropriate stencil and add a suitable symbol to represent any lantern in stock. A clear legend must be included on every plan [plot] (see section 15.7). Stencils for letters and figures can be useful, particularly if your handwriting causes confusion, but they can be time-consuming.

15.5.3 Drafting Pens

These instruments try not only my draftmanship but also my patience. They have me completely bluffed, and instead I use felt-tipped pens. (Warning: some felt-tip pens do not copy well under ammonia technique; test a sample beforehand). Whichever pen you use, you need fine, medium, and medium/large nib sizes to improve differentiation between symbols: fine for lantern outlines and lantern numbers, medium for colour and patching details, and medium/large for dimmer numbers and representing bars [barrels, pipes].

15.6 Plan [Plot]: Scale

The standard scale for your lighting plan [plot] is 1:25 [½":1'], but you need concern yourself only with maintaining a precise scale along the length of the bar [pipe, batten]. The relationship between each bar is fixed by the configuration of the theatre; and, so long as you identify each clearly on the plan, you do not need to represent their relationship one to another. This enables you to "explode" the drawing and include detailed information without cramping. Example: Figure 15.1 gives a plan view of a cluster of fixed bars that

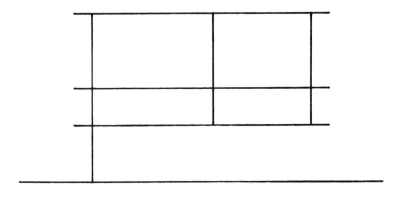

Figure 15.1
Bar Arrangement.

evolved over an end-stage. These bars generally carried forty or more lanterns, and to include complete details would make the plan utterly unreadable. But "exploding" them (see Fig. 15.2) allows space to include every item. This applies to any arrangement of bars: proscenium, thrust, or in-the-round. Since you need concern yourself only with scale along the bar, where you draw bars on the plan page is a matter of convenience.

You may see plans [plots] that include features of the theatre (such as proscenium arch, apron, and so on); but, if each bar is clearly labelled, there is no necessity for this. It merely takes up space that may be better used for clarifying the information. If necessary, include a version of the set layout that details precise positions for every bar, boom, and the like.

15.7 Plan [Plot]: First Draft

To ensure that the final version of the plan is pristine, prepare a first draft. Start with the centreline and leave space for legend, colour, and title blocks; then lay out all lighting positions so that

Figure 15.2
Exploded Bar Arrangement.

they are relatively evenly spaced. You may leave extra space below a bar that you know will be heavily rigged and for floor electrics, booms, and separately flown specials (such as chandeliers). Arrange the space between bars so that patching details can be added behind lanterns, generally towards the bottom of the sheet. Mark any obstructions that prevent the hanging of lanterns; also mark areas where the size of lantern needs to be limited. Example: You may have speakers on the orchestra bar, or there may be minimal clearance between lanterns and flying scenery—if it's impossible to brail [breast] the bar, you may be forced to use small lanterns only.

Establish a clear symbol for every item in your lantern stock, including fittings and accessories. Figure 15.3 gives an example for the STRAND Pat 23 in all its various forms. For clarity, use graphic symbols rather than written, but leave space within the lantern for colour information, gobos, and so on. Most stencils include a small mark to either side that defines the outside dimension of each lantern, and including this as part of the symbol ensures clearance on a crowded bar (see section 15.8). When a stencil does not exist for a lantern in your stock, create an appropriately sized (scale 1:25 or [½":1']) symbol that follows the international conventions outlined

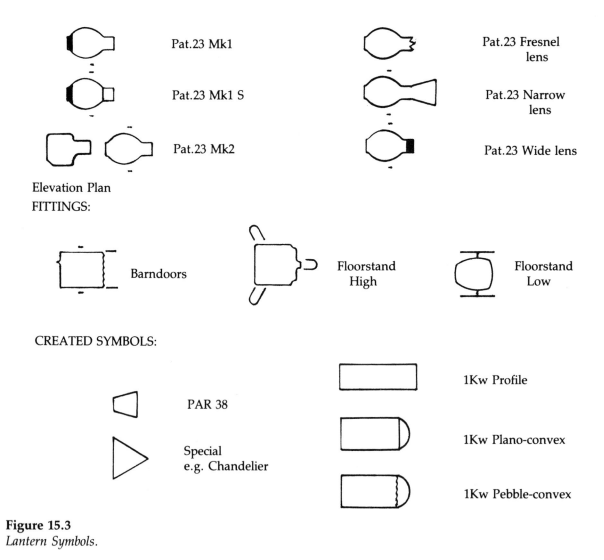

Figure 15.3
Lantern Symbols.

in sections 11.6 to 11.9. Figure 15.3 gives some possibilities for created symbols.

Returning to your 1:100 [⅛":1'] circuit sketches, do a final check of lantern types, coverage, accessories, stock, and patching. It's important that you are clear concerning these details now. Otherwise, your focus session will be experimental, trying to discover what a lantern will do instead of giving it the coverage and shape you know it must have to fulfill its purpose. Sort the circuit sketches into descending order of placement precision. Example: Near the top will be highly directional specials that can be placed in only one position to achieve what you intend. Next may come the acting areas and directional fills, since they, too, need relatively precise placement. Lower down will come the fills, colour washes, nondirectional textures, and floods.

Add each circuit to the draft in descending order so that you get the important items down early and can automatically make the necessary compromises where two lanterns compete for the same position. At this point you will realise the advantages of circuit sketches; the important process of arranging lanterns on the bar is simplified tremendously.

As you add each lantern to the plan, you must identify it or you will soon be utterly lost. Figure 15.4 illustrates how lanterns look once complete identification is made. At this stage you are unable to complete anything other than colour and dimmer identification, but you should add bar identification and counterweight line number. The remainder will be discussed shortly but are included in this diagram so that you are aware of their existence and will allow room for them. The identification number for colour is included inside the lantern symbol. Some standards insist that it be encircled, as illustrated in Lantern No. 16; but, particularly with smaller lanterns, this clutters the symbols unnecessarily. If you are using a variety of brands (for example, Cinemoid, Lee, Rosco), you may need to add further detail.

The impression given in Figure 15.4 is that the plan will be cluttered by a confusion of numbers. That is not the case, and in further sections you'll see how simplification occurs. Already, though, you should appreciate the advantage of various nib sizes to help differentiate the purpose of each number. Continue the process until all your circuit sketches are transferred to the plan [plot]. Compromises will continue, but the priority ordering ensures that they occur in the lower-rated circuits; there they least affect the concept.

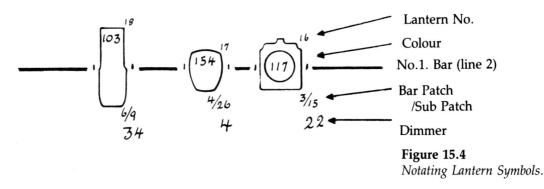

Figure 15.4
Notating Lantern Symbols.

When drawing plans [plots], should you give some indication of the direction in which lanterns point? If you merely indicate *position* and point all lanterns dead front (that is, flat hung), you miss seeing the problem that shows up in Figure 15.5. A small profile [ellipsoidal] is placed next to a large flood, which will interfere with the beam of the profile. This means that you must either reverse the order of lanterns or separate them further. Since this situation occurs frequently, try to discover problems in advance and correct them on the plan by drawing the angle of each lantern—it's better than shifting lanterns during the focus. However, doing this may add other problems, particularly when lanterns are closely packed. The two lanterns in Figure 15.6 are highside; and if you include them on the plan at the correct angle, you get an exaggerated idea of how much space they occupy on the bar.

Remember, you have already done a weight calculation assuring you that the counterweight or winch was capable of lifting all you intend (see section 10.14), but, as you draw the plan, you may have difficulty fitting them all on. If you can't draw them on the plan, it is unlikely you'll be able to squeeze them on the barrel without causing horrendous fouling problems that make the focus very difficult. Using the stencil lantern dimension marks (see section 15.7) reduces this likelihood, but you may need to cut or reposition lanterns onto less crowded bars.

When a show demands large amounts of highside or your lanterns are clustered in small groupings, the bar may distort, particularly if it is suspended at widely spaced intervals. Consider a recent example: Our bars were lifted with winches by three lines regularly distributed over the 11 metre [35'] length, and a single pipe tended to distort badly, particularly on the ends. Since the winch had sufficient capacity, my head of technical production devised the arrangement illustrated in Figure 15.7. A shallow welded gate-batten, using standard 50 mm [2''] o.d. steel pipe, was used; and smaller sections of pipe created saddles, which spread the pick-up points over a metre-and-a-half [5'] or so. Note the inclusion of insulators onto each line, a necessary safety precaution on all lighting bars.

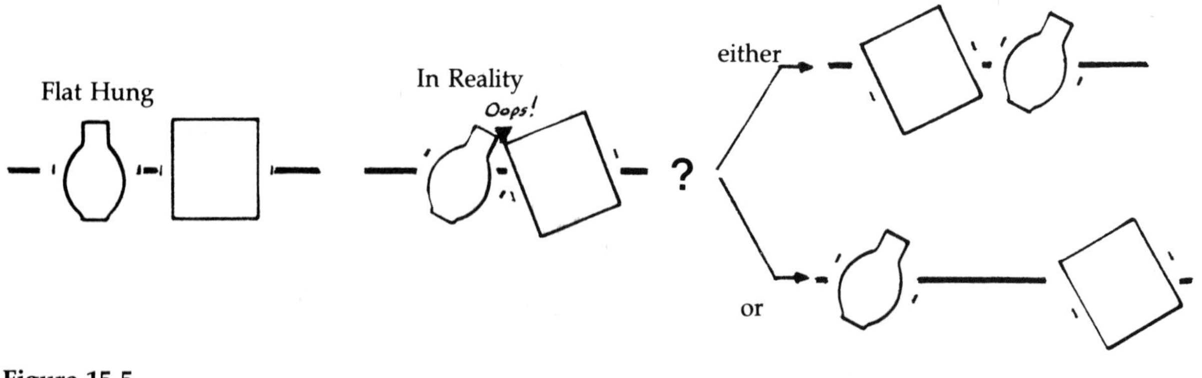

Figure 15.5
Advantages of Indicating Horizontal Angle on Plan.

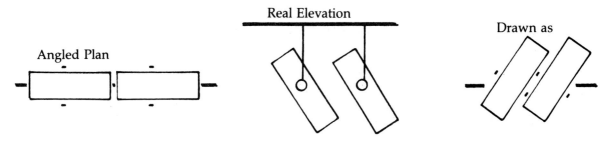

Angled Plan

Real Elevation

Drawn as

Figure 15.6
Attempt to Indicate Vertical Angle on Plan.

15.9 Patching: What Is It?

Now that you have lanterns specifically placed, you must make electrical connection between associated lanterns (thus grouping them into circuits) and their dimmer, using extension cords, looms, multicore, or in-house wiring. (A "loom" describes a group of extension cables numbered at each end and bound into an easily handled cluster.) This is known by the general term *patching* and is illustrated in Figure 15.8.

If you are able to plug an appliance into a G.P.O. (general power outlet) using an extension cable, you can arrange the patching for a rig! You also need some talent for figures and organisation, but

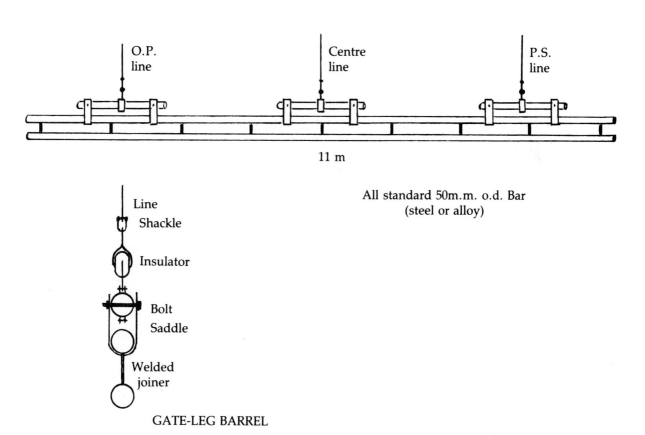

O.P. line

Centre line

P.S. line

11 m

All standard 50m.m. o.d. Bar
(steel or alloy)

Line
Shackle
Insulator
Bolt
Saddle
Welded joiner

GATE-LEG BARREL

Figure 15.7
Suspension of Lighting Bars.

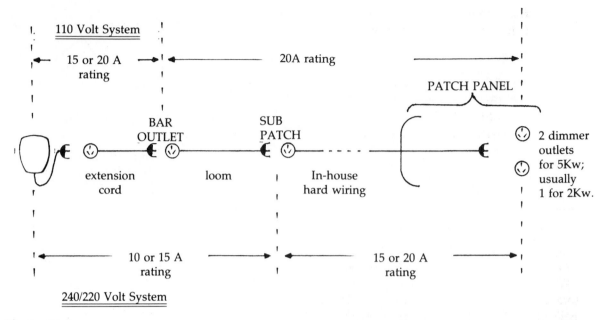

Figure 15.8
Simplistic Patching.

the skills are not really difficult. The only complication is whether the patching system is capable of delivering the power required by each circuit. Note the usual rated amperages for both 110 volt (U.S.A.) and 240 volt (U.K./Aust.) systems illustrated in Figure 15.8; and make certain you never overload. Example: In a 240 volt system most 5 kw dimmers outlets appear at the patch panel as two 10 amp rated sockets. If the house system is rated at only 10 amperes (the standard capacity) or if you are uncertain of the rating of any section, you must provide two pathways, each rated at 10 amperes, to supply those lanterns safely.

Figure 15.9 illustrates the layout for a more complex circuit, which has an alternate backlight achieved by switch-repatching. The keylight on the No. 2 front-of-house (FOH) bridge patches direct to a nearby outlet (7), which can be thought of as a permanent extension cord from the patch panel to the bridge. The same identification code (7) will appear on each end, and, at the panel, it appears as a tail that can be plugged to dimmer 16. Similarly, the fill on the orchestra bar uses outlet 22, which services this position. (The number of patching outlets installed in each position will vary from house to house, and details are available from the head electrician. Most use a patching layout diagram to detail their system.) Both these examples are relatively straightforward; neither lantern draws more than 10 amperes (240 volts), and you need not concern yourself with overloading.

The O.P. [stg. rt.] lantern of the No. 1 bar deckle circuit joins with the P.S. [stg. lft.] via an extension cord, and both plug to outlet 4 of the No. 1 bar loom. This continues along the bar, together with other loom components, and has sufficient length to reach the sub-patch with the bar flown to any height (stage level to grid). A sub-patch is usually found on the fly floor adjacent to each bar, which groups a number of outlets from the patch panel that serve exactly the same purpose as those already discussed for the front-of-house

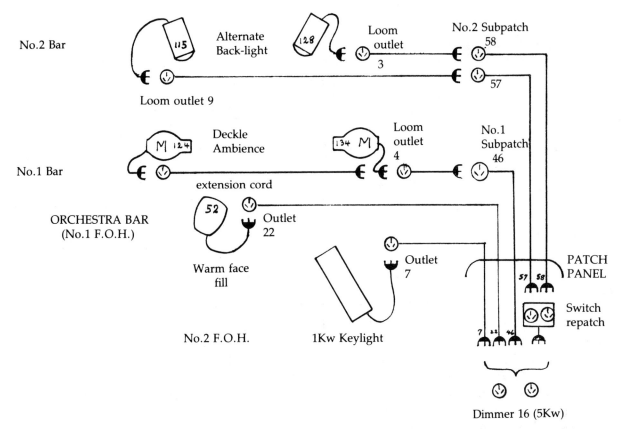

Figure 15.9
More Complex Patching.

positions. Selecting one (46), you use it to connect your lanterns to the patch panel.

On the No. 2 bar you have two lanterns, which you want to use independently via a switchblock; you may choose either or both. Remember, this was one method of retaining flexibility without requiring three dimmers to control one circuit (see section 10.11). Each lantern therefore needs a separate run via the loom and its associated subpatch back to the patch panel. There the tails (57 and 58) are plugged to a switchblock, which, in turn, plugs to dimmer 16. Check power ratings using a 240V system as an example. No portion of the circuit draws more than 10 amperes, and thus we have no overloading of cabling. However, the total amperage may total 14.6, and you must use both outlets from dimmer 16 to ensure that no plug carries more than 10 amperes. If you use adaptor plugs—one into another and all into one outlet—the pins of the bottom plug must be carrying 14.6 amperes, which is well over their 10 amperes rating and dangerous!

Before you patch a rig you must be very familiar with the system. The layout diagram should show most details of numbering and position, but you must be sure you understand all the details. Often, because the patching system has been added to in a piecemeal fashion, these additions may not be fully documented. Although convenience, simplicity, and minimal labour are the hallmark of good patching, careful recording of the information is also essential (see section 15.16).

The example in Figure 15.9 is soft patching: dimmer outlets are centrally located, and a patch panel enables you to allocate any of the scattered outlets to any dimmer. This is not always the case. Often, a patch panel will not be included; each of the outlets scattered about the theatre is, in fact, a dimmer outlet. This is known as hard patching.

Consider the circuit in Figure 15.9 in a hard-patched theatre. If you could afford no more than one dimmer, you must run extension cables to wherever the dimmer is accessible. This is labour-intensive, and, generally, it's easier to allocate onstage elements to one dimmer and front-of-house elements to another. Thus, a hard patch, if it is to be as flexible as a soft system, needs more dimmers allocated around the theatre (see section 9.3). As the profession is in the midst of a change of thinking regarding patching systems, you need to be familiar with both formats. The soft system was developed when dimmers were expensive and labour costs were low, which made patch panels relatively cheap and convenient. Modern installations tend to use hard patches, since the price of patch panels has skyrocketed while the relative cost of dimmers has fallen.

You may be required to rig in a space where there is absolutely no patching. The process is exactly the same, but you will need to purpose-build a system using extension cords. Familiarity with the theatre will lead you to the simplest approach, and clear identification of every extension cord is the secret of accuracy.

15.11 Responsibility for Patching

Since familiarity with the theatre is important, it may be that the head electrician is better qualified to organise the patching. You need to consult well in advance of the rig and to reach agreement on your approach. If it's the head electrician who will complete the patching, your plan must be prepared so that his job is made easy; and you must deliver it in time for him to complete the process. Even so, you, as lighting designer, must make yourself familiar with the system so that you don't present the head electrician with impossible problems. Example: Fifteen circuits in the front-of-house bridge will be very difficult to patch if there are only twelve outlets. The head electrician may be forced to request that you cut three circuits because fire regulations forbid the running of extensions through the fire wall formed by the proscenium arch.

When the head electrician accepts responsibility for patching in a hard-patched house, Figure 15.10 illustrates the manner in which you should prepare your plan. Clearly illustrate the manner in which lanterns are grouped; in this case, twelve lanterns are paired to form six circuits. You may not even allocate dimmers. It may be simpler for the head electrician to arrange extension cords and outlets to be least labour-intensive and get that information back so that you can make up numeric/alphabetic lists and state-of-the-board sheets for

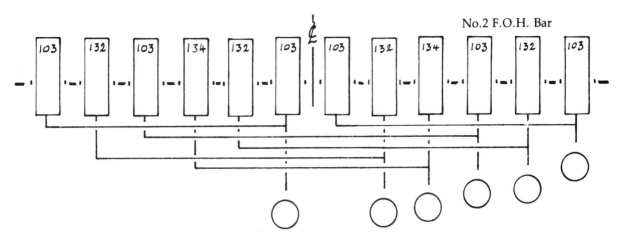

Figure 15.10
Plan with Nonspecific Patching.

the plotting [dry tech.]. In many theatres it is common not to detail patching until the rig, when precise lantern position enables allocation to the nearest outlet (see section 15.16). However, this means that the patch panel cannot be plugged up until the rig is completed—a waste of time. This implies that the lighting designer has no self-confidence in predicting lantern positions precisely. In either case, you must still ascertain that all patching is feasible *prior to the rig*.

15.12 The Process of Patching

Frequently you will detail the patching yourself, and the best way of illustrating the process is by example. Figure 15.11 gives an example of a heavy front-of-house rig with limited patching facilities. What the various lanterns are is unimportant; none is over 1 kw, and total amperage never exceeds 10. First, add the lanterns and circuits, and compare this with the number of outlets available. In this case you have twenty-four lanterns, plus a power supply for a

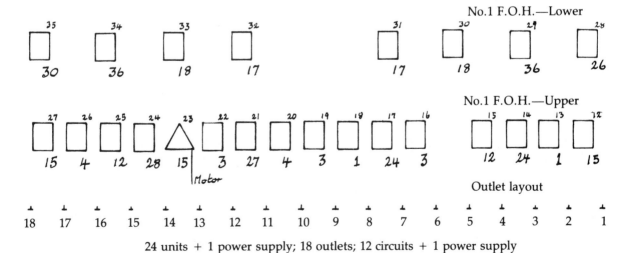

24 units + 1 power supply; 18 outlets; 12 circuits + 1 power supply

Figure 15.11
Patching Example.

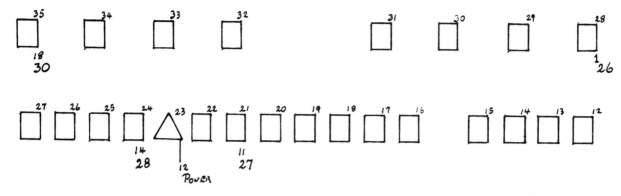

Figure 15.12
Patching Example—First Stage.

special effects motor but only eighteen outlets; one-to-one is obviously out of the question. However, until you know the number of circuits, you are unable to say whether the rig is feasible. Twelve circuits plus the power supply total thirteen—yes, it's possible with eighteen outlets; and by using the surplus five outlets, you will save running some extension cables, grouping lanterns at the patch panel instead.

Identify those units that are not paired with another unit in the front-of-house bridge and therefore must be run separately to the patch panel. Allocate them to the nearest outlet, as illustrated in Figure 15.12. You now have thirteen outlets remaining, with twenty lanterns to be arranged in eight circuits. You need to pair any seven lanterns with another that is allocated to the same circuit; and, to minimise labour, you look for pairs that are close. Figure 15.13 suggests one possible selection. These groups are allocated to the nearest available outlet, as shown in Figure 15.13, but details are marked only on the lantern nearest the outlet. This minimises confusion on the plan and, further, indicates to the riggers the need for seven extension cables with an estimation of length. There are now seven lanterns to be allocated to seven outlets; each goes to the nearest, and any further grouping will be done at the patch panel. Figure 15.14 illustrates the completed plan. This process is repeated for every lighting position in the rig.

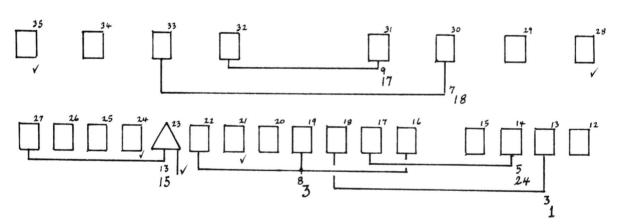

Figure 15.13
Patching Example—Second Stage.

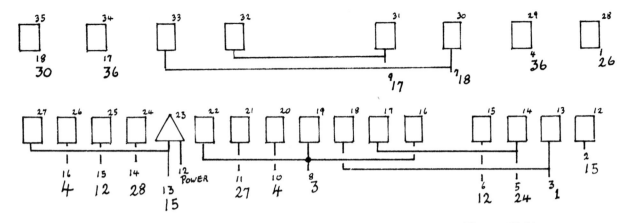

Figure 15.14
Patching Example—Final Stage.

Comparing Figure 15.4 with Figure 15.14, you will note that there are figures associated with the patching that do not occur in Figure 15.14; they indicate bar patch or subpatch details. This occurs usually with onstage bars where you have both loom and subpatch details to record (see section 15.16).

The skills associated with effective patching are difficult to study. They depend much on familiarity with a system and a keen appreciation of the work involved in running a cable. Until you've run cables under difficult conditions, you cannot know how much sweat it costs and how easy it is to make mistakes. The simpler the lighting designer's demands are, the more accurate and fast it will be.

15.13 Lantern Number

Figures 15.4 and 15.14 give examples of lantern number. This is merely a convenient way of referring to a particular lantern without needing to describe it by type and position. Wait until all lanterns have been included on the plan in their final positions before you number them; thus, you will not have confusing out-of-sequence numbers after last-minute alterations and additions.

Conventions differ around the world—even between theatres—and lantern numbers are no exception. In the U.S.A. the convention is to number each position separately, whereas in Australia and U.K. the entire rig is numbered consecutively: from prompt to O.P. [stg. left. to stg. rt.], from top to bottom, and from front-of-house to upstage. Thus, the sequence of positions when numbering the entire rig tends to be: front-of-house bars/bridges and their associated box booms; then onstage bars followed by booms/ladders/transverse bars and, finally, the floor. Hence, the highest lantern number is likely to be on the floor in the upstage O.P. [stg. rt.] corner of the stage, whereas the lowest should be on the P.S. [stg. left] of the farthest front-of-house bridge.

Now return briefly to the question raised in section 15.4: is there any advantage in producing two plans [plots]—one for the riggers and the other complete? Two sets of numbers are of little use to the riggers (the lantern number and the dimmer number in a soft-patch house), since the patch list will detail what is to occur there. It is up to you to weigh the advantages of these simplifications against the effort involved.

15.14 Completing the Plan [Plot]

The plan [plot] is now complete in all its major detail. You need add only the title block and legend. The title block should be included in the bottom right-hand corner, where it will be obvious when the copies are folded to fit your briefcase. (When carrying different plans, it's frustrating to unfold each before you can identify it.) Figure 15.15 gives an example of a title block. Note that your drawing should be checked if possible, and you must indicate when more than one drawing is required to detail the rig fully. Example: A section may better specify some odd position (also see 15.6). If there is space available, include a detailed legend. Many lighting designers use symbols and the associated lantern type, but Figure 15.16 gives more. Its third column includes the stock being used and, in the corner, the spares available. You will find this useful when you need to replace an unserviceable lantern or have an unforeseen requirement for another. You can quickly check what is available and select the most suitable. A breakdown of colour and a column for gobos, barndoors, and so on gives the riggers a clear indication of total requirements without checking other documentation (such as the lantern schedule). A colour breakdown must be done at some stage (the head electrician needs it to cut colour); you can do it as a check of lantern numbers (individual colours + open white = total stock), and include the information where it is available to all. With an inexperienced crew you may also add a version of Figure 15.4, which clearly indicates the purpose of all identifying numbers.

If you prefer to ink the drawing, you will find it convenient to use a new sheet overlaid on the pencil version. It's easy to shift up and down to correct the spacing between bars if your first draft was a little disproportionate.

Figure 15.15
Title Block for Lighting Plan.

PRODUCTION:	"ANNIE"	
DIRECTED by:	DI CREASE	
DESIGNED by:	IAN McGRATH	© FEB '85, *[signature]*
Drawn by: I McG Checked by: —		Scale: 1 : 25
Date: 19/2/85		Drawing No.: 1 of 1

Lighting Design Documentation

LEGEND   COLOUR (LEE)

SYMBOL	TYPE	No/REMAINS	GOBO	O/W	103	104	106	117	118	124	134	147	156	159	165
[symbol]	Pat. 264	18/4				4		2	2		2	2	2	2	2
[symbol]	Harm. 15°-28°	14/1		2	4	2				4	2				
[symbol]	Harm. 22°-40°	4/NIL	2									4			
[symbol]	Pat. 223	1/1			2	5							1		

Figure 15.16
Lighting Plan Legend.

15.15 Plan [Plot]: Printing and Distribution

Now, about Wednesday afternoon, it's time to print (ammonia or Daizo) at least five copies of the plan for distribution as soon as possible. You need a copy for your own use, since the original is bulky and inconvenient; further, you should keep the original as pristine as possible. The next, the master copy for the theatre, goes at once to the head electrician, who should keep this copy up to date, as it will be the definitive copy once you have departed (see section 21.12.1). Another copy goes to the stage manager/production manager to check details. (For example, has space been left for speakers, and is the weight within the capacity of the counterweights?) This copy may also become part of company records (see section 21.14.1).

Depending on the size of the rigging crew, at least another two copies will be required. The head electrician may cut them into convenient elements, called cardboards (for front-of-house, onstage, and so on) to make better use of them. You need to ensure that there are sufficient copies so that the crew members won't have to search the stage for information.

15.16 Lantern Schedule

This document is nothing more than a numeric summary of all the lanterns contained in the rig and, since most of the information is contained either on the plan [plot] or in the patch list (see section 15.17), you might question its validity. However, as an easy-to-handle summary that is particularly helpful during the focus and for maintaining the rig, it continues to be useful.

The lantern schedule's purpose is to record each lantern individually and to summarise details of patching, colour, accessories, and focus. It must be kept up to date as the show develops, but at this stage it will look similar to the extract illustrated in Figure 15.17.

Lantern No.	Type	Lee Colour	Patching		Dim	Accessories	Focus
			BAR	SUB			
31	Pat. 223	103	8	52	22	B/D	A/A 4. P.S.
32	" 264	"	4	57	27		CENTRE (U.S.) SPECIAL
33	" 223	"	9	58	28	B/D	A/A 6. O.P.
34	" 264	165	11	56	26		NYC BOX CENTRE
35	" 223	103	12	55	25	B/D	A/A 5 CENTRE
36	" 264	"	13	59	29		O.P. (U.S) SPECIAL (DESK)
37	" 814	118	14	60	30		COOL SIDE from O.P.
38	" 223	104	15	58	28	B/D	A/A 6 O.P.

Figure 15.17
Lantern Schedule.

The first column lists the lanterns by number, and it's convenient to prepare the schedule so that each page details one bar or position. The next two columns list type of lantern and colour. It is from this list that the crew preparing and framing colour would work if you had not included the summary as part of the legend. The next three columns list patching (bar and sub) and dimmer, thus tracing the delivery of power from dimmer to lantern. This information is useful when patching faults occur during the rig. Also you can use it for quick repairs of accidental dislodgments during the run—a frequent occurrence in floorwells [dips, pockets] and gallery subpatches, where passing traffic is heavy. When the head electrician prefers to allocate patching during the rig (see section 15.11), the lantern schedule is used to record the details and plug-up at the subpatch. Details of subpatch and dimmer may be used to plug up the patch panel, but an extraction may be more useful (see section 15.17). Three columns are generally sufficient, but you may vary the number to suit the patching system in the theatre.

The accessories column summarizes all the equipment needed to complete the rig, such as barndoors, gobos, safety chains, boom arms, floor stands, and extension cords plus estimated length. Some designers say that the last column should be left for the head electrician to detail during the focus, but those who take this position tend to be experimental focussers—they don't quite know what the lanterns are going to do. This is contrary to the principles of design. You should certainly know enough about them to detail as much as is given in Figure 15.17. The head electrician may record more specifics, but you are shirking your responsibilities if you leave it entirely to him or her.

It's difficult to define a single purpose for the lantern schedule, which can be useful in a number of modes: a summary of the rig, a means of recording details, a tool to assist in preshow checks, and an aid to maintaining the rig after the designer's departure. Yet this is the document often left out, forgotten, or passed on to an assistant!

Imagine yourself at a 60 dimmer/150 outlet patch panel. Your lantern schedule is in hand as you try to patch quickly and accurately. If you work numerically down the schedule, the cables will lie all over the place—on top of one another, twisting through, pulling down on sockets. Tracing faults in such a mess will be difficult, and you find that plugs can be dislodged by weight of cable. Frequently, two or more lanterns use the same subpatch (see Figure 15.17), and you will be looking among the unplugged tails for one that has already been patched.

Use the lantern schedule to extract a patch list, but be careful; the process of extraction needs to be checked for transcription mistakes. By listing the dimmer and extracting all the associated outlet numbers, you will be able to remove duplications and arrange the subpatches in numeric order. This allows for the task at the patch panel to be achieved quickly and neatly (see section 17.8.1).

15.18 Plotting [Dry Tech.] Preparations

You have completed the documentation required for the rig, but your task as lighting designer is not yet finished. You must look ahead to production week and prepare yourself and the board operator for the plotting [dry tech.], technical rehearsal and beyond. The remainder of this chapter looks at the process of predicting the level of each dimmer required to reconstruct your original vision and shows how a draft cue sheet can be written well in advance.

Many would ask, "What's the point? The director's going to change everything anyway." The reply is, "Time!" Every second saved now solving mechanical problems and preparing your operators can be devoted to shaping your lighting to fit the production better. Why waste time in the plotting [dry tech.] devising methods of handling cues when you can outline them beforehand? This is particularly so when plotting a complicated show on a manual board. Although the technology of computer boards relieves the pressure of inadequate mechanics, it does not remove the need for the lighting designer to have conceived each intensity required to re-form the vision. Further, if your estimation of the director's requirements is so badly off, your communication has been—to say the least—poor.

The task is to produce preliminary state-of-the-board and cue sheets that will improve achievement rates during the plotting session, which should be just that—not a cue sheet writing session! You should be concentrating on the stage picture, not on mechanical details (such as choice of master or whether there is sufficient time for a preset). Even if your communication with the director is at fault and you deviate from the planning or, as is more usual, you happen upon an exciting new approach, then it's easy enough to take the extra time and return to the preordained format as soon as possible.

There is another advantage. The process of dissecting cues ensures that both you and the board operator are fully prepared for the plotting [dry tech.], are using the board to best advantage, and are encouraging comprehension of the purpose behind each cue.

15.19 Updating the Cue Synopsis

At the end of Chapter 9 you returned to the cue synopsis to pencil in dimmer numbers to be used to create each state. It's now time to revise that; but, before doing so, be certain that all alterations from the rehearsal room, together with any variations you have devised, are included. The run you attended at the end of last week will form the basis of these changes.

Once you've updated, it's—at last—time to number the cues for easy reference; then publish at least three copies. The first is for your own use, while the second is for the deputy stage manager and director as an aid to preparing them for the plotting [dry tech.]. They can check details against what is happening in rehearsal, and the deputy stage manager will enter cues into the prompt copy in preparation for the technical rehearsal. The third copy goes to the stage manager/technical director, who must have details of all cues well in advance of the technical rehearsal so as to continue the complex process of combining each element into a whole.

For the lighting designer the major purpose in updating the cue synopsis is to make a partial step towards the development of state-of-the-board sheets. Some say a partial step is a waste of time, but you will probably find that processes are simpler if you reduce the size of the step being taken on each occasion.

In the last column of the cue synopsis (see Figure 8.1) ensure that you list all circuits required to achieve your original vision. You may be forced to revise your ideas in the light of more recent developments, but don't feel guilty! Fluidity is part of the process of refining ideas and developing a shape that matches the latest information from rehearsals. Go a step beyond: estimate the level each dimmer should be set at to form the balanced picture you intend. Start with the keylight, perhaps, and work outwards. Return, in your mind's eye, to your experiments on the model; this may give you further indications of the balance between dimmers needed to form a centre of focus and balanced tonings in the ambience.

During your first attempts at this process an eraser will be a major item of equipment. As you'll always be changing your mind, progress will be slow; however, as you gain more experience, your speed and accuracy will improve. (These days I'm able to predict to within about 15 percent for the majority of circuits—but often I'm wildly out.)

Figure 15.18
Cue Information for Cue Synopsis.

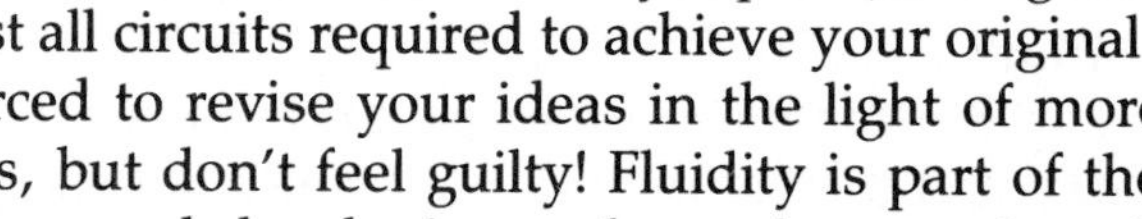

$$\frac{1,6}{60} \quad \frac{10}{F} \quad \frac{28\text{-}30}{35} \quad \frac{32}{F} \uparrow \quad REMAINDER \downarrow$$

Use the method in Figure 15.18 to record your estimations. This example is gross in its detail, but don't forget that this is merely the first step; it's preferable to be bold at this time and leave refining to the next step.

15.20 Preliminary State-of-the-Board Sheets

You have already used this format in section 9.10.4 to assist in organising repatching; the current use is similar but demands far greater detail. Your purpose is to predict the movement of every dimmer as you shift to each new state outlined by the cue synopsis. The information may be transferred directly to the memory of a computer board or used to prepare cue sheets for a manual board (see section 15.21). Figure 15.19 illustrates the format.

Down the two left-hand columns you list the page number of the script and the cue number from the synopsis; across the top you list each dimmer by number, including repatch circuits; for example, 8A and 8B. You may also include the dome (follow-spots) and, perhaps, a column for special effects—anything you feel will be useful in the formation of cue sheets.

Simply transfer the estimations of level from the cue synopsis to this alternate format. (*Note:* ▓▓ indicates zero) Allow yourself plenty of space, as this document is likely to be used under minimal lighting conditions. Try to indicate the various stages of a cue. Example: Cue 5 has dimmer 1 and 2 moving during the first part and dimmer 3 during the second, while dimmer 11 is involved throughout. As you transfer from the cue synopsis to the state-of-the-board (SOB) sheet, you will certainly discover more detail that had not previously occurred to you; that is the benefit of working this document through. The format of a state-of-the-board sheet is similar to a computer printout; it presents the contents of memory in this form at the touch of a button and becomes the permanent record of the show's cues. On a manual board you need the same record, but, unfortunately, you must correct preliminary state-of-the-board sheets or rewrite new sheets once the plotting [dry tech.] of the show has been completed.

Final state-of-the-board sheets and printout copies should be included in company records (prompt copy) and also retained by the board operator as an aid to the running of the show. If the computer dumps its memory, you can use the printout to reprogramme the machine. With a manual board, state-of-the-board sheets may help to trace transcription faults when cue sheets are rewritten; they are also useful during the rehearsal process as an aid to returning quickly to earlier states.

Don't be too reserved as you plan the board operation. It's better to overestimate at this stage and to simplify from here on; in that way you prepare the board operator for the worst, then reduce the workload to a manageable size if you have been too ambitious. Remember, you are out to challenge, not destroy, the board operator.

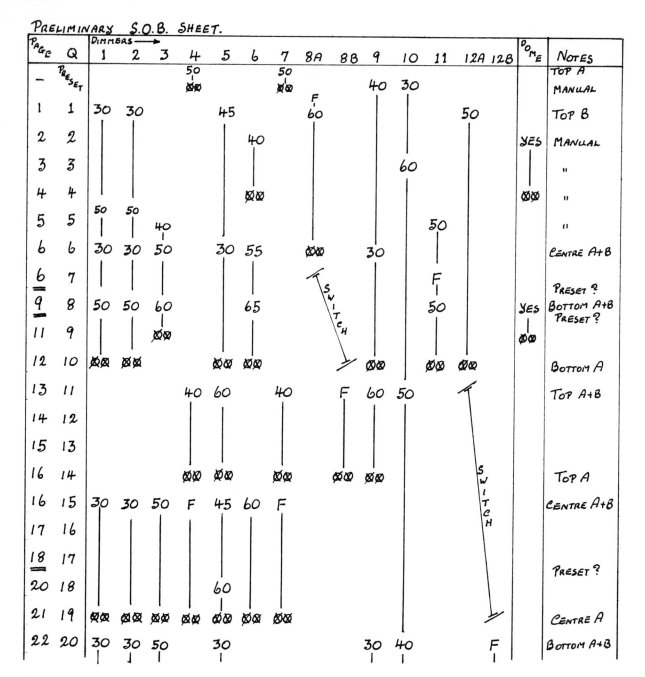

Figure 15.19
Preliminary State-of-the-Board Sheet.

15.21 Preliminary Cue Sheets

As was already mentioned, the plotting [dry tech.] session is frequently pushed for time (average rate of 8–12 minutes per cue). You must establish a method and outline limits to the operation before drafting (in pencil) cue sheets sufficient to allow the plotting to proceed with the emphasis on the stage picture—not on the board! The method of writing cue sheets will vary from person to person, board to board. Anyone using a manual board should sit at the desk during this process, as this is the easy way to visualise operations. The board operator should write the cue sheets because he or she will be the one trying to read them under pressure. Further, it's beneficial if the board operator takes a major role in the process for better understanding of each cue's purpose; much of the work to be done during technical and dress rehearsals will be given a firm basis at this time. With experienced operators you may notate the state-of-the-board sheets and leave them to devise the method of operation themselves.

Consider Figure 15.19 in terms of a manual board (3 preset, A and B switching). First, define where there is sufficient time for a preset: between cues 7 and 8, 8 and 9, 17 and 18 there are two or more pages of script completely free of cues that may be useful for major presets. The Notes column suggests an approach to each cue that seems appropriate to the complexity of operation; in other words, by assessing the entire cue, you've made a decision whether it's possible to achieve the effect by movement of individual dimmers (manual) or whether a master is more suitable. Since dimmer 10 was continually in operation, though the levels change, you resolved to retain all except dimmer 10 on A master while 10 was allocated to A + B.

The preset, both in front of the curtain (4 and 7—warmers) and behind (9 and 10), was on the top A master, and you decided to take the curtain-warmers out manually. Dimmers 1, 2, 5, and 12 were temporarily switched to B; and, to create the sequential feel with dimmer 8, you added it manually on the A submaster, then followed with the remainder on B. Cues 2, 3, and 4 involved the movement of one dimmer only and were quite easy to handle on the top master manually. Cue 5 was a little more complex but could still be achieved manually. Cue 6, however, required a number of dimmers to shift simultaneously and demanded a master crossfade between centre (A and B) and top (A and B), since you still have some dimmers switched to B and A + B.

After cue 7 you have time available for a preset. You can adjust the switching back to what you consider standard for this show (all to A, except 10 to A + B), and you can clear the top preset, which is no longer in use, and set up cue 11. The switch repatching for dimmer 8 can also occur during this period.

Cue 9 again involves a master crossfade, though it may be easier to operate as an add of the upcoming master with an adjust of dimmer 11; on completion you can preset the centre with cue 15. Try the remaining cues yourself. The examples illustrate how an understanding of the workings of the board, together with a clear concept of how the lighting is shaped moment by moment, enable you to predict how the operation might best be arranged, with due regard to pressure of time and complexity. If you leave it to the plotting [dry tech.], you might well "paint yourself into a corner" and produce cue sheets that are unduly complex. Under these circumstances you frequently scrap the whole lot and rewrite with time pressing.

This whole approach may not remove all problems, but it should enable you to consider them calmly and with least pressure. Not only are the advantages to the lighting designer sufficient to justify the time required, but also most board operators find it beneficial to have these preliminary sheets and, perhaps, the desk at a rehearsal. This approach enables them to judge tempo-rhythms precisely, ensures they have sufficient time to complete all that is required of them (presets), and gives them advance warning of pressured times or impossibilities (the lighting designer may need to simplify and cut). Consider the problems of a board operator. Actors have been in rehearsal for weeks; yet, with one technical rehearsal, the board operator is expected to match them in precision and subtlety. Any advanced experience you can give, any understanding of cue shapes, any appreciation of pace must be to the operator's advantage.

15.22 Final Preparations Before Production Week

It's now Friday and you may still be working on cue sheets, though you already realise the advantage of the board operator's having them for the final run today. Instead, you will need to continue working over the weekend and allow the board operator to attend any rehearsals on Monday while the remainder of the crew is rigging. In either case, you both must attend this last rehearsal to pick up any developments that have occurred during the past week. Timings will have changed, even staging, and you need to incorporate them. It's important for the lighting designer to spend time with both the deputy stage manager and board operator during this run. They need to begin appreciating the relationship between their documentation and what is happening on the floor. Get to see the head electrician sometime today to talk through the problems of the rig and to ensure that you're working as a team. Acknowledge your mistakes with good grace—there may be many or a few—and invite suggestions. Inexperienced designers tend to isolate themselves, but they should remember that the head electrician is as much in the service of the production as the designer is.

Check to see that all orders have arrived and that the manufacture of special effects and props is completed. Prepare your crew as much as possible; give them the chance to see the plan, and find time to discuss the details with them. This is not always possible when using a free-lance crew, but you may be able to leave a copy of the plan somewhere central for viewing. During the past week you have been in partial isolation; now you need to get out among the others of the production team. Only by doing this are you fully prepared and working together before the stresses of the production week commence.

15.23 In Summation

The paper war is completed, but you still don't have a design. You have created a blueprint for efficient transfer of your ideas into fact—the means of clearly communicating details to all concerned and preparing them for their part in the process. You still want to allow for flexibility; and, despite the hours you spent preparing detailed documents, you dare not get overly protective of your efforts.

Some of your colleagues may find it more convenient to keep all information in their heads and work during production week from adrenaline and inspiration; but, in so doing, they leave a trail of ill-prepared and nervous people behind them. A large part of your job is to weld together a team that can continue the run after the lighting designer departs on opening night. If you withhold information to the last possible moment, you may be working contrary to that aim.

It's been a big week, and a bigger one is coming. If possible, take a weekend's rest!

CHAPTER 16

Production Week Programming

The time available before opening night is now reduced to days, hours, even minutes! The schedule outlined in chapter 2 is no longer sufficiently detailed to control the activity of so many different departments all needing to work within the same facility. The stage manager/production manager therefore publishes a bump-in [load-in] schedule that details every activity between now and opening.

The production's size and complexity dictates how long you have between getting onto the stage and the opening. On tour with a medium-sized piece, you may have two days, whereas a premiere production is likely to need until Friday. Whatever the circumstances, management attempts to keep this "dark" period short, since the overhead for this time is enormous and the receipts zero.

Following are example bump-in [load-in] schedules for both types of production. Fine detail not pertinent to this book is not included, and there is a strong bias towards the electrics department, but you should realise that every department has responsibilities and schedules as tight as yours.

16.2 Opening Friday, 8:00 P.M.

The example given below is based upon a premiere production involving an orchestra and a major technical commitment. The musical element makes little difference to the lighting department except that this type of show requires additional labour to set up the orchestra pit.

Bump-in [Load-in] Schedule

Monday	8:00 A.M.	Commence lighting rig (downstage) Fly masking and set pieces (upstage) Bulk of set arrives, loading bay

Staggered Tea Break

Monday	11:00 A.M. (approx.)	Set construction (concentrate on major items required for focus) Rig front-of-house lighting

Staggered Lunch Break

	2:00 P.M.	Rig onstage, side, and floor; flash out

	6:00 P.M.	Lighting dinner break
		Set deads [trims]
	7:00 P.M.	Focus (finish by 11:00 or before)

On Completion Focus, Paint Stage

Tuesday	8:00 A.M.	Complete set construction (detail)
	11:00 A.M.	Scene change rehearsal (worklight)
	1:00 P.M.	Lunch break
		Continue set construction if required. Rig communications and production desk
	2:00 P.M.	Plot sound
		Props and wardrobe set up
		Lighting prepares for plotting [dry tech.]
	4:00 P.M.	Lighting plotting [dry tech.]
	6:30 P.M.	Dinner break
	7:30 P.M.	Continue lighting plotting (finish by 11:00)
Wednesday	8:00 A.M.	Stage available for technical work; lighting trim rig
	9:00 A.M.	Scene change rehearsal (stage lighting)
	10:00 A.M.	Technical rehearsal act 1—piano only
	1:00 P.M.	Lunch break
	2:00 P.M.	Technical rehearsal act 2—piano only
	6:00 P.M.	Dinner break
	7:00 P.M.	Technical run acts 1 and 2—piano only (finish by 11:00)
Thursday	8:00 A.M.	Detail painting
	9:00 A.M.	Set up orchestra pit lighting
		Trim rig and focus
	11:00 A.M.	Drill board operation, plus deputy stage manager and sound operator
	1:00 P.M.	Lunch break
	2:00 P.M.	Full run or Sitzprobe (orchestra and performers downstage of house curtain; *very* quiet work may continue upstage)
	6:00 P.M.	Dinner break
	7:00 P.M.	Dress rehearsal (invited audience)
		Notes to finish by 11:00
Friday	9:00 A.M.	Stage available for technical work
	11:00 A.M.	Run act 1 and notes (piano only)
	1:00 P.M.	Lunch break
	2:00 P.M.	Run act 2 and notes (piano only); finish by 4:00
	7:25 P.M.	Half-hour call
	8:00 P.M.	Premiere performance

16.3 Opening Tuesday, 8:00 P.M.

This schedule would be expected on tour with a medium-sized production where you are re-mounting a familiar piece or for a premiere production with a minor technical commitment (for example, a single box-setting with twenty lighting cues and eight sound cues).

Bump-in [Load-in] Schedule

Monday	8:00 A.M.	Lighting rig onstage, commencing downstage
		Unload truck (lighting toolbox packed to be first off!)
	9:00 A.M.	Set construction and flying, commence downstage
		Wardrobe bump-in to dressing rooms
		Rig sound system and communications (lighting to rig speakers)

Staggered Tea Break

		Lighting rig front-of-house, then onstage, sides, floor
	12:00 A.M.	Lighting lunch break and two mechanists
	1:00 P.M.	Mechanists' lunch break
		Set deads [trims] (stage manager and two mechanists)
		Lighting focus commences
	2:00 P.M.	Set detailing (available light only)
		Sound check
		Props set up (assistant stage manager (A.S.M.) to organise worklight through head electrician)
	6:00 P.M.	Dinner break
		Sound plot
	7:00 P.M.	Lighting plotting [dry tech.]
	10:00 P.M.	Paint floor/trimming
	11:00 P.M.	Finish
Tuesday	9:00 A.M.	To be advised (T.B.A.); board operator check cue sheets at motel
	11:00 A.M.	technical rehearsal; top-and-tail
	1:00 P.M.	Lunch break
	2:00 P.M.	Dress rehearsal (panniers and basic items only); on completion, set back to opening
	7:25 P.M.	Half-hour call
	8:00 P.M.	Opening performance

16.4 Amplifying Notes

The following (16.4.2 to 16.4.6) are amplification to the above schedules.

16.4.1 Similarities

Both schedules are basically the same, the only real difference being the duration of each segment. Whatever size the show or whatever degree of technical commitment, the same processes must be completed before you can open.

The production manager has built into the first example a certain latitude that allows for inevitable slight departures from the schedule. The second example, however, has no room for mistakes; should something go wrong, the only way to compensate is to truncate other activities or to extend into overtime. It is for this reason that all would-be lighting designers should attempt a one-night-stand tour as a test of their skill.

16.4.2 Interaction between Departments

No department can have exclusive use of the stage. You must learn to share facilities, abiding by the bump-in [load-in] schedule, which gives priority to each department in turn. During these times you should not expect to be alone onstage, but you do have the right to ask those with a lower priority to suspend activities temporarily while you continue with yours. Example: during the sound plotting the lighting department can be focussing upstage (quietly), and the scene painters can be trimming downstage.

16.4.3 Additional Demands on the Lighting Designer

Besides attending all activities involving your department, you need to attend other events to fully prepare yourself.

It's imperative that you attend the setting of the deads [trims], which the stage manager/production manager will achieve in association with the set designer and flymen. It involves masking all flown items; and, despite the best estimates from the section, there are sure to be minor problems for which the lighting designer must be available for consulting. Try to attend the sound plotting, particularly of cues with interaction between lighting and sound. Similarly, scene-change rehearsals may be of interest, since you need a feel for their tempo before you can plot the board operation with confidence. By remaining aware, you will quickly realise where else your presence would be appreciated.

16.4.4 Departures from Schedule

At all costs you must organise your department to complete tasks within the time given, but the unforeseen does happen—minor departures from schedule are inevitable. It's imperative that you keep the production manager informed with realistic estimations of your progress so that he or she can adjust in minor ways to compensate for delays or take advantage of time savings.

16.4.5 Staggered Breaks

The production manager may stagger regulation breaks to ensure the stage is used to maximum effect and is at no time "dead." The lighting crew may take an early lunch while the mechanists carry on; then they take lunch while lighting continues unimpeded. You are always regulated by union rules, but within the theatrical profession there is a healthy regard for common sense. Everyone is aware of problems and is prepared to shift minor details around to compensate, but those who are in management must always request and never expect the rules to be bent in any way.

16.4.6 Demarcation

The second schedule requires a greater degree of interaction between departments, interaction that in a more rigid unionised theatre could form the basis of demarcation disputes. Such softened attitudes and more willing cooperation is common among smaller touring companies and is a further example of the healthy attitudes mentioned in 16.4.5. However, you need to ensure that no one abuses the privilege or puts to the test the goodwill of colleagues.

CHAPTER 17

Rigging

The shift into the theatre involves not only a change of pace for you as lighting designer but also a change in your responsibilities. As the emphasis shifts away from art and very firmly onto the craft, you no longer have the freedom of an individual artist working whatever hours suit you best. While remaining responsible for the achievements of the lighting department, you accept additional responsibility for the safety and well-being of the crew, in partnership with the head electrician. The degree to which you are forced to compromise your artistic endeavour depends largely upon the quality of your preparation, your ability to foresee difficulties before they eventuate, the cooperation and trust of your crew, and your ability to think quickly on the run.

17.2 Safety

Before anyone steps onstage, you must realise that it's a dangerous location, particularly when there are individuals about who are unaware of the fact or choose to ignore it. In the lighting department you have responsibility for heavily weighted bars over performers and audience; individuals working on ladders at great heights; electricity and the ever-present risk of fire—all or any of which can kill.

This book doesn't have the space to give first aid, safety, fire control, and basic electricity courses, nor can it instruct in basic tools and equipment; you must obtain this knowledge elsewhere. Without that basic knowledge you are dangerous to yourself, your colleagues, and your audience (and I wouldn't want to work with you).

17.3 Organisation and Authority

You're all onstage, and it's 8:00 A.M. What should you, as lighting designer, do to get things moving? Nothing! Remember that in a professional/union house the designer is not in charge—the head electrician is. Theoretically, you are not permitted even to touch a lantern; you're not there as a worker but as the final arbiter of what the design requires.

Chapter 15 said if the plan [plot] is sufficiently detailed, the designer need not attend the rig. That is the theory; this is the practice! You're onstage with absolutely nothing to do, waiting for the crew to discover unforeseen problems. If you like to combine theory and paperwork with sweat and dirty hands, you'll find this time extremely frustrating. You'll want to pick up a lantern and push ahead to opening; but you must resist the temptation, since in a union house you are considered part of management. Union members may be deprived of jobs if you carry out their functions; and, besides, you cannot be available for consultation onstage if you're swinging from the farthest box boom. But once everyone sees that you understand the situation—that you are trying to make the crew's job easier and that you are happy to be part of the team—then they are prepared to accept your contribution, and you may touch lanterns when necessary. It may take a couple of rigs for the head electrician and the crew to know you well enough to understand your motives, so don't expect immediate acceptance.

In any event, you have latitude to work only as a designer—not as a member of the crew. You may pick up a lantern to demonstrate a point, or you may see the need to adjust the position of a lantern by 100 mm [4"], which will make it easier to focus; and you may be able to point out a mistake or add an accessory. That's not rigging; you haven't taken a crew member's position or responsibility. Rather, you are adding another dimension, a further check that the head electrician and crew will generally accept and welcome. But if you try to usurp anyone's position or authority—particularly that of the head electrician—whether your actions are deliberate or unwitting, you're asking for trouble.

In an amateur or semiprofessional house there will be unwritten rules just as rigid and sometimes more difficult to understand; tradition, convention, and personalities are likely to be far more influential and, possibly, more restrictive. You must try to understand or, at least, to cope with the situation and to establish a working relationship that will see you through the production. It's still 8:00 A.M.—and it's time to start work.

17.4 Preparation of the Crew

Ascertain that all members of the crew understand the plan [plot]. Every symbol, method of indicating patching, colour identification, and the like must be clear to them before they start; and, since they are likely to have worked under all sorts of systems, they need to familiarise themselves with your approach and its peculiarities. Make yourself available for questions, and try not to become defensive if you are subjected to a certain amount of banter.

There are universal requirements for a rig, and there are others in which designers differ in detail; all of them need mentioning during the briefing before you start work. Sections 17.4.1 to 17.4.7 list a few; you may add those that have specific application to your show.

17.4.1 Colour

It is advantageous to fit colour during the rig. That way you're able to check if sufficient has been cut, and you can detect errors early.

It's easy for the focusser to remove colour to assist your vision of the beam during the focus.

17.4.2 Gate Accessories

You'll want to fit gobos, irises, and so on during the rig because it's often difficult to locate them correctly while working at the top of a ladder.

17.4.3 Finger Tight

At this stage all adjustments and locking devices should be no more than finger tight. Once they have been correctly positioned and angled, they can be firmly locked off so that they remain unmoved throughout the run.

17.4.4 Barndoors and Shutters

All barndoors should be fitted and fully opened, whereas shutters should be free and fully withdrawn. If either is closed there is a danger of heat damage, and you may have difficulty in seeing whether lanterns are functioning.

17.4.5 Looming and Cabling

There needs to be latitude in the cabling from the lanterns to the loom/trunking to allow for minor shifting of the lantern, but be sure that no cable can brush against its own or any other lantern, where it may become heat-damaged. It could short-circuit, a dangerous situation. The bar [pipe] arrangement in Figure 15.7 makes separating lanterns from cabling much easier. (See Figure 17.1 for examples.)

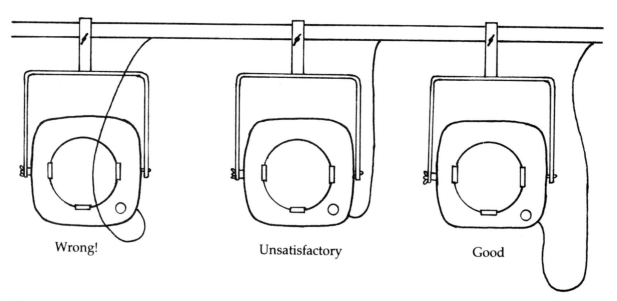

Wrong!   Unsatisfactory   Good

Figure 17.1
Power Cables to Lanterns.

17.4.6 All Lanterns Spotted

A good way to start is with all lanterns either zoomed or spotted to their narrowest beam angle. It is easier during the focus to position the lantern while spotted; then flood to the minimal coverage required.

17.4.7 Rough Angling

Figure 15.5 showed the advantage of indicating angle on your plan [plot]; for the same reasons, lanterns should be roughly angled during the rig. You discover problems that can be solved simply at stage level instead of up the ladder during focus—where every action is much more difficult. Ask permission of the head electrician to adjust lanterns finely once each bar [pipe] is rigged.

Other designers may consider some of the above detail unnecessary, and there are two points that they may dispute. Many prefer to colour the lantern after it has been focused; these designers are also likely to "flat-hang" all lanterns (angled up-and-down stage and horizontal). In this way they prevent too many confusing lights onstage during the focus; only those lanterns that have been correctly adjusted will be apparent, and the remainder will be lighting the border overhead. Try both approaches and select which appeals to you.

Now that you've answered all the crew's questions, it should be no more than 8:15 A.M. and it's time to get dirty!

17.5 Preparation of Equipment

Whether you start with your lanterns in storage, on the floor, or still in the air where they were used by another show, your first task is to strip, check, clean, and sort all lanterns. If possible, this should be done in the previous week, but you may have neither time nor access and are forced to undertake maintenance just before you start rigging. Even if the equipment is superbly maintained and regularly cleaned and serviced, you will need a quick check to ensure that every lantern you put into the air is safe, functioning correctly, and performing according to specifications. It's far easier to work on lanterns at stage level with a full range of tools and test instruments than to make corrections when lanterns are in the air.

Apart from the obvious dirty mirrors and lenses, faulty lamps and unserviceable wiring, seized shutters and nonstandard lens arrangements, you're looking for oddities such as that illustrated in Figure 17.2. (Why lanterns end up in this condition so frequently I'll never know!) As you curse, keep in mind the group to follow you and make sure they don't have reason to do the same. It may still be 8:15 A.M. if you were able to achieve the strip and lantern check in advance; if not, you hope you haven't lost too much time. Sufficient time to carry out the check needs to be anticipated carefully, however, and included in the bump-in schedule—about an hour to ninety minutes should be sufficient.

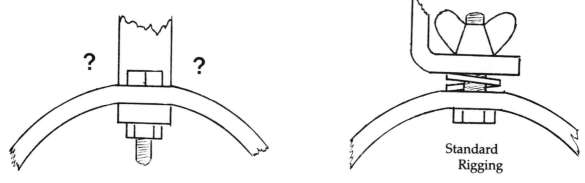

Figure 17.2
*Correct Suspension of
Lanterns.*

17.6 Allocation of Tasks

Once the lantern check has been completed, the crew can be split into teams and allocated tasks. Team sizes will depend upon the magnitude of the task, difficulty of access, and safety considerations. Union rules—and common sense—state that, wherever a ladder is being used, a minimum of two of the crew should be made available: one up the ladder and the other at the base.

17.7 Where Do You Start?

The setting and space dictate which rigging sequence will be most beneficial, and the stage manager/production manager needs to consider all ramifications and consult carefully before publishing the schedule.

Your lighting department is trying to get its equipment into the air and working as fast as possible without causing too much delay or obstruction to other departments; that, however, must be a *mutual* aim. There's no point getting the set up early if it's going to take four times as long to rig the lighting off ladders. And it would be stupid to position booms early, since they are sure to inconvenience every other department.

Generally, you start with overhead bars [pipes] downstage and move up so that you get off the stage as soon as possible and move front-of-house while the mechanists do most of the flying and set construction. Once that is well under way, the lighting department can return onstage to rig sidelighting and floor. That's only a loose rule-of-thumb; compromise and cooperation are also required. Perhaps the lighting department needs to accept a greater degree of difficulty for one or two hanging positions to accommodate another department. Conversely, elements of the setting may be left off until after the focus so that ladder access and movement will be faster. There are no rules; every show must be looked at in the light of its own problems.

Now that the crew is working, the immediate pressure is off both you and the head electrician; but, because you must remain accessible, you cannot slope off to coffee. Always listen to suggestions from your crew, since they are the ones with immediate experience of the problem; but available time and the requirements of the show will be your paramount considerations in making decisions.

17.8 Specific Jobs, Problems, and Points to Watch

As your crew will be scattered all over the theatre, you may need to move from one activity to another with nimbleness of wit and body. Sections 17.8.1 to 17.8.6 look at some of their tasks in isolation.

17.8.1 Patching

The patch list (see section 15.17) should be given to one of the crew with a talent for precision. Figure 17.3 illustrates the task at a patch panel with 96 outlets from 40 dimmers (1–30 rated at 2 kw, 31–40 at 5 kw). The approach will need to be varied to suit each facility, but, in the one illustrated, dimmers 31 to 40 should be patched first, then 21 to 30, 11 to 20 and finally 1 to 10. In this way you layer the

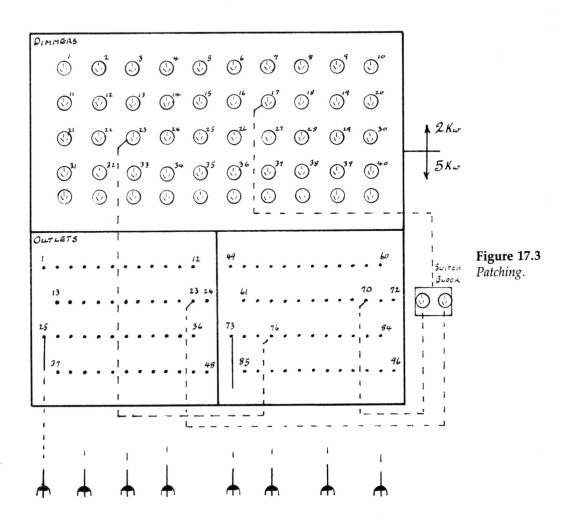

Figure 17.3
Patching.

cables one on top of another so that the weight of cable maintains each in position. Further, cables are neat and easy to trace if you take each tail behind the hanging tails, then vertically up to the dimmer outlets you require as illustrated in Figure 17.3.

This seems very logical when discussed in isolation; but, when next you are able take a good look at a show's patch panel, see what a mess some people can make of them. It's impossible to trace cables, and plugs may pull out with the slightest disturbance—it looks awful!

17.8.2 Fixed Grids

Recently a group of students faced with a fixed grid (see Fig. 15.1) and a short rigging period chose to spend time precabling the grid, marking outlets with masking tape and marker pen; thus, at the rig all they needed to do was place lanterns, plug, and flash out. Not only was the positioning of lanterns simple and the looming [cabling] safe and easy to trace, but also the double process was shorter than the usual simultaneous rig-and-loom, since obstruction by the lanterns in the cluttered grid was less.

You need to be precise with outlet positioning, but you can accommodate by adding a loop of extra cable at the outlet to lanterns whose positions you may be unsure of.

17.8.3 Excess Cable

A simple yet powerful electrical component is a coil of wire; it forms, in association with a metal core, the heart of every electric motor and generator. You may know it better as an induction coil. You have the same basic elements—which can be dangerous or the cause of appreciable power loss—with every lighting bar and coil of excess extension cable. Your accidentally formed device will generate heat, reduce efficiency, and, in the extreme, cause insulation to melt resulting in short-circuit and fire. Although it's difficult to avoid excess cable in a rig, you must make every attempt by careful selection. You can't keep chopping extensions down to exact sizes, but you must minimise the dangers. A coil performs in proportion both to the current and to the number of turns in the wire; you have no control over the current in a practical situation, but you can reduce the number of turns. See Figure 17.4.

17.8.4 Cable Ties

You need to secure cable safely and cheaply, yet only temporarily. Do you use insulation tape, gaffer tape, string? Perhaps you prefer nylon ties, which can only be used once and must be cut off? Why not try toggles? (See Fig. 17.5). They consist of a heavy-duty elastic

Figure 17.4
Coiling Excess Cable.

Don't coil!

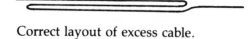

Correct layout of excess cable.

Rigging

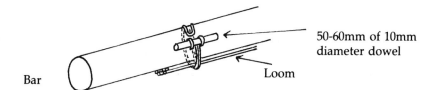

Bar   Loom

50-60mm of 10mm
diameter dowel

Figure 17.5
Reuseable Cable Ties.

band (car inner tubes) with a section of dowel fitted as illustrated. They can be reused, are cheap yet effective, and can support a loom of twenty or more cables to a standard bar.

17.8.5 Safety Chains

All lanterns should be fitted with safety chains; but, if you have insufficient to service the entire rig, you must identify lanterns in positions where they endanger cast, crew, and audience. (An example would be a lantern suspended over the audience or on bars where flown scenery moves in close proximity.)

I've never yet had a lantern fall, but I have had certain types of barndoors come crashing down. I suggest that you also determine those accessories that are at risk and safety chain them to the lantern.

17.8.6 Bar [Pipe] Fittings

When rigging a bar [pipe, barrel], try to ensure that the locking wing nut is on the downstage side, since it makes location easier for the focusser. Also consider the fitting illustrated in Figure 17.6. This type of barrel clamp is fitted to some larger lanterns; and, if you arrange them all on the same side, the bar will tend to rotate, since the weight is to one side. As you release and adjust one lantern, it will vary the torque, adjusting the angle of every other lantern. Alternate this type of clamp so that the weight is evenly distributed either side of the barrel.

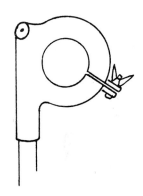

Figure 17.6
Off-Centre Barrel Clamps.

How often have you wanted a lantern with a longer yoke to get under another lantern or, perhaps, highside lanterns to be much lower? The devices illustrated in Figure 17.7 are simple (bent and drilled sill iron) yet I've found them very useful.

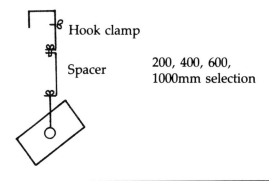

Hook clamp

Spacer

200, 400, 600,
1000mm selection

Figure 17.7
Lantern Spacers.

17.8.7 Overhanging

How do you position a lantern so that it sits above the barrel, thus allowing a larger number to be fitted onto the same length of bar? The answer is, don't! In the same way that the clamps illustrated in Figure 17.6 placed the bar under a rotating torque, so do overhung lanterns. Furthermore, irrespective of the type of clamp you use to secure the lanterns, the clamps are always working against gravity, and repeated heating and cooling may loosen their grip.

There are many tricks and devices that electricians and designers have developed over the years. Take note of each, assess it for safety and reliability, then try it yourself. It may not be right for this show but may be the solution for some future problem.

17.9 Staying on Schedule

By now it's well into the morning, and most of the onstage bars should be nearing completion.

During the crew's tea or coffee break, the head electrician and lighting designer should review their progress. Who is ahead or behind? Can you shift staff to take up the slack? To some degree you can make only an educated guess, but you must try to make it a realistic estimation that keeps the production manager fully informed. If you're behind, there's little to do except to see that all facilities are used to their maximum effect. You may need to establish priorities; perhaps minor items can be achieved during the focus, or you may need to cut elements. If you're ahead, maintain the momentum and don't let the work stretch to fit the time; the production manager will be grateful for any minutes saved. Don't keep crew members in the dark regarding their progress; if you include them, perhaps they can make suggestions or give a better insight into their difficulties.

Be careful getting back to work after the break, particularly later in the week when people are tired. With energy low, returning to a productive pace is often slow and time is wasted. You and the head electrician may need to be firm, and it's best to set an example early in the week to establish a pattern.

17.10 Checking and Flying Onstage Bars

As the onstage bars near completion, both the head electrician and the lighting designer should give each a visual check—the designer while roughly angling each lantern, and the head electrician during supervision of the patching process. If he prefers to leave patching until all the lanterns are positioned (see section 15.16), the head electrician will usually take the lantern schedule and, with one crew member doing the plugging, travel along the bar, recording the information.

The bar is now ready to fly or winch; but, before it goes, use a portable dimmer at the end of the loom to check each circuit against the plan [plot]. Let me emphasise that, particularly with lanterns of 1 kw or above, it is advisable to fade—not switch—to avoid blowing lamps. Since you checked each lantern before rigging, it's unlikely that any faults are due to inoperative lamps unless they've been roughly handled. The problems are most likely in the patching. If each bar goes into the air fully operational, you will be able to narrow down any further problems quickly to the patch panel or subpatch.

Now the head flyman can counterweight the cradle and lift the bar out of the way while the tail of the loom is taken to the subpatch and plugged according to the lantern schedule to complete electrical connection to the dimmer. However, you must also concern yourself with the *mechanical* connection between bar and subpatch. (See Fig. 17.8.) The loom needs to be lashed both at the loading gallery and at the end of the bar, since there is considerable weight involved and you need to ensure stability. You cannot allow weight to drag directly on the subpatch, where it may cause plugs to pull out. It's also convenient to pick up the centre of the loom from a high point; that way you can lift it out of harm's way, yet still allow freedom to adjust the bar height. (See Bibliography for *The Colour Book of Knots*, which gives simple, safe knots for the purpose.) A similar check of each hanging position should be conducted throughout the theatre.

The same care for the mechanical soundness and safety of cabling that you took with overhead bars must be exercised wherever passing traffic is anticipated; for example, on the floor where cables run for some distance. Whenever possible, take cables up-and-over or include them with structural items that provide protection. When forced to lay cabling across the stage, the usual solution is to employ vast quantities of gaffer tape to secure the cabling to the floor. A better solution is that in Figure 17.9. The cables need to be arranged

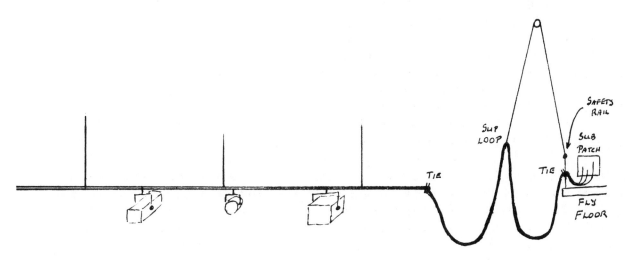

Figure 17.8
Suspending the Loom from the Bar.

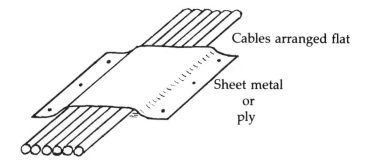

Figure 17.9
Protecting Cabling on the Floor.

Cables arranged flat

Sheet metal
or
ply

so that they do not override, which causes chafing of the insulation. Sheet metal can be noisy and must have the edges rounded to prevent chafing; therefore, use off-cuts of flexible plywood or carpet scraps secured with flathead nails.

17.11 Flashing Out the Completed Rig

Toward the end of the session the rig will fall together quickly as each position is checked and subpatched. Since the patch panel has also been plugged up (see section 17.8.1), the rig is complete and can now be tested from the board [control desk]. Set all dimmers at about 30 percent and bring the master to 100 percent; this should warm through all the lanterns and enable you to check each one visually. Make sure that, if you're using switch repatching, no dimmer is overloaded.

As you know from earlier checks that each position and bar was correct, problems are most likely in the patch and subpatch; a multimeter and lantern schedule will aid in locating mistakes. You need to check further, however, to make sure every lantern is not only powered but also controlled by the correct dimmer. This is best achieved by bringing each dimmer to full and checking that only those lanterns you have allocated to it are operating—it's also a convenient time to check switch repatching. (This same process is carried out prior to each performance as a preshow check.)

You can now safely congratulate the crew and yourself on achieving a successful rig, but there are still a couple of points to check. Particularly when on tour, ascertain that the power supply to the system is sufficient to service the entire rig; that is, with all dimmers at full, ensure that no phase is overloaded. Run at full power for about ten minutes, since the breakers are substantial and may need some time to heat sufficiently to trip. If no problems occur, a performance is likely to be safe unless foyer urns or air-conditioning are also on the same power supply—you can never be sure in some older theatres. (Alternatively, use a caliper ammeter [amp probe] that fits around each phase's active supply to measure current.)

A full load test is reassuring in *every* theatre on completion of the rig, despite the fact that all calculations and precautions tell you there should be no problems. After all, you're looking for anomalies; and, unless you check all possibilities, something is sure to go wrong—and always on opening night!

The final check requires a blackout onstage while you check that each dimmer is trimmed correctly. With all masters and faders at zero, kill worklight and be certain that all lanterns are producing no light. There is an adjustment on each dimmer or group of dimmers that controls the output. It can vary over time and may be affected by the different composition (loads) of this rig, causing trimming problems that were not evident in the previous show. (*Note.* If you are not qualified, you cannot trim dimmers. You must know exactly what you're doing if you are not to electrocute yourself. Usually the head electrician is properly qualified.) Trim alterations must be made *before* you commence plotting [dry tech] or you may need to replot every circuit you adjust. The rig is now mechanically and electrically safe and fully operational.

17.12 Surveying the Damage

Ask the board operator to run quickly through the circuits while you try to get an impression of what you've achieved. It's amazing how much you can see of the final results even when there is little set and the angling of lanterns is rough-and-ready. Also, it may give advance warning of problems to be coped with during the focus. For instance, there may be faded colour on the cyclorama that needs replacement, as it is not matching the remainder of the circuit. Or you may forsee that a lantern is not going to perform as you imagined, and you can thus prepare a suitable replacement to use during the focus.

Allow yourself time to view each circuit, and compare it with what you had foreseen. At last there is something concrete to look at, which may be at odds with what you imagined. Do you scrap the circuit? No, not at this stage. Instead, note how the circuit may be altered during the focus to achieve what you had foreseen. As this book has stressed throughout the planning processes, the lighting designer must remain flexible; now that flexibility will be tested. For example, you anticipate that a circuit of multidirectional texture will not cover the area you intended. You may convert the profile [ellipsoidal] lanterns to wides or perhaps replace some with Fresnels so that you get at least coverage with colour, but you will need to adjust your preliminary state-of-the-board and cue sheets to compensate for the loss of intensity.

In summary, now that the rig is complete, you should take a moment to feel satisfied with the results you have accomplished; but remain sufficiently analytical to predict necessary changes of detail or purpose for the tools you have created.

The crew should be sent on its way—with thanks—since only a selected few will remain for the focus. You should try to get a little sunlight before returning for setting the deads [trims].

17.13 Setting the Deads [Trims]

As mentioned earlier (16.4.3), the designer, stage manager/production manager, and head flyman will have attempted, using the section, to predict the height of every flown item but during its realisation they'll discover anomalies. As lighting designer you need to understand the process and to be present to look after departmental interests or to suggest ways you may assist in solutions. Keep your eye open for problems such as bar heights in excess of what you can comfortably reach with a ladder, borders too low to obtain backlight, or masking leg-returns (where the offstage end is brought downstage to improve the masks) that obstruct lighting positions such as booms and ladders.

The production manager/stage manager will usually sit in the front row of the stalls (orchestra seating) with an assistant in the dress circle (balcony) to check the viewpoint from that angle, but both individuals need to be mobile to check masking from either side. Start with every flown item at the grid or well above its anticipated height; then commence by flying in to their correct height all the items—excluding borders—that remain fixed throughout the performance: for example, cyclorama, legs, and some items of set. Once these items are set, they should be marked [spiked]. Beginning upstage, bring in each border to form the overhead canopy as high as possible while still achieving a mask of all supporting pipes and equipment; the borders may then be temporarily marked. Next, check that the border canopy completely masks all flown items at their out deads [trims] and, similarly, that the barrels supporting each item are masked when the object is set at the height required in performance. Lighting bars can then be positioned so that lanterns—including barndoors!—are masked from all members of the audience. (It's helpful to have a few of the larger lanterns burning during this process.)

17.14 In Summation

At last you have something to show for your efforts, thanks to the craft of the crew and head electrician. You may need to reconsider some elements in light of what you have seen, but remember that the clock is ticking relentlessly and that any changes you make must be brought about within the schedule and available resources. If it is too late, you must make the best of what you have—but sometimes this can work for you in unexpected ways. You may have created a "divine accident" that, if recognised early enough, may be incorporated into your design to give it a dimension you had not contemplated.

CHAPTER 18

Focus

As lighting designer you are about to embark upon the first of two stressful sessions: the focus, then (in the next chapter) the plotting [dry tech]. Try to be calm, clear, and precise without being fussy. Your purpose is to refine further the tools you have designed for the service of the show; you will be shaping them to fit within the action, setting, and stage-house.

Again, the major workload will fall upon the crew, though they'll need clear, detailed, and frequent directions from you throughout the process. But no one can efficiently conduct a focus without having had sufficient experience up a ladder on the receiving end of instructions: it is important that the lighting designer approach the focus with a clear appreciation and understanding of the focussers' difficulties on top of the ladder.

18.2 What Makes a Good Focusser?

While the lighting designer's place is comfortable centre stage, the focusser's is usually hot, awkward, and dirty. Balance is precarious, hearing instructions is difficult, the lanterns [instruments] seem red-hot, and it is hard to see the work being done. Some would say that tenacity, perseverance, resolution, and stoic indifference to pain should be high on the list of qualities for a focusser, but my own prescription for success at the top of the ladder is made up of the three following considerations.

18.2.1 Lantern [Instrument] Knowledge

Both the lighting designer and the focusser need intimate knowledge of the lanterns [instruments] in use. They both must know the function and purpose of every adjustment and be aware of the limitations of each lantern before they can communicate clearly. Only then can the lighting designer appreciate the problems of the focusser and not insist upon the impossible.

18.2.2 Correct Positioning of the Ladder

This is the most important consideration in the speed and the precision of the focus. The same lantern may take three times as long to adjust when the ladder is in an awkward position, making the focusser unable to see the results of the adjustment and/or causing difficulty in reaching each of the control functions.

A recommended position is illustrated in Figure 18.1, though this may differ from person to person. Ideally, the ladder should be positioned so that the focusser's head is behind and to one side of the lanterns with the top of the ladder at about waist height. Under these conditions the focusser can add stability by leaning against the ladder or, if necessary, crooking one leg through a rung while supporting weight on the other. With head to one side of the lantern and both hands available to adjust controls, the focusser can look down the beam of the lantern to see the results of fine adjustments.

Standards of safety and stability for ladders have improved dramatically; no one is obliged any longer to suffer the discomfort of, for example, the combination A-frame/extension ladder illustrated in Figure 18.2, which was common until not so long ago. Although minimum safety procedures while using ladders are basic knowledge for lighting personnel, accidents continue to happen. I know of a serious injury that occurred when a stage trap was lowered while the footing of a ladder rested on it. Make sure your ignorance or negligence is not the cause of a similar occurrence.

Figure 18.1
Position for the Focusser.

18.2.3 Locking Off

It's most important that the focusser firmly lock off all adjustments in each lantern. There's no point in precisely focussing a lantern if the lens shifts or if the lantern swings across stage when the air-conditioning is turned on. In addition to lantern knowledge, the focusser needs a shifting spanner [crescent wrench] as an aid when his or her own strength is insufficient. The lanterns don't need to be welded to the bar, nor is a sledge hammer necessary to remove them at the end of the show; they need to be firm only. In most cases, finger tight plus half a turn is sufficient. There are tricks to locking most lanterns. For example, the lock between the yoke and a hook ["C"] clamp (assuming it's correctly arranged as in Figure 17.2) can be firmed as illustrated in Figure 18.3. Point the lantern roughly, swing it back 30 degrees or so, and finger-tight the wing nut; then swing the yoke to the position required to tighten against the spring washer. A locked lantern can be released by the reverse action. The firm grip resulting is quite sufficient for the run of most shows, though you may choose to tighten very firmly on booms and ladders where passing scenery may dislodge lanterns accidentally.

Of course, the three points above are nothing unless the focusser has your cooperation as lighting designer. Unless you know precisely what you intend, how can you expect the focusser to create the magic?

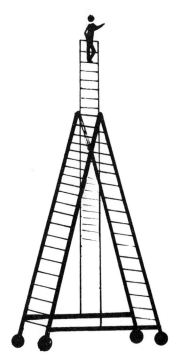

Figure 18.2
Old-Style Ladders.

18.3 Crew

Although the size of the crew will vary—according to the size of rig, the time available, the space and its facilities—generally it comprises the following:

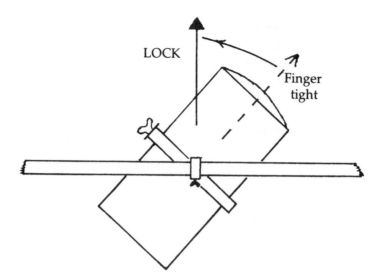

Figure 18.3
Locking Off Lantern Pan.

LOCK

Finger tight

Two crew per ladder in use; one on top, the other for safety at
stage level.

The board operator, controlling the circuits by dimmer.

The head electrician, floating as required.

The lighting designer, also floating.

Support staff, such as deputy stage manager and mechanists/
flymen.

You already realise the need for two per ladder, but also remember
to rotate personnel so as to alleviate the boredom of the individual
at stage level and the fatigue of the other. When teams are working
in locations where both have access to the lanterns (as in front-of-
house bridge), higher achievement rates can be maintained.

The number of ladders will vary according to the size of the
stage and the ability of the lighting designer to organise them effectively. There's no point in having more than two ladders on a
small stage, since they get in each other's way. On a larger stage
you may be able to cope with three or more so long as you are able
to keep them all fully occupied.

To this point you have been concerned with the capabilities of
other individuals, but now, during the focus, you will be put to the
test yourself. The efficiency of your operation depends largely upon
your ability to organise time and activities so that you make maximum use of the available crew. You need concentration and single-
mindedness as you shift from lantern to lantern, crew to crew. You
must retain sufficient grasp of what all are doing to give them clear,
precise directions, check on their progress, and anticipate where
they should go next.

The head electrician, who should not be expected to carry out
any specific function, acts during the focus as safety number, trouble-shooter, and support to both the crew and designer. Although
likely to change a blown fuse or maybe to organise a replacement
lantern, the head electrician is meant to be onstage keeping an eye
on safety and efficiency. He or she can also take notes on the lantern

schedule regarding fine details of focus so as to confidently maintain the rig as designed. (This is a possible exception to the no-specific-function rule.)

In the past you would have needed the board operator to bring up the circuits required in turn, as there was no other way of controlling them. It's a dreadful, boring task and, if you still require this in your facility, make sure that the operator is made to feel part of the team. More modern facilities include infrared riggers controls or a focussing block in prompt corner, which allow for bypassing the board and calling up circuits at will. Since the head electrician may choose to operate the device from onstage, the board operator could be better occupied attending a run in the rehearsal room, writing preliminary cue sheets, or blind-plotting the board from preliminary state-of-the-board sheets.

It's beneficial to have the deputy stage manager available to position furniture and props, mark spots, and detail the movement of performers onstage—all of which assists in obtaining an accurate focus. Why guess (then waste time adjusting during the plotting [dry tech.] or technical rehearsal) when you can be precise the first time? You'll have a skeleton crew of mechanists available to position items of set needed for precise focussing, but be selective. Make do with minimum requirements and don't demand unnecessary items—setting a near-complete stage will take time that you can better use for focussing (also see section 18.8).

18.4 Equipment

Given the above personnel scattered about a medium-sized or large theatre, you can appreciate the difficulty of communicating during focus. Reliable walkie-talkies or radio headsets assist, but they often add to the problems of a focusser in an awkward position. In-house systems, particularly Stage-com, aid communication with the biobox [lighting control box] and backstage; however, you need frequently to revert to a good, loud, clearly enunciated human voice capable of filling the theatre. Since communication is so important, you must impress upon all other departments working in the vicinity the need for keeping extraneous noise to an absolute minimum. Apart from obstructing communication, noise and static make concentration for extended periods very difficult.

Sometimes you see that another ladder, perhaps a different type or size, would be more suited to a particular task. To cover as many circumstances as possible, you need available extension ladders and A-frames of various heights in addition to the more expensive mobile work platforms. A company should obtain a reasonable range of the conventional types before going to the expense of a Tallescope or scissors lift, which, though convenient in many situations, can also be quite limited. There will always be an odd position that you can't reach with available equipment; it may be too high or impossible to support a ladder beneath. This is an important point needing consideration when you first see the plans and model for a set design during production concept meetings.

You and the production manager must try to eliminate problems before they are built into the set, though that's not always possible or desirable. You may accept responsibility for difficult access since you see the importance of the troublesome element to the design, or, while on tour, cope with problems caused by the space. As you may need to develop safe yet effective methods of coping with these unusual focussing situations, Figure 18.4 illustrates a number of ideas that may convert to your purposes. Most solutions require you to make temporary structures and, again, you should see the reason for all members of the electrics department to be familiar with a range of effective knots and lashings. However, don't allow your enthusiasm to trap you into trusting the lives of your crew to temporary structures that could fail a safety inspection.

Rocking-the-bar is a frustrating and time-consuming solution to the problem of bars set far above the reach of any ladder or when the setting makes it impossible to use a ladder. If the bar is coun-

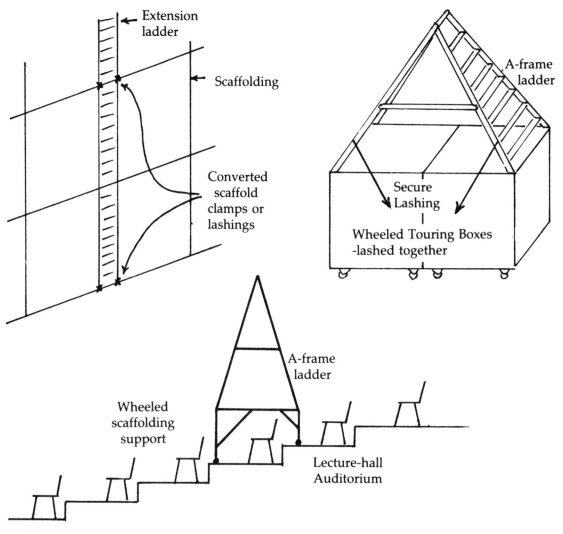

Figure 18.4
Unconventional Ladders.

terweighted or even winched, it can be dropped to working height, where you take a guess at the correct angle and shape. The bar is then flown, and notes are taken of the results before the bar is dropped once again for further adjustment. The process can take an age and should be avoided unless absolutely necessary.

18.5 Preparation by Lighting Designer

Before stepping onstage to begin the focus, you must do your homework. All the points, though mentioned before, are worth being repeated, with emphasis on the most important items.

Know the lanterns in stock sufficiently well to refer to each adjustment specifically; then you won't confuse your focussers by asking them to use imaginary or inappropriate controls. Refresh your familiarity with the theatre and the problems involved with each of the lighting positions. It's easy when you're onstage to forget how difficult movement in the front-of-house bridge can be or how much effort is involved in shifting a ladder. A lighting designer who exhibits frustration and impatience during focus will achieve little other than ulcers and ill-will. Go through the lantern schedule and return to your 1:100 [⅛":1'] sketches to be certain you know precisely what you intended for each lantern. The focus is not the time to experiment. When a crew discovers that you don't know what your lanterns are doing, they are the ones to become frustrated.

18.6 Communication and Terminology

Before you begin the focus, be sure that you are all talking the same language. Phrases and terminology do differ between theatres and persons; but, because the lighting designer is the one under the greater pressure, you should not have to change your terminology. Explain to your crew what you mean by each term; however, you must remain consistent if you are to avoid confusion and frustration. The following (18.6.1 to 18.6.5) will help you to establish terminology that is generally recognised throughout the profession.

18.6.1 Vertical Angle

You can range from up-and-down to flat by asking the focusser to lift or drop, tilt up or down.

18.6.2 Horizontal Angle

Movement in this direction is generally referred to as panning, and you need to clarify by adding a direction such as upstage/downstage, prompt/O.P. [stg. lft./stg. rt.]. Just "left" or "right" are confusing, since you could be referring to the lighting designer's or focusser's left or right.

18.6.3 Field Angle

The field angle applies to an increasing number of lanterns (pebble-convex, plano-convex, zooms, and so on), but the old phrases used for Fresnels can apply to all: spot down or flood out.

18.6.4 Focus

In a profile [ellipsoidal] lantern you need to indicate the sharpness of the image; the terms *hard* or *soft* are generally accepted.

18.6.5 Shutters and Barndoors

The image from a profile [ellipsoidal] lantern is inverted and reversed; you need to use the opposite shutter to alter the onstage image, but this does not apply to barndoors. You should explain that your phraseology applies always to the *image*, whatever the lantern in use; the focusser can translate where necessary.

Besides the above points about communication, never forget the strength of body language. A strong, clear indication with a point or sweep of an arm is easier for the focusser to comprehend than any jumble of words you may be able to put together. Since you can be clearly seen in the light of the lantern, communication from the stage to, say, front-of-house bridge will be much easier if you use body language.

18.7 Focus Pattern for Lantern Types

Particularly with an inexperienced crew, you might find it worthwhile to demonstrate focus patterns (18.7.1 to 18.7.3) for each lantern type; if everyone adheres to them, achievement rates will improve. Try to share work between the experienced and inexperienced until time presses. You have an obligation to pass on your knowledge in order that the profession will grow; this sharing of experience is part-fulfillment of that obligation.

18.7.1 Floods

The simplest lantern to focus is a floodlight. First, ensure that the clamp is firm on the bar; tilt and pan to the required position, then lock off both adjusting points. Also illustrate what it means to flag a lantern and pull colour.

These two practises aid the lighting designer, who must work almost entirely from shadows, to see what lanterns are doing, especially when there are more than two lanterns involved. You will stand with your back to the lantern watching your own multiple shadow, since to look into the light serves no purpose other than to blind yourself and to slow the process.

Pulling colour assists by allowing you to see more clearly the open-white lantern against the remainder of the coloured circuit.

When you ask for a "flag," you are requesting that the focusser's hand be waved across the front of the lantern; you can then detect the extent of the beam spread by watching the shadow of the passing hand.

18.7.2 Fresnel, Pebble-convex, and Plano-convex Lanterns

All these lanterns, plus the beamlight, take the same pattern while focussing; it is similar to the pattern with flood lanterns, but with a couple of extra steps.

Start with the lantern spotted down, barndoors opened wide (see section 17.4.6), with long barndoors rotated to where the lighting designer expects to need them (for example, top or sides). Make sure that the clamp is firm on the bar; then finger-tight adjust the tilt and pan until the spot is located where required by the lighting designer. Flood the beam until you have sufficient coverage; then finely adjust tilt and pan—in this way you ensure maximum intensity and minimal loss by the shaping of barndoors. Now the clamp, tilt, and pan can be locked before adjusting the barndoor housing so that the most precise cut-off (such as along the apron or down a flat-line) is serviced by one of the long barndoors. Next, adjust each door until the beam is shaped as desired. Point out that the focusser is often able to see "damage" better than you can and may be asked to use discretion to trim off borders, out of orchestra pits, and so on.

Note. The inexperienced designer especially must realise that barndoors are suitable only to trim and shape. The beam spread control must do most of the work while the barndoors nibble at the edges, if you are not to waste light.

18.7.3 Profile [Ellipsoidal] Lanterns

Completely withdraw all except one hard-edged shutter, and obtain on any convenient surface an approximation of the sharpness you require; if you're using a gobo, adjust the focus to it and not a shutter. Check the firmness of the clamp; then adjust tilt and pan until the beam is located where it's required and lock these controls. Adjust the zoom to maximise power over the field required. Using both soft and hard shutters, shape the beam as desired; if necessary, trim the focus again.

These general patterns produce maximum effect for a given field, but they are not rules. You may vary them to suit the purpose to which the lanterns are put, but establishing a routine assists all concerned to forge ahead without precise directions for every step.

18.8 Routine and Organisation

As you know how many lanterns there are in the rig and the time available, you can calculate the minimum rate required to complete the focus on time. You dare not allow yourself the luxury of fussing over minute details. Quickly get the lantern into position, shaped, and locked off; then move onto the next. You must also allow extra time to check what you have achieved (see section 18.11).

Assuming that there are three ladder crews working, disperse them so that they cover a different section of the stage. You want to avoid clashing (putting light into the same area) as much as possible. Usually, one team starts front-of-house, prompt [stg. lft.], and moves to the orchestra bar and box booms, while Team Two starts onstage No. 1 bar O.P. [stg. rt.], then moves to the other onstage bars. Team Three should probably start upstage, moving down the booms, ladders, and structure; then it would shift to floor-rigged and in-set lanterns. The teams should rarely clash, since they begin work far apart.

When teams do overlap badly, send one off to a staggered coffee break to allow for smooth coordination; and, if individuals get more breaks than is minimally required, what does it matter? The lighting designer won't get a break, but perhaps in this special case the stage manager will allow you to have your coffee onstage (generally, food, drink, and smoking are not allowed onstage because they cause accidental damage).

Team Two, allocated to onstage bars, has an enormous load compared to the others; that's unavoidable, since there is probably only one ladder capable of servicing these high bars. However, this team is likely to require less time to shift from one lantern to another and should achieve a higher rate than Team Three does. If front-of-house is serviced by catwalks, both members of Team One can be actively involved; this should allow them to achieve rates as high as Team Two. Thus, the availability of ladders, size of the rig, and its distribution all must be considered as you and the head electrician assess the problems of the theatre and allocate the teams accordingly. No matter how many teams you have working, you need to share your time between them so that each has a continuous flow of work and none is left without direction. Example: While Team One is being given clear directions, Two should be adjusting according to directions just received, and Three may be shifting the ladder to the next location. Spend brief moments with each on a continually rotating basis so that each knows its next task and can accomplish that while you are occupied elsewhere. The required lantern should not be illuminated until the focusser is in position to ensure that the lanterns are as cool as possible and to minimise the number of confusing blobs of light onstage.

Don't allow the pressures of the process to fluster you; keep your instructions clear and precise. You're sure to slip out of synch every so often, but ask the crews to give you a gentle reminder if they think you've forgotten them. Wherever possible, allow the teams to continue ahead with minimal direction; clear instruction for a lantern may consist of nothing more than "It has the same focus as the last lantern you did; only it's a different colour." They can continue without further instruction while you return to a team with a more complex problem. Give your teams credit, and don't treat them as your puppets; if you allow them to use their skills and intelligence, your task as lighting designer will be greatly reduced.

Don't get fussy and bogged down by any one problem; you need to keep moving at three to four minutes a lantern. Keep your eye on the rates of achievement for each team; and, if the individual up the ladder is getting slow, change over so that you capitalise on the freshness of the other member. If they've been in a difficult position (for example, box boom), make sure their coffee break comes immediately after, since they will be far more useful to you after having rested and recuperated. Above all, don't "circuit-hop." Lanterns in the same circuit are rarely together, and it's faster if the ladder is moved in sequence along the bar, adjusting each lantern in turn rather than shifting back and forth endlessly. You need the mental agility to hop from circuit to circuit, but you have lantern schedules, the plan [plot], and circuit sketches to assist you. It's also faster if the front-of-house team working on a bridge each does a lantern when a pair of units are focussed into the same area. It might be simpler to direct one, while the other unplugs a lantern, then reverse the process; or you may choose to give directions to both.

Remember that you have mechanists, flymen, and possibly the deputy stage manager awaiting direction. Since they are sure to have other responsibilities, it's unreasonable to expect them to wait on you continually. You must organise yourself to give sufficient warning for changes; thus, no department wastes time waiting for the other. You can also ensure that all circuits are focussed to a piece of scenery at one time to remove the need for your requesting that item constantly. It's a matter of compromise; if the item is massive and difficult to shift, it makes good sense to position it once and circuit-hop as much as necessary; but, if it's a simpler matter to fly the item whenever required, you should ask the head flyman to leave a flyman with you for the duration of the focus session.

18.9 Function of the Lighting Designer

In the years that lighting has been used in theatre, there still has not been developed a method for precisely indicating the intent for each lantern. The best achieved is the plan [plot], but that gives nowhere near the detail required; therefore, as lighting designer you are onstage to communicate to the focusser the intent of the design. As was stressed before, the focus is no time to experiment; it is the time to point lanterns in their preordained position, have them do what you intend, and then move onto the next. You need to see in your mind's eye your original vision and make it happen. This book has reiterated that point, but now reality slips in beside it. Sometimes you must admit (quietly) that the vision isn't always happening. You miscalculated the field or, perhaps, the colour doesn't work. What do you do?

Every wit and facility you possess needs to be working overtime, and you must call on past experience—your own and that of others. Keep half an ear cocked to your intuition and gut reaction while the other one-and-a-half listens to the relentless ticking of the clock. With every lantern you need to make value judgments at an exhausting rate. Is this lantern going to work? If the answer is *yes*, tell the crew precisely what's needed and get onto the next. If *no*, can you adapt it to salvage something of the effect, and can the adaptation be done in time? If the answer is *yes* to both, then do it;

but if *no*, you may need to start another chain of thought. Cast about for some other weakness in the rig (maybe there isn't enough texture), and judge whether this equipment can be converted to provide a solution—but remember you've got only about four minutes per lantern. If nothing resolves itself in the decision-making process, cut your losses and get on, or come back to it at the end of the focus.

The ratio for an experienced designer who's open to experimentation should be, depending on the show, that about 94 percent of lanterns are a definite *yes*, while another 4–5 percent can be salvaged and the remaining 1–2 percent need conversion. Your greatest attribute at this time is a workmanlike attitude; you don't have time to be a perfectionist and fuss about or to be artistic and precious with your creation. If an experiment works, great; if not, try it again next show.

18.10 Focussing an Area

This section explores the process of focussing a group of acting areas into an even, dipless cover. You've looked at the theory before (see 12.6 to 12.8); every theoretical factor discussed then is valid during the focus. Remind yourself of the area each circuit must cover and, in particular, the points at which they intersect. If the stage manager will allow, use chalk or tape to mark the stage as a constant reminder of these important points.

You are not lighting areas, but an actor standing within them (see Fig. 18.5); therefore, you must hold your hand above your head at all times to ensure that the hand is lit and that you don't commit the crime of foot-focussing. Assume a Fresnel coverage for the area illustrated in Figure 18.5. Stand with your back to the lantern, hand on head at the point where you feel the "centre of weight" of the area to be; it won't be the geometric centre unless the light is straight up-and-down; and the flatter the angle of the light, the farther towards the lantern that point will be. The point you're looking for (see Fig. 18.6) is the place about which the beam of the lantern is evenly distributed—it's difficult to visualise in three dimensions but

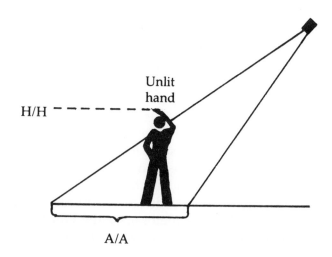

Figure 18.5
Foot-Focussing.

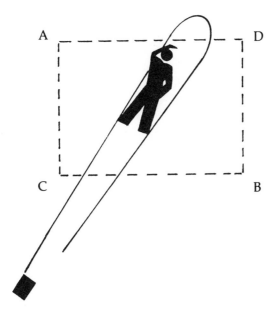

Figure 18.6
Pointing the Lantern.

you need not be precise. Having made a guess at the point, ask the focusser to locate the spot of the lantern on your shoulders; then both tilt and pan can be finger-tightened. Now move to the point marked A, still with your back to the lantern, and ask the focusser to flood the lantern until you are just covered by the light as illustrated in Figure 18.7.

If your guess at the "centre of weight" was correct, you will find yourself equally well lit at point B; but, if you are out of light, the lantern needs to be flooded and the pan adjusted so that you have sufficient beam width to cover both A and B. If you are well lit initially at B, check that the light does not extend far beyond; if so, the lantern must be spotted slightly and the pan adjusted towards A. The pan adjustment can now be locked off. Still with your back to the lantern and working from the shadow of your hand, move to point D and be certain your hand is lit. If not, the lantern needs to be lifted but then you check at point C to ensure that you're lit from about crotch up. Your aim is to place the hot-spot of the lantern at head height, and you're not really interested in feet unless you know that within this area there will be important action at floor level. (You'll have noted this at rehearsals—it's an important point to look for.)

Generally, coverage from C to D is easier to achieve when the lantern is at 35 degrees or more. At any steeper angle or when the area is very deep, you may need to adjust the flood and tilt to obtain an even coverage from C and D, knowing that the beam spread will now extend beyond points A and B. There's nothing to be done about that until you get to trimming with barndoors. When you are satisfied that you have covered the area C to D, the focusser can lock off the tilt adjustment and make sure that the flooding control is firm.

Don't be too fussy; know the four points and quickly check between each one while keeping a constant stream of directions flowing to the focusser. To ensure even blending with neighboring

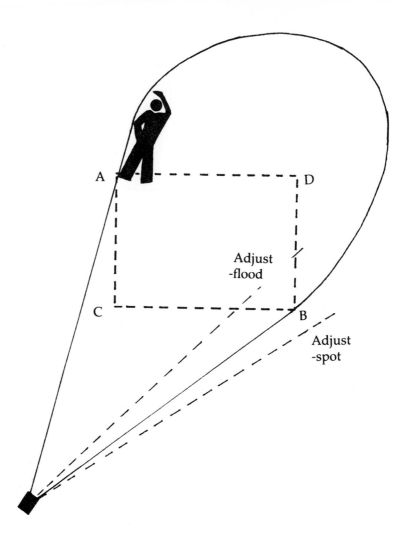

Figure 18.7
Adjusting the Lantern's Flood.

A

D

Adjust
-flood

C

B

Adjust
-spot

areas all four points should be within the half-peak beam of the lantern, not the tenth-peak, though this depends to some degree upon the isolation you require.

Using barndoors, you can roughly shape and trim off excess spill, but you cannot expect ellipsoidal performance. Selecting the edge that needs most precision, ask the focusser to rotate the barndoor housing so that a long door is servicing that edge. Example: A to D in Figure 18.7 may be near the cyclorama and you wish to remove the excess bounce; but remember that you can't cut off along A to D, but along the projection of A to D at head height. Trim along the selected edge carefully; then adjust the three remaining doors as close as possible to the other three edges (with fixed-hinged doors this trim can only be rough—see Fig. 11.16). Do a final check of all four points; ask the focusser to check that light is not catching borders or anywhere else that he or she can see better than you can; then get onto the next lantern. You will eventually come to other lanterns also focussed into this area, and exactly the same process occurs with each new lantern. You can differentiate between various shadows if the focusser pulls the colour and occasionally flags the lantern under consideration. As was mentioned before, with front-of-house lanterns the units already focussed may be unplugged for the same purpose; but that's unlikely onstage, since the time taken will be wasteful.

As you focus the last lantern into the area, quickly check the whole of the perimeter to ensure that you are lit by all lanterns at all times. To do this, it's easier to forget about watching your shadows; instead, hold your hand up-and-down stage at head height to simulate either side of actors' faces (see sections 12.6 to 12.8); then watch it as you move around.

Young designers need to practice the craft of focussing until every aspect becomes second-nature, while speed and accuracy continually improve. There are no shortcuts; the process has only slight variations for each lantern type, and you must develop a firm grasp of the routine before you waste the time of your crew.

18.11 Blending Acting Areas

As you finish focussing each position (such as front-of-house bridge)—before your crew leaves it—check that all the acting areas rigged in that position blend. It's easier to detect problems if you bring the circuits only to about 50 percent; at full the bounce sometimes disguises faults. Move along the front edge of the areas with your hand up-and-down stage looking for holes and humps, as discussed in section 12.7. Don't adjust until you are absolutely sure what the problem is, as you can fuss and nibble away at circuits until you ruin everything you've achieved. You may find that the positioning of lanterns wasn't too bad but that you were too drastic with the amount of barndooring or shuttering. Once you've identified which shutter is doing the damage, ask the crew to adjust it while you stand in the hole watching the hand.

You can't afford to waste much time, and you are looking for gross errors only. Remember, there is time between the technical rehearsal and opening for trimming and finely adjusting circuits once you have seen them doing the job for which they were designed—lighting performers. Lighting designers tend to be too precise during focus and risk running out of time; yet, when they see actors onstage, they find it impossible to detect the fine tuning they attempted. Just make sure there are no holes!

As you complete each position, you need to check not only for blending across stage but also for ensuring that each group blends with the adjacent areas upstage (see section 12.8).

18.12 Focussing Spots, Specials, and Washes

Make sure the crew members are given breaks at times convenient to the process and within union rules. The attention span of most people is limited, and beyond about forty minutes it requires increasing effort to achieve the same results. For this reason you may want to start with front-of-house and No. 1 onstage bars, as it's there you find the more difficult acting areas. Because the easier backlights, washes, and spots are scattered, it's better to attack them in the latter half of the session, when fatigue has taken its toll on both you and the crew.

As washes, textures, spots, and the like are unique to each show, there's not much to be said about the manner in which you should approach their focus. The basic sequence outlined in section 18.9 applies to every circuit; and, when you combine that with the patterns listed in section 18.6, you should be able to achieve what your vision demands. Sometimes, of course, you can't work from your own shadow (for example, when lighting the cyclorama), so ask the the focusser to flag the lantern while you stand well downstage or even in the auditorium where you'll see better. Don't forget the assistance the deputy stage manner can give when positioning spots or furniture, and remember to keep your eye on the clock.

18.13 Surveying the Scene

If, happily, you finish with a few minutes to spare, invite the set designer to join you to survey what you've done. Now that you've completed the focus, you finally have something concrete to show your colleague. You may need to be selective because many circuits seen in isolation can be harsh and may startle the unprepared set designer. Despite this, the viewing can frequently be exciting and helpful to you both. Not only are you able to share the successes but also you may be able to define problems and determine how they might be handled. For example, you discover that the results of a colour filter on a section of the set are different from what your early experiments on the model indicated. You may agree that a variation of colour filter will assist in creating the effect you are both searching for, or the set designer may decide to alter the paint shade to bring it closer to the model tonings.

There may be occasions when you and the set designer take opposite viewpoints. You may try persuading and referring to the production concept meetings that formed the basis for the lighting. This may convince the designer that what you have achieved is necessary for the production—and just as frequently the same argument will convince you to alter the rig. Keep in mind that it's generally easier for the lighting department to change a colour than for the set to have a complete repaint; but, in any case, the requirements of the production must be paramount. During such differences of opinion, the most important skill to develop is the ability to listen. Too often you can find yourself trying to drown out the other person's argument instead of reminding yourself of the need for collaboration. Rosenthal implies (see chapter 3) that you should respect the other opinion and learn from it, while the other party should respect your authority within your department. Don't be frightened of differences of opinion; in practice, successes far outweigh the problems.

Don't forget to keep your eye open for practical problems such as a clipped border or an unwanted spill on the proscenium. You may also foresee that estimated levels for preliminary state-of-the-board and cue sheets are wildly out. Although you may not have the time to solve problems now, you should take notes of tasks that need doing. The list will grow during the plotting [dry tech.] and technical rehearsal, but you may not have the opportunity to tackle any trimming until both sessions are completed. Try to arrange your list in some order of priority so that you knock off the gross and distracting mistakes first; this saves the director, designer, and even the general manager from repeatedly drawing your attention to the same problem.

18.14 In Summation

You still don't have a completed design, merely the tools particularly selected and manufactured for the job. However, you are much closer, and you should be able to estimate how the end product will differ from your original vision. You may need to consider how these differences may be minimised before the plotting [dry tech.] session—which isn't far away! Try to relax and compose yourself before it starts.

CHAPTER 19

Plotting [Dry Tech.]

It's time for the trio discussed in chapter 4 (director plus set designer and lighting designer) to meet again with the same rapport that existed during the production concept meetings. Since that time all have been obsessed with their own difficulties and tasks. Each has been—at best—a remote observer of the others' problems. Partly because of these differing paths, this reunion could have its ups and downs. You may happen upon combinations of setting and lighting that exceed everyone's expectations; but there's the other end of the spectrum, where the lighting designer produces a cherished creation that the others consider to be junk!

Before you commence plotting [dry tech.], try to get the trio together semisocially; five minutes over coffee in the greenroom can help to revive the original objectives of the production concept and get your relationships and achievements back into perspective. You and they need to remind yourselves of the ethics of a collaborative venture but, more important, you need to reach agreement on the objectives for the plot [dry tech.].

19.2 Realistic Goals

Even in the hands of experts, the plotting session cannot realise a finished product. You are working under makeshift conditions to produce lighting suitable for performance, but without every performance detail (actors, complete wardrobe) the results can only be an approximation. Moreover, you're trying to use time and money efficiently and, with only a handful of people, produce cue sheets and lighting states that work without having the entire company waiting on you. It means that you go to the technical rehearsal with a semirefined product that can be shaped more quickly. Some directors and lighting designers feel plotting is a waste of time, preferring to extend the cue-to-cue element of the technical rehearsal—but that can be a greater waste of time for more people!

You need to consider how a plotting session differs from performance so that you have a better idea how the plotting [dry tech.] may be distorted. Given the number of cues and the time available, you can calculate an achievement rate in advance, but that process distorts performance time badly. You'll spend the same time on a state that will hold the audience's attention for thirty minutes as on those that are nothing more than fleeting impressions. This is necessary, since the operational considerations for each state are the same, irrespective of how long each remains onstage. The danger is that during the plotting you may become distracted by details that are unimportant or may ignore others that, with long exposure, will become really important. An example would be in the case of underlit performances; during the plotting you set a state in about ten minutes but view it for a couple of minutes only. You are apt to forget that this underlit, dingy scene must hold the attention of the audience for, say, forty minutes. Alternatively, you can finely adjust elements for each state in a sequence that flashes past so fast in performance that even you can't see the differences you so painstakingly added.

It's a waste of money to use the full company as little more than dressmakers' dummies to decorate the stage while you plot lights. Instead, use one or two walkers (assistant stage managers usually), together, perhaps, with a representative costume on a dummy if the wardrobe department can spare it. But, under these conditions, it's not possible to form a complete stage picture, and you may make the mistake of emphasising the setting to compensate. *Never forget that your primary purpose is to light performers.*

None of the above conditions is conducive to a perfect plot [dry tech.]. But you can, at least, agree to stick to schedule, accomplish as much detail as possible, provide accurate documentation, and establish a comprehension of the shape and feel of cues for both deputy stage manager and board operator. You can leave the fine balancing of the stage picture to the technical and dress rehearsals.

Sometimes the director or designer, or both, are under the mistaken impression that the lighting is complete once the plotting is achieved. They forget that, just as a performance or wardrobe needs fine adjustment right up to opening, so too does the lighting department. For example, you need to trim and adjust the rig to catch every performer, but you must see actors under performance conditions before you can detail precisely what's required. The board operator also needs time to develop confidence, to integrate with other departments, and to learn by making mistakes.

By the end of the plotting session, each member of the production team should have notes on any shortfalls they perceive in mood or appearance for each cue, the direction in which the lighting must develop or, perhaps, how the painting or staging can be altered to complement the lighting. All then go their various ways to concentrate on departmental problems but undertake to meet formally (before the final dress rehearsal) to compare notes, to discuss how closely they've achieved what they intended, and to decide what more should be done before opening. This approach is based on the premise that the lighting designer needs time under performance conditions to develop the plotting and operation and that the plotting session is merely one step along the way.

19.3 Environment

Before commencing the plotting session, you need to arrange carefully the environment of the production desk and also the auditorium/

house. There is no point in trying to balance lighting levels delicately under anything other than performance conditions, as any extraneous light will distort your impression of the stage picture. All extra worklights should be off, and those to be used in performance should be correctly shielded/coloured. The blue safety-lights around the stage perimeter should be on, as should the deputy stage manager's desk light. If you're working with musicians in the orchestra pit, establish light levels there with the musical director before the plotting session and, further, undertake the session with sheet music on each stand (bounce light from white pages will be greater than from black-painted stands).

The production desk is nothing more than a convenient tool where all the facilities required by the production team are to be found; but, since it's in a fixed position, you must never assume that what you see from the desk is representative of the whole auditorium. As you spend so long there, the environment should be comfortable and workable but must not intrude upon the purpose for which the desk was constructed. Worklight levels, for example, must be kept as low as possible to approximate the blackness that normally surrounds an audience; they should not blaze out in competition with the stage.

19.3.1 Production Desk Location

Generally, the desk is located midway back in the stalls [orchestra seating] (see Fig. 12.13) in a cross-over aisleway, if possible, allowing for easy access to the stage and both extremes of sightline. Sometimes a bridge across the orchestra pit improves stage access.

19.3.2 Facilities

In a trap that protects them from the general public, you need outlets for power, headset communication, the lighting board, and perhaps a microphone input to the sound system. A number of general power outlets and headset outlets will be convenient, since there's a tremendous amount of traffic around the production desk; the fewer the extension cables, the less likely you are to have accidents. Generally, three headsets are sufficient—one for the stage manager/technical director, one for the lighting designer, and a spare for deputy stage manager, sound, or any other visitors you have. Particularly in a large theatre, have a microphone connected to a public address system. This improves communication between the desk and the stage; it may be impersonal contact, but it's useful if voices fail with time.

Access to the lighting board may take a number of forms. If the desk is portable, it can be brought to the production desk; that makes for easy communication between the lighting designer and board operator but may introduce problems to be discussed shortly. Alternatively, the lighting designer may have headset communication with the biobox [lighting control booth] and, perhaps, a V.D.U., which displays the output from a computer board.

19.3.3 Arrangement and Access

Figure 19.1 shows an arrangement of the production desk that you may find convenient for plotting, though this is a matter of taste and will vary between teams. Both the designers and the director need to be in close proximity to confer easily, but it's unusual for the set designer to need light and desktop space for documentation. The deputy stage manager, stage manager/technical director, and director also need to confer regarding the precise placement of cues, and the deputy stage manager requires light and desk space to update the prompt copy. The lighting designer and operator need close contact, but remember that you, the designer, are not entitled to touch the board without permission of the operator—it's not your job. You must understand the board sufficiently to explain what you intend, but you must accept the right of the operator to achieve the desired end-results in whatever way he or she is able. The b⸍ ard operator will require additional light and space for cue sheets and, perhaps, an assistant to help document the board and to update state-of-the-board sheets.

Each group needs to confer easily without disturbing the work of any other, and you may sometimes require a degree of privacy while a problem is settled. The lighting designer, director, and deputy stage manager all need free access so that they can check the stage from different aspects or get to the stage.

19.3.4 Worklights

Both the board operator and deputy stage manager require ample worklight for accurate and clear documentation; however, the lighting designer, director, and set designer should have little or no light—just as the audience has none. The time required for your eyes to adjust from a brightly lit page to the stage picture will make

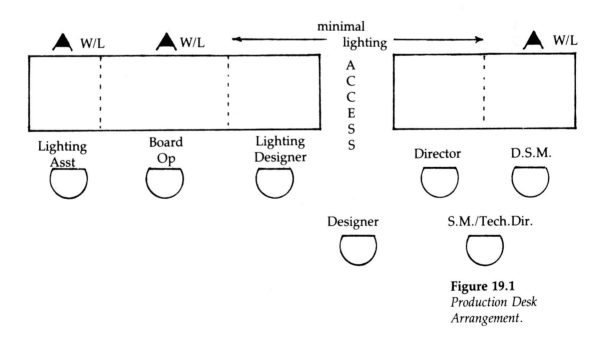

Figure 19.1
Production Desk Arrangement.

for a very slow session; but, as it's expecting a great deal of you to memorise every detail of the rig, you will occasionally need to refer to documentation. Generally, you're able to see sufficiently well in the spill from the board and deputy stage manager's lights. Each worklight needs to be fitted with its own dimmer, masked down to only the area required, and fitted with a blue gel.

I've tried a number of different arrangements to that illustrated in Figure 19.1, but I've yet to find one that allows for better access, light, space, and communication.

Try to make everyone as comfortable as possible, since the hours spent plotting can seem endless. You don't want luxury, but you should supply chairs of an appropriate height and ensure that all have sufficient space to do their job without clutter and inconvenience. Ask the cleaner for a garbage can nearby, and insist that all use it. Everyone must be careful not to spill drinks, which could cause permanent damage to the board and documentation.

The desk and its facilities must be set up in advance of the plotting session with each device checked to ensure it's fully operational—all this so that you are ready to *start* at the scheduled time. It's useful to have a spare headset handy in case of failure during this or subsequent sessions at the desk. Similarly, the entire rig needs to be thoroughly checked prior to the plotting. It seems impossible in the short time between the focus and the plotting for anything to have failed, but you dare not take the chance.

19.4 Ancillary Staff

Besides the staff at the production desk, there are likely to be two other groups associated with the plotting: backstage crew and walkers. The mechanists and flymen need the same consideration during the plotting that you gave them at the focus (see sections 18.3 and 18.7). The scenery changes are likely to be more detailed now than at the focus; since you don't have the benefit of the cast nor the full range of costumes, it will be helpful to have as much of the setting as possible. However, since you're likely to have a skeletal crew, give them every assistance possible (for example, sufficient warning for changes).

Walkers must have the worst task in theatre. Generally, they have little idea of what's going on, they're bored out of their minds for most of the time, and then they're shouted at and shifted about like shop mannequins for the remainder. Before commencing the plotting, take a few minutes with them to explain the purpose they are fulfilling. Tell them why you'd like them to keep their heads up and into the light, why you need them to face front, and why there are the long periods of boredom between frantic activity. Make them realise their importance to the plotting, and allow them to share in the achievements; it may help to bring them out in rotation to the desk to watch what you do.

Although the most qualified person to give detailed staging, the deputy stage manager is required at the desk to position cues in the prompt copy. At times he or she can take a few moments onstage to explain movements to walkers but not at the risk of missing detail at the desk. On occasions I've had the luxury of having the assistant to the director onstage, and the rapport between the stage and the desk was a joy. There was no need to waste time explaining; I merely mentioned the moment and allowed the assistant to organise the walkers. Generally, the assistant finds this arrangement constructive and at the same time gains a thorough appreciation of the process of plotting.

19.5 Commence with Communication

There is a further reason for the arrangement of personnel illustrated in Figure 19.1. You must be careful that the collaboration represented by the director and two designers is not interpreted as a committee by either the deputy stage manager or the board operator. Proximity makes it easy for the director to make a suggestion directly, but the board operator cannot afford to split attention among three or more individuals. There can be only one voice, that of the lighting designer, to which the board operator listens, disregarding all else while concerned with the accurate and detailed recording of the operation. The board operator experiences the same kind of pressure during the plotting as the lighting designer did during the focus. If his or her attention is continually pulled in many different directions, the stress will eventually reduce productivity.

An aid to clear communication is establishing a precise and consistent routine that everyone adheres to throughout the session. Of course, there must be variation occasionally; but, if everyone recognises that fact, copes, then returns to the recognised pattern, achievement rates will be easier to maintain. You can base your routine on the following steps:

1. Establish clearly with the board operator the state with which you are starting. It could be a blacked-out stage upon which you intend to build a picture, or you may start with a previously plotted state and vary it. Be sure that the operator retains the last plotted state (either on a manual preset or in memory) for comparison.

2. Refer to each dimmer by number and indicate what movement you require: "Up . . . up . . . stop!" or "Down . . . stop!" Note that the board operator will usually adjust to the nearest 5 percent, unless critical, to facilitate presetting. Often, a lighting designer will ask for the level at which the dimmer is set before indicating the change required. What does it matter what level the circuit's at? If you want it up, say so—the actual figures don't matter. Continue altering circuits until the state is close to what you intend.

3. Allow the operator to relax while the state is discussed with the designer and director and checked from different positions in the auditorium. It may help to compare the new state with that last plotted. Adjust and experiment—with the walkers substituting for the performers—to ensure that actors are lit up to the point where the next cue is expected.

4. Once final approval is obtained from the director, tell the board operator and the deputy stage manager to plot or record the state. The walkers should be told to rest. While the operator and assistant record the state on cue and state-of-the-board sheets, the director and deputy stage manager can position the cue in the prompt copy with your assistance and that of the stage manager/technical director. The deputy stage manager and operator should inform you when the function is complete.

5. Use the previous state to determine take-up levels (the point at which the upcoming lights begin to be perceived onstage) and make certain they are noted in the cue sheet. Detail the shape and timing of the cue and briefly explain its purpose. Try the cue with the deputy stage manager calling to the board operator. Repeat as necessary. Seek the director's final approval and note details.

6. Retain the newly plotted state on the board and return to step 1 above; recommence the sequence for the next cue.

Usually, the above process takes from six to twelve minutes, depending on the difficulty of the cue.

The mixture of "artistic" and mechanical details, the fluctuating activity from person to person, and the breadth of expertise involved demands that there be a single controlling influence. That individual must be aware of the entire process and be able to ensure that each stage is complete before continuing. It's not a job for a committee but rests firmly with you, the lighting designer. This should not be an excuse for you to exclude or subdue any member of the production team. Full discussion needs to take place, and, if necessary, the director must arbitrate on artistic matters. But the entire team needs to be aware of time restrictions and the need not only to create the lighting states but also develop documentation that has sufficient precision to ensure an accurate repeat of the sequences decided upon during the run of the show. A plotting session is a mixture of mechanics and "art'"; you must retain a balance between the two.

19.6 Associating Documentation with Circuits

Prior to the plotting you should give every member of the team numeric and alphabetic lists of circuits. Now, at the plotting's commencement, you should view each circuit so that all not only discover what the lighting designer has created but also associate circuit name and number. As a result, for the remainder of the session you will have a common terminology. When you ask the operator to bring up each, describe its purpose and indicate the scenes for which you believe it will be useful. Get the walkers to describe the limits of the light, and don't try to disguise problems. Don't rush through the circuits; keep in mind that many at the desk have never seen them before and, for the first time, will have something concrete to evaluate. Since the process should take no more than about twenty–thirty minutes, it's not a time for prolonged debate, but the comments made in section 18.13 concerning the set designer's first viewing also apply here. Do not stifle debate; if something is obviously wrong, it should be either noted or dealt with immediately, since it may continually hinder you throughout the remainder of the plotting.

This same dilemma may arise at any point during the session, as you discover glaring errors. For example, a spot might be 2 metres [6 feet] out of position. Do you take time focussing in a plotting session? Yes, because this is a major item that should be changed. The head electrician should have ladders and crew readily available for just such an emergency. Make the change quickly and get on with the plotting. But if it's a minor trimming point that does not affect the substance of the rig, it's not worth the loss of time; take detailed notes and correct it as soon as possible.

This chapter seldom mentions the head electrician; it's not that he or she is absent, but rather is in the role of trouble-shooter. The head electrician will be responsible for ensuring that the rig is fully operational and remains so throughout the plotting; will keep a check on the environment (such as worklights); and will also be available for advice on, say, a tricky board operation or focus detail.

19.7 Detailed Plotting Procedure

Using the example illustrated in Figure 15.19, take a detailed look at plotting procedure. As is often the case, the initial preset behind the curtain is an extraction of cue 1, and you need to determine that state before you can commence. Set up the state of cue 1 detailed in the preliminary state-of-the-board sheets, and adjust it for a better match with original vision (see section 19.11). Once the state has been achieved to the team's satisfaction and within the time available, ask the board operator to use this information to correct the preliminary cue sheets (see section 15.21); this will enable an accurate preset of both top masters. Now you can return to the beginning of the show.

Bring house lights to full and the curtain in. Check that your estimation for curtain-warmers (dimmers 4 and 7 at 50 percent) balances against the house lights; then have those levels recorded in the cue sheets. You are now fully preset. The first board operation is house-to-half; it's usually not given a cue number but is referred to by name. Using the house faders, find the level at which auditorium illumination is sufficiently subdued to pull attention to the curtain-warmers. This will settle the audience, raise their expectations, and focus their attention on the musical director, who is about to enter. The deputy stage manager can now write the cue into the prompt copy: "H to ½ as MD enters pit." (This example assumes a conventional opening.) The operator should be told to shape the fade to finish slightly abruptly as the musical director reaches the podium, probably triggering applause from the audience. You could try the cue with a walker replacing the musical director, but, in a cue as simple as this, it's not necessary. Check that the director is happy with the "artistic" aspects of the cue before proceeding.

Both the calling of the deputy stage manager and the timing of "house-out" need to be closely associated with the beginning of the overture. If able to see the musical director's beat, the deputy stage manager can anticipate the downbeat slightly so that the cue commences with the music. The board operator needs to be familiar with the music to be able to match the fade—for example, to the first bar of a fanfare. It will be beneficial if the board operator can listen to a tape recording before the technical rehearsal if not sufficiently familiar with the rehearsal room. "Curtain-warmers out" will be called at a point within the music, and the timing will be regulated by, say, four bars of music. (Already you should see that both board operator and deputy stage manager benefit from some knowledge of music.)

Now ask the flyman to raise the house curtain so that you can plot the next sequence. Cue 1 is conceived as a sequential fade (one element follows another) with dimmer 8 highlighting some element on stage before the remainder of the state builds. Do the sequence in stages. Raise dimmer 8 until a satisfactory level is found and adjust the cue sheets. Since you already have the follow-on preset, you can skip ahead to shaping the sequence, though that would normally be the next stage in the process. Explain to the deputy stage manager and board operator that the cue should be called with the house curtain and that dimmer 8 "rides" the movement of the curtain; that is, you don't want any light on the front of the curtain, but it should appear at the earliest opportunity.

Find a take-up level for both dimmer 8 and the top B master (see section 19.5), and detail the timing for each fader and also the flyman. Try the cue once without the curtain and check that it matches the director's concept of the cue. If it does, try the cue again with the curtain and the deputy stage manager calling; if all works well, proceed. If the cue shape fails to meet approval but the problems are simply a matter of practice, explain the required improvements to the deputy stage manager, board operator, and flyman; then proceed on. Time for rehearsal will come with the technical rehearsal, drilling sessions, and so on (see chapters 20 and 21).

As lighting designer, you must listen carefully to the detail of the production team's comments. Perhaps the solution to their reservations is that not only should the timing of each element be tightened but also that the shape of the cue needs changing from sequential to progressive (not one after the other, but overlapping). This function is, perhaps, your greatest responsibility throughout the plotting. You are the interface between art and mechanics, that is, between production team and board operator.

Clearly announce that you are now plotting cue 2 and that the flyman is no longer required. Remind the board operator that cue 2 is merely an addition on the same master, then determine the level of dimmer 6 so that the operator can record it in the cue sheets. Figure 15.19 also includes a dome cue at this time, and you need to set iris, focus, pick-up, and fade time for the follow-spot. Once the levels have been set, approved, and noted, return to the state of cue 1, establish the take-up levels for cue 2, and explain the purpose of the cue to the deputy stage manager, board operator, and dome.

Try the cue; you might want the dome trailing, and this might best be achieved by separating the call. If all approve the trial, the cue can be noted while the director and designers discuss a colour problem or the mood for the next state.

The plotting of cues 3 to 5 will take exactly the same method as cue 2, but don't allow yourself to run ahead under the pressure of time. Do each separately; make sure each is completely noted and that all concerned have sufficient information to approach the technical rehearsal with confidence. The state of cue 6 was planned to be similar to that of cue 1; and if you believe that cue 1 is sufficiently similar to what you had preplotted, then you should also use the preplotted state for cue 6 as a basis from which to start. If not, it may be easier to ask the board operator to "transfer" the state of cue 1 onto the centre preset, since it will require less adjustment than the preplotted version, and the process will be considerably faster. "Transfer" means to copy the settings of one master onto another. It doesn't mean that you wipe the original; rather, you now have two versions, one to alter and the original, against which to compare the altered version.

You must continue to explain the shape of each cue. Cue 6 is to be a snap, which must coincide with a visual cue onstage; that is, as Miss Hannigan pulls the imaginary light-cord. The board operator would normally take this as a visual cue since from the control position he or she is able to see the action just as clearly as the deputy stage manager can; thus, the reaction time of one more individual is eliminated. This is not to negate the importance of the deputy stage manager but is to ensure that the lighting is perfectly in tune with onstage action. You still require a "standby," and with that call the deputy stage manager should remind the board operator what and where the visual cue is, in much the same way as a pick-up is described to a follow-spot operator. Try the cue once with a walker, but emphasise to the board operator that fine coordination with the performer is a matter for the technical rehearsal.

You now no longer need the preset on the top master; and in the preliminary cue sheets the board operator will find a replacement preset to set up, since there is nothing so far to suggest that your original estimations are going to be too far out.

Cue 8 is a fade up to daylight from night/tungsten lighting, and the same patterns outlined above are used to set the state—but don't forget to check the picture from different sightlines around the auditorium (this scene needs a good skyline). It's a slower cue and needs to be carefully located in the dialogue so that action and lighting blend. Try it with the director reading from the script and deputy stage manager calling; a stopwatch can be useful to check the exact time for dialogue.

When you are plotting, you must realise the importance of both the artistic and operational aspects. Without detailed notes of cue positions, times, shape, and take-up levels, the deputy stage manager and board operator cannot approach a technical rehearsal with any degree of expertise or accuracy—they simply are not prepared. Of course, details may change once you see all elements working together in the technical rehearsal, but you need to make sure that the plotting provides them with a good basis from which to work. A person with a strong input during the plotting is the stage manager/ technical director—the only one aware of what every department is doing and how the lighting must blend. For example, he or she can inform the deputy stage manager what the clearing cues for mechanists will be at the completion of a scene change or can guide the lighting designer as to what minimal level of light is required onstage to carry out that change. The stage manager/technical director will have timings for sound cues and will have devised a shape that combines all the elements contributing to the moment. If you can impose that shape on the lighting now, the coordination process during the technical rehearsal will be much easier.

19.8 Achievement Rates

Until you settle into the routine, achievement rates will be slow. Maintain a firm pressure, knowing (hoping) that pace will improve once you've ironed out communications and become familiar with one another's method of working. You may need to curtail lengthy discussion or to pressure a decision—perhaps the best that can be achieved is agreement that a particular state is unsatisfactory—but time has run out and you must continue if you're to plot the entire show. If necessary, you can return to these early cues and adjust them if the team later discovers, say, a scene change state that eluded you early in the plotting. But, for the moment, push on! The focus and plotting are similar in that once you're started and are into a routine, the rates improve. And, not surprisingly, so does the product.

19.9 Maintaining Awareness

Two people at the desk sometimes find the plotting difficult when the lighting designer is forced to forge ahead under the pressure of time. The set designer may feel that there is nothing to do except watch the ruination of a dream at the hands of lighting. Elements of set that have taken hours to create disappear in a mist of gloom, while some uninspired element is a blaze of light; yet all the set designer can do is to say, "But . . . !" The problem stems from the fact that the set designer has nothing active to do now; this, combined with a history of poor collaboration between the two designers, makes him or her feel helpless.

It would be easy for you as lighting designer merely to placate or fob off the designer—or to cut off the comment. Instead, you need to include the set designer as much as possible, listening carefully and taking time to explain your purpose with the lighting. It's important that you continue communication from this point right up to opening, and there is a danger that pressure of time during the plotting could damage that rapport irreparably.

The board operator may feel as the set designer does, but for entirely different reasons. The relentlessness of the process is wearing on the operator, who may feel like nothing more than underpaid computer equipment. Spend occasional moments to check on how the board operator is coping and maybe to help with some difficulties. Example: Perhaps dimmer 26 at 35 percent, 27 at 45 percent, and 28 at 40 percent could be altered to read dimmer 26–28 at 40 percent, since it makes little difference onstage but is part of a fast preset. Remember that, compared with many of the others, the board operator is very raw. Without having had the benefit of weeks of rehearsal like the actors, he or she will be expected, within a rehearsal or two, to tune the board performance to match. Whatever the lighting designer can do now to assist that process and to preserve the sanity of the operator will benefit the show as a whole.

19.10 Management of Personnel

The routine of plotting should by now be well set, and you can afford to ease the pressure. If you're plotting a scene where only one walker is required, send the other for a break. When a state is proving difficult, the atmosphere is tense, and a solution cannot be found, call a coffee break. Insist that all get up out of their seats and go away from it all for a few minutes. The solution will probably come as the tension eases. No show is worth getting ulcers over; if any one of the team is at risk, make sure they get relief.

All this may sound melodramatic, but now the thoughts of reputations and careers creep in as the production team sees the end product looming. In the past it's been on paper; but now, when there is something concrete, everyone tends to leap forward, expecting everything to happen *now!* In the process an individual—a board operator, set designer, deputy stage manager—can be hurt. Since each individual is integral to the success of the show, this damages the chance for success.

19.11 Painting with Light

So far this discussion has been about only the mechanical aspects of plotting and has emphasised these frequently neglected details. But you also need to consider the delicate process of painting a stage with light, shade, and colour.

Where do you start? Again, there are no rules; it's what works for you. If you are like me, you would find that everything originates with the cue synopsis vision, and you would recall it once again. You would trace the apparent source and feel the colour balance, the ambience, and each highlight. If you're lucky, the predicted state onstage will be close; even though it's distorted, unbalanced, too bright, or dull, the essence will be there. Continually comparing it with the vision, you must force the image onstage to shape to your will in the same way you made the lanterns comply during the focus.

Perhaps the cyclorama is too bright at the top—bring it down until it doesn't offend, or alter the balance to create a less vibrant colour. Perhaps the stage is too bright on O.P. [stg. rt.], where you know there's no action—the acting areas need to be brought down —which creates a dull spot that must be filled with ambience. The central character, now represented by a walker, does not seem to be part of the scene but seems superimposed upon it—perhaps the keylight representing the apparent source is too dull and the acting area too bright? Adjust them both until the character is brought into the scene and linked to it by the dominance of the apparent source.

The manner in which you balance a state varies according to the show's style. If it's naturalistic, you will probably start with the ambience and adjust the elements until the time of day is clear, the mood is apparent, and the shape is inclined towards the centre of action. Then you will ensure that the time of day is clearly reflected on the set in terms of colour and direction. You want the audience to see the elements they need for full appreciation of the locale, and you want the remainder to echo the mood you require. Finally, you will attend to the centre of focus—the performers. They must be included within the setting and be lit by the same apparent source that bathes the stage, but that light must touch them more firmly. By adjusting the acting areas so that actors are not only lit by the apparent source but are also lifted slightly into relief against the set, you will make them part of it yet still dominant.

With a stylised piece you can change the approach to suit, such as starting out with the keylight on the performer and radiating out in concentric circles until the picture is complete. You are creating a black stage with pools of light in which one or more actors are performing and the keylights are at levels that match the degree of focus and character dominance required. Each face is filled with light from acting areas or washes to ensure the audience sees all that you intend. Finally, an ambience is overlaid on each to form the mood and quality each character demands.

The above illustrates how one designer works, but you must vary and adapt until you find a method that guarantees achievement rates from yourself and your team. However, no method can substitute for your intimate knowledge of every circuit, its precise coverage and toning. It's time-wasting, frustrating, and confusing to pot-luck your way through circuits, hoping to happen upon something that feels right. Once you decide a circuit may be useful, ask the operator to bring it to full; check that it does what you anticipated and then adjust it to balance with the remainder of the state.

19.12 Seeing for the First Time

The secret of fine plotting lies in your ability to see the onstage picture for the first time *every* time. Avoid the tendency to stare at a problem, trying to define what's wrong with it. This seems to imprint the mistake more firmly. Instead, close your eyes, wipe the picture from your mind, and replace it with the original vision. After a few seconds open your eyes at about the centre of the stage picture and note two things: the differences between your vision and reality and the points to which your eye is pulled.

Behavioural psychologists have discovered that the eye does not absorb a whole picture; rather, it scans very quickly from point to point. In everyday life you don't realise that this is happening, but if, as a lighting designer, you can train yourself to recognise the random movements of your eye, you can quickly recognise the points to which your eye is pulled and how this differs from the intended focus of the scene. Pick up a magazine of glossy advertisements, close your eyes, and open to any page. Feel how your eyes scan the picture. As the psychologists discovered, not only will you trace intensity, shape, and form but also your eye will tend to search out what you find pleasing.

Now try the same technique on a stage picture, and compare results with what you believe the production team intended to be the centre of focus. It's surprising how often your gaze is pulled to the cyclorama, to the set, or to a bright patch of furniture—anywhere except to the performer at the centre of the action. In this phenomenon you're concerned not just with intensity, although it is a major consideration. The form and shape of the stage setting, colour, arrangement of the performers onstage, height, and movement all add to the centre of focus. You must ensure that the plotting of the show echoes your intention or, occasionally, adds an ambivalent quality. Refresh your memory of the Don José and *Carmen* example discussed in section 13.12. That's what is meant by ambivalence—where you use your skills to draw the attention of the audience not only to the performer at the centre of the action but also to another who may be commenting upon the action. There can be a number of focal points onstage for a given moment, but each must be selected and shaped to mirror the intention of the production team.

There's another trick you may find useful. The "see-for-the-first-time" technique is telling you there's something wrong, but you aren't quick enough to define the reason. Use anything appropriate—hand, finger, thumb, ruler—to block out each element of the scene in turn. Part A of Figure 19.2 involves removing everything except the performer; in this way you check that there is sufficient light for seeing details of facial expression clearly. You now need to eliminate those items of setting that may be competing with the performer for attention. Section B shows the hand being used to remove the cyclorama/backdrop; if this improves your reaction to the whole, you infer that the background is too bright and must be reduced. Sections C and D use fists and fingers to remove smaller elements.

If you are unable to find fault with any particular element, reverse the intention of section A and use a finger to eliminate the performer. If the picture holds well under these circumstances, it implies that you must either raise the intensity of the performer or reduce the intensity of the remainder with respect to the performer. Before deciding, check your diagnosis from a different sightline.

This technique can help explain lighting problems to the set designer. When you have an actor standing near an object and both are within the same acting area or keylight, it is impossible for the lighting designer to separate them. The finger test (as in Figure 19.2,

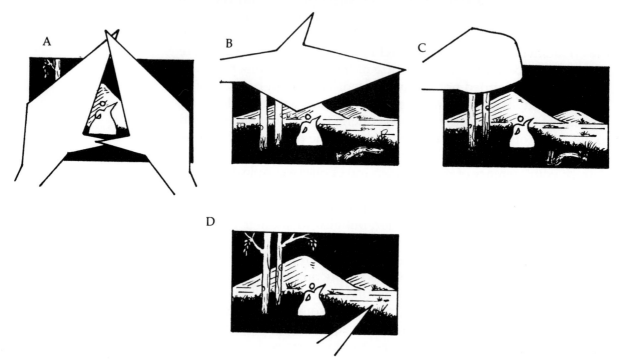

Figure 19.2
Analysing the Plotting.

section D) proves that the picture would be improved by reducing the dominance of the object by texturing (also see section 21.23).

19.13 Breaking an Impasse

What happens when you've tried every trick you know, yet still are unable to find the balance or mood that you're looking for? Or perhaps some other difficulty creates an impasse in your plotting; maybe you continually run out of "ceiling"; that is, you need 130 percent on one circuit to balance with the remainder. It's easy to get trapped into a set way of thinking, forget about time, and keep gnawing away at a problem with far more determination than skill.

When blocked in this fashion, try an entirely different approach; instead of starting with the background, start with a black stage and the circuit causing difficulty; or put the clouds onto the cyclorama before filling in with washes—anything to break the preconceived idea that's restricting you. If time presses, leave it and come back later, or pencil in a preset plotted for an earlier sequence that you know is close enough. By the time you get to the technical rehearsal, you may be unable to detect that the plotting is the same.

19.14 Designer, Know Thyself!

Try as you may to be guided by nothing other than the production's requirements, you are an individual, and your tastes and biases will be apparent in every plot [dry tech.] you embark upon. The same colour will reach out to you, similar textures will appear whatever the naturalistic justification, gloomy scenes may be underlit, and the same midnight sky will appear whether the piece is set in the tropics or Antarctica. During a plotting session you may need to trick yourself into correcting for the faults to which you are prone. What devices you use, what deceptions you require to change your usual patterns depend upon the problem, but you cannot begin to correct until you learn how others see your work and recognise the recurring problems. The objective opinion of trusted colleagues—particularly if it's often repeated—must receive your careful consideration.

19.15 Failure to Meet Schedule

What happens when you run out of time or, more realistically, when you realise that there is still half the show to plot [dry tech.] but only a third of the time remaining? The usual reaction is to tell the production manager at once that you must go into overtime, but this is the least productive solution. The entire plotting team has been sitting at the desk for hours—they're tired, their attention span has long since been exhausted and, to put it bluntly, they're bored with the whole process. Overtime is likely to be both unproductive and expensive. The Union Award recognises that these circumstances sometimes occur, but the prohibitively expensive rates are designed to minimise the likelihood.

An in-between solution is to continue for the time remaining, achieve as much as you are able, but inform the production manager that you may need extra time prior to the technical rehearsal—perhaps during the mechanists' lunch break, early morning, or wherever else it can be squeezed in. You will be amazed how productive that extra time will be. When, after a good night's rest, you approach the same problems that your tired brain was unable to encompass, they are solved so easily that you wonder what was the cause of all the fuss. Because the act of sleeping on the problem alone may enable you to formulate solutions, you don't need to ask for overtime. In the time available, you may be able to truncate the plotting procedure, since scenes are often repeated later in the piece; and you can "blind-plot" the same states into the cue sheets.

Alternatively, you may dispense with the cuing details and merely plot the differing states on state-of-the-board sheets, then work out the cuing problems when you meet with the board operator and the deputy stage manager. This may be a more suitable option because it does not demand exclusive use of the stage; you can work over the top of, say, a scene-change rehearsal. Remember, however, that this work must be done prior to the technical rehearsal. If you aren't given the opportunity to complete the process, the technical rehearsal degenerates into a very expensive plotting session.

19.16 In Summation

You now have a shape for your lighting that you believe will suit the stage once it's fully populated by performers. It won't be perfect, but the challenge of a plotting session is to get as close as you are able to your original vision in the time available, while retaining a reasonable degree of sanity for yourself and everybody involved.

CHAPTER 20

The Technical Rehearsal

The technical rehearsal is a most important act of intercourse: it's the first occasion when both cast and crew are together in the theatre; and, in all probability, it will also be the first time when every element of props, scenery, and wardrobe has been gathered together. This occasion has the flavour of the wedding night in an arranged marriage, where the couple have never before seen each other. The mood of both the bride from the rehearsal room and the groom from the workshops is tentative, yet full of expectation; and each partner is determined to impress, yet secretly afraid of being hurt. You know that the marriage must be made to work, and you hope that the matchmakers have done their part with skill, sensitivity, and an eye to the future, as the show could run for years!

20.2 The Runaway Technique

Everyone knows that a marriage night must be carefully stage-managed, yet too often a technical rehearsal is allowed to degenerate into a run of the show, which forges ahead like a juggernaut with actors, technicians, stage management, and director alike clinging desperately to it. Even if the organisation, preplanning, and communication have been perfect, the run-at-it technique doesn't work because, for everyone concerned, there are so many new components to comprehend and incorporate. The actors see a huge, empty auditorium and lighting instead of the blank walls of the rehearsal room. As costumes now have live mannequins inside them, life is difficult for wardrobe; and props people are stumbling about in a backstage traffic jam the likes of which hasn't been seen since the last technical rehearsal. The confusion is the same in every department—and no one seems to care!

The technical rehearsal must never be considered as just another run at the show. It is an entirely different process in a completely foreign environment with a range of mechanical problems that are quite unfamiliar. To expect either technicians or performers to "wing it" is to invite an air of desperation into the production that may take weeks to dissipate and will certainly not be gone by opening.

The paramount purpose of a technical rehearsal is to blend all the disparate elements of the production into a unity and to introduce all members of the cast and crew to their part in that process. You'll know how the lights, setting, and costumes blend into a sequence of images that flow from the show's beginning to end, along with the responsibility of each individual in the formation of those images. You'll know the tempo-rhythm of each moment and how each person must match or counterpoint that rhythm to form a complete orchestration. Most important of all, every individual needs to be confident that his or her contribution is feasible, can be achieved within the time available, and is accurately documented. Much of the fine detail that will form the basis of a performance may not be seen during the technical rehearsal, but all involved must receive a clear indication of the ideal so that they can commence the task of building a performance. They also need an objective summation of their work so that they can learn to assess for themselves what's required and become their own harshest critic. Too often, criticism degenerates into destructive carping that gives little or no guidance to the way in which an individual's efforts can be improved.

20.4 Who Runs the Technical Rehearsal?

Some individuals are confused and inattentive during the technical rehearsal; and this is aggravated if, in addition to everything else, there is more than one voice of authority to attend to. To whom should this voice belong?

In theory, the technical director is responsible, though the title behind the voice may vary from company to company, depending on the personalities involved, company structure, budgets, and the type of show. He or she is responsible for coordinating and integrating the show once it reaches the theatre and is charged with its care up to opening night. In many companies the position of technical director is not filled, and the responsibility is shared among the production manager, stage manager, director, and the various designers. So, which one speaks? It should be the individual best able to communicate the shape and form of the moment to both actors and technicians and who has all the relevant information and facilities, such as the following:

1. Access to current information—must therefore be connected with the headset communication system.
2. Easy communication with the stage.
3. A clear appreciation of the artistic intent of every moment.
4. Details of each department's contribution and an appreciation of the complexities involved.

5. The ability to communicate freely with every individual involved in the process, from the front-of-house manager to the props person.

When a company does not have a technical director on staff, the individual best suited to this position is the stage manager. This doesn't mean the type of stage manager who is backstage calling the show (that's the deputy stage manager); rather, it refers to that person who has been with the show from its inception and has been responsible for the coordination of the rehearsal process and technical preparation. During the run the stage manager is required to maintain production standards and must therefore be thoroughly attuned to the artistic and mechanical requirements of the director and designers; during the technical rehearsal this same person must be at the production desk and be party to all discussion. This is not to suggest that the stage manager should be able to execute every technical function; on the contrary, an appreciation of, and ability to communicate with, every department are sufficient. He or she delegates responsibility for any segment to the appropriate departmental head and, once the problem has been solved, picks up the reins again and carries the process forward.

These days theatre is considered to be a director's medium, and you may find that your director feels obliged to control the technical rehearsal. A director must retain artistic control but is seldom in a position for clear communication with, and coordination of, all departments. That is why it seems preferable to let the stage manager, who is at the apex of communications, organise, regulate, and control the technical rehearsal. The director must always retain power of veto over matters of artistic content; and, as in the plotting session, nothing is fixed until approved by the director, but these are matters of end results and final products. The stage manager has the clearest understanding of how the various departments need to mesh and of the dangers inherent in the process. Communication-intelligence indicates how well that meshing is taking place moment by moment. To know what is required to improve the results requires an appreciation and understanding of the problems of performers, the calling difficulties of the deputy stage manager, lighting, sound, musicians, mechanists, flymen, props, wardrobe, front-of-house, set construction—and on and on!

Consider a different company structure, though. The stage manager is in the corner calling the show; the production manager has been required to act as workshop supervisor in addition to the administration of staffing and budgets—he or she has rarely been seen at the production desk because of the weight of responsibilities elsewhere. The only two people remaining at the desk are the director and the lighting designer. It's very difficult for the stage manager to control the process from prompt corner, since there is enough to do calling the show from the prompt copy; the director, with enough problems handling the performers, doesn't wish to be tied to the production desk by headsets. That usually leaves the lighting designer in the hot seat. For this reason you need to be very familiar with the process of a technical rehearsal; then you can accept these responsibilities when called upon to do so.

The precise role of technical director or stage manager in this role is difficult to encapsulate. You might say that the juggernaut of a major production surging forward needs to be converted by sheer force of the technical director's will into a nimble two-wheeler that can stop on a dime, back up five stages, and recommence at the same tempo-rhythm—then skip ahead four pages and perform intricate manoeuvres before continuing on to the next challenging spot in the script.

There are three major functions involved: controller, analyst, and delegater. The technical director uses the authority of the "single voice" to stop and restart the action at will, to analyse and define areas requiring attention (in consultation with the director and other department heads), and then to delegate responsibility for solving problems to the appropriate department before continuing. Example: "Stop, please. We'll do that sequence again starting from . . .? [pause for consultation] This time let's (A) because (B). . . ."

(A)	(B)
1. Increase speed of lighting cue.	1. Actors are entering before their light is up.
2. Run the sequence again at performance pace.	2. The lighting operator didn't complete the preset in time and needs to ensure that it's feasible.
3. Alter staging for actors.	3. They must avoid incoming flown elements of scenery; someone's going to get hurt!
4. Extend the rate of actors' exit, descent of rag (house curtain), or lighting cue.	4. They must all phrase exactly with musical director.

When each departmental head has acknowledged that necessary changes have been made and that all operators are standing by for the rerun, the deputy stage manager will take control and repeat the sequence. Note the use of "Stop, please." It follows the rule of always being polite but firm, clear and consistent, even though the tone may vary to encourage a suitable attitude within the company; for example, a brisk tone may keep achievement rates high. Next, the voice gives clear directions regarding the point from which to recommence so that all departments can reset and be ready to go again as soon as possible. The deputy stage manager needs to be involved in this process and will usually organise the detail (as "... from Doctor's line, Help!"). Too frequently, someone busy with corrections will forget about the intricacies of operation and expect other people to pick up on the instant. That is possible only with computers, not with people and heavy equipment.

Instructions regarding problems and solutions should be clear and concise, but details should be left to departmental heads, individual operators, and performers. All are capable of altering their performance to suit if they know the required results.

The quick public summary outlined in the examples above has at least two other advantages. First, the entire company are aware of, and sympathetic to one another's problems. This helps break down barriers between departments and starts to weld the group into a company that can survive the length of run. Second, the statement of problem and solution allows for objections to be raised if difficulties are created for some other department. Example: If a sequence is speeded up, a performer may give warning that a fast costume change will become very difficult and additional dressers could be required, or the board operator may find that a preset that has always been fast will now be impossible (also see section 20.7).

Here's another common reason for the technical director to call a halt: "Stop, please. The lighting for this scene needs adjusting. Actors, please hold your position as we're lighting you. We'll continue from this point immediately the lighting designer has finished." Again, it's firm, polite, clear; everyone knows what the problem is and how to contribute to its solution. Let me narrate, for example, how a fine performer took advantage of a well-run technical rehearsal. The scene required her to prepare a family breakfast; and, since we were performing in-the-round with the audience close to the action, she had to cook real eggs. Two children and an adult performer were involved in a complex staging sequence that needed to be precisely arranged. The technical rehearsal for this ten-minute scene went on for well over an hour, but at the end of it Judi was able to say, "Yes, the eggs will cook in time." At every pause in the process she would take the eggs off the stove and replace them only when the action was again continuing at pace. That performance encapsulates the essential elements of a technical rehearsal. Judi was not only concerned with her own problems but was also aware of how she had to blend with other production components. Even so, she could not have succeeded without the control of a technical director who was able to shape complex details into a performance.

20.6 Location of the Technical Director/Stage Manager

Where is the best position from which the technical director/stage manager can operate? Answer—the production desk, since it is the centre of communications and allows access to the director and designers; however, there are problems with the desk to which chapter 19 has already alluded. First, it limits the technical director to only one perspective of the stage, but this can be overcome if the director and designers are free to move about and feed information back to the technical director from differing vantage points. Second, the convenience of the headset system presents a danger—the technical director may ignore the stage and broadcast only to technical departments. This risks alienating performers from technicians; the performers hear "Stop" but not the explanation. For a while they'll make the effort, but eventually frustration and annoyance will cause them to give up and behave no better than they are being treated. They may become slow, uncommunicative, uncooperative, and petty; they may even demand attention by manufacturing silly problems and minor annoyances. When acting as technical director, I prefer to switch off the headset microphone and use a clear voice or the microphone mentioned in section 19.3.2 to reach not only the stage but also the stage-com microphone; thus, everyone is made party to the process. In this manner you keep the technical rehearsal from becoming a mechanical exercise of correct timing and documentation. Instead, it is a major opportunity for forging a company from the separate departments, which, to this point, have been working in splendid isolation.

20.7 Departmental Authority

Given the organisation and structure outline above, how does the technical director/stage manager know when to stop the action? Neither the headsets nor the stage picture will give complete information; therefore, the stage manager needs a representative in each department to whom responsibility is delegated for requesting a halt when necessary. Generally, the head of department is nominated, though the technical director may choose to add anyone considered necessary (for example, deputy stage manager).

Before the rehearsal begins, the organisational structure should be explained to the entire company. All must be aware that only the technical director or representative may call a stop and that they should continue with the run until they hear that pronouncement. A company member should feel free to approach any departmental head with a problem but must realise that this may not automatically result in a stop. Some companies accept a democratic approach, with anyone allowed to request a halt; but this approach can work only in a small group. In a larger group every member cannot be aware of what others are doing and may invite frequent stops for minor problems that will result in inefficient use of time. Example: A halt could be called because a prop is wrongly positioned during a sequence involving critical timing for other departments; once that sequence is broken, they are forced to start all over again.

The technical director must study cuing patterns carefully to know which sequences must be considered a unit and, therefore, should not be interrupted. The actual pauses will be frequent enough, and at that time every individual must be encouraged to raise points of concern. No problem should be dismissed; each must be acknowledged and dealt with, if only by promising to discuss it during the break or saying "We've taken a note. Thank you." To many people this regimentation and organisation are unnecessarily authoritarian, and they prefer a looser, more relaxed structure. Unfortunately, the time available for the technical rehearsal is far from loose—it must stay on schedule if it is not to eat into the processes of technical runs and dress rehearsals.

20.8 Responsibilities of the Lighting Designer

As lighting designer, you sit at the production desk with the authority to request a stop—but for what do you stop? As in the plotting session, your concerns include both the manner in which your lighting services the whole stage picture—including actors!—and the necessity for the operators to develop accurate cue sheets. Thus, reasons for calling a halt to the rehearsal tend to fall into three major areas. First, you need to establish a firm working relationship with performers and to counteract a lighting designer's tendency to treat them as inanimate objects—canvas to paint, objects to light. Such an attitude is counterproductive, and at the technical rehearsal you must work toward a relationship based upon mutual understanding and common objectives.

Second, you must ensure that department members who will carry the weight of performance not only have accurate documentation but are also confident of their ability to blend with other performers onstage. As lighting designer you must get the design out of your own head and into those of the board operator, dome crew, and floor lighting person if it is to have any chance of succeeding.

Last—and perhaps this is the least important reason to request a stop—you need to trim and finely tune the stage picture to match as closely as possible your original vision. You are gently urging your audience to select only those portions of the stage picture you intend and to see each of them clearly and with sufficient detail to understand the intent of the production concept. For any of these purposes you may request a stop when you are unable to achieve results with the action continuing at pace or when a second attempt may improve your team's understanding of the cue.

20.9 Relationship with Performers

For many performers the change into the theatre can be disorienting, since the large reinforcing stimulus of the rehearsal room environment has been removed. Actors who have known their lines perfectly will hardly recognise their fellow performers, let alone know what line comes next. If you add to this unfamiliar environment a group of seemingly uncommunicative technicians who thrust unknown props into their hands, mutter gibberish into microphones, or shout numbers, then the performers may feel like pawns in a madman's game of chess.

Remember that the technicians comprise the first "audience" the nervous performers have. You need to talk to performers and to encourage them to feel free to talk to you. Make sure that they know what each one of your team is doing to contribute to the performance and assure them that you are in the service of the same production. In no way, however, are backstage crew servants to performers—that's a mistake too many performers have made! They need to be careful not to upset backstage crew, as their performance can be made or broken by the crew—you've all heard of itching powder in costumes and sabotaged props. I've known occasions that justified the itching powder, but I have also known technicians to behave equally poorly. Whatever the cause, both attitudes must change. The idea of "mutual service" forms a basis of respect from which working relationships can be built.

20.10 Finding a Light

With permission of the technical director/stage manager and director, begin the technical rehearsal by taking ten or twenty minutes to show performers the spots and special lighting that will be used during a performance. Ask the board operator to bring them all up together so that you can explain and demonstrate where necessary. With performers who are familiar with finding their light, simply point out their spots and indicate the moments when used. With less experienced performers, though, you should explain how the light can be located and how it may best be used. Example: Figure 18.5 shows how a raw performer may be tempted to fall into a lighting trap. It may be easier to demonstrate where to stand so that the face is lit but the feet are not. Many performers mark a spot onstage, but finding that precise spot in performance is sometimes clumsy. Instead, you should explain triangulation; for example, if performers place themselves on a line with the first set of legs and between seats 15 and 16 of the front row, they will be sufficiently close to find the light by "feeling-the-heat" on their faces. While searching for these markers, the performers are able to keep their heads up, and the mechanics will be less obvious.

If any circuit has particular problems, you should explain the best method for performers to present themselves for the benefit of the audience using that source, for example, the cone of light from a single overhead source as illustrated in Figure 20.1. Actors tend to use the centre of the light, which will result in deep shadows being cast on the face. If you require the audience to see more detail, you should explain that the best position is the extreme upstage edge of the cone, which maximises the angle of light on a performer's face. When two performers use the same source, they share the light between them so that neither is upstaged and both are equally well lit.

Figure 20.2 illustrates another example involving a façade with windows at varying heights and a low proscenium. When performers at upper windows play down to their fellows at stage level, section B of Figure 20.2 illustrates the problems if the actor faces directly downstage. The *only* place to light faces successfully when their heads are at this angle is from footlights, since it was decided that overhead lanterns had to remain masked by the proscenium

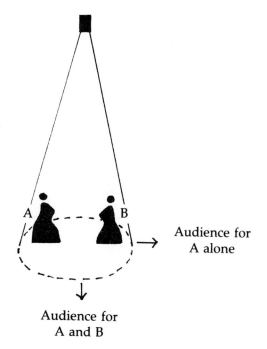

Figure 20.1
Actors under Light.

Audience for
A alone

Audience for
A and B

arch. The lighting designer should demonstrate both the problem and the solution in section A of Figure 20.2, where the performer presents a profile to the light.

With certain personalities it may be better to ask the director to handle the performer, since a director is more aware of the artist's idiosyncrasies and may be able to choose a more appropriate explanation. You need to remember that, up to this point, the only artistic authority the cast members have known is the director; some will feel more comfortable adjusting their staging to coordinate with lighting if the director is actively supporting the process.

Many of these problems will have been apparent to you for some time. If you were able to visit the rehearsal room frequently to suggest solutions as early as possible, it may be unnecessary to go into too much detail now that you've reached the technical rehearsal; the actors would be sufficiently prepared.

20.11 Welding a Company

At the beginning of the technical rehearsal, you should also introduce the head electrician to the cast and point out other members of the electrics department, in particular those at the biobox [lighting control booth] and dome positions. The reasons for this are twofold. Between the technical rehearsal and opening, much learning will occur, but a settled company may not be a reality until some weeks into the run, when the lighting designer is long since gone. As performers need to know who is responsible for lighting then, it is your responsibility now to open those avenues of communication. Note that you introduce the electrician only and point out the others. This is to minimise a problem referred to as "giving unauthorised notes." (A "note" is the very theatrical term describing comments

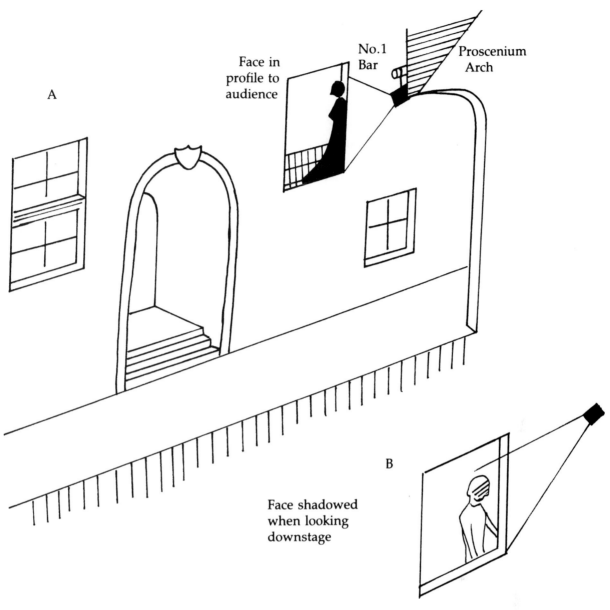

A

Face in profile to audience

No.1 Bar

Proscenium Arch

Face shadowed when looking downstage

B

Figure 20.2
Light Angles on Actor's Face.

from usually the director or head of department concerning another company member's performance—it may be either oral or written.) Example: One actor suggests to another that they change the staging or rearrange some detail of performance. Their stated reasons seem quite valid; however, as a byproduct of the action, one upstages the other. Something similar can occur between performers and, say, floor electrician and we therefore introduce the head electrician in the hope that all electrical matters will be referred to him.

The correct procedure for giving notes is for the plaintiff to approach the stage manager, who will pass it on, if valid, to the head of department and down to the individual concerned. This sounds convoluted and contrary to the prior-stated aim of improving communication; but in a long-running show, where personalities become ruffled and clashes of will occur, such detailed organisation serves to protect individuals and the production.

The comments above cover the negative side of relationships, but you also need to consider the positive side, which is frequently neglected. Often, technicians complain that performers know nothing about their technical support, yet it is rare to hear an invitation extended to performers that encourages them to expand their horizons. If the head electrician and management approve, you could, when you point out the biobox [lighting control booth], invite any of the company to visit at a mutually convenient time arranged with the head electrician. It's important to have some appreciation of what others are contributing to the production. To complain about the ignorance of some without making an effort to educate—and learn yourself—is short-sighted and counterproductive. Example: When performers have difficulty finding a light or seem uncomfortable with a scene, replace them onstage and invite them to view the scene from out front. It's very difficult to conceive the whole when you are an element of it. Similarly, with performers who have make-up problems: arrange to have onstage the lighting state, the performer, and a mirror so that they can view the results of light on make-up under performance conditions. Such demonstrations cost the lighting department very little, but the benefit to performers and to interdepartmental relationships is great.

20.12 Top-and-Tail [Cue-to-Cue]

In a presentation of two and a half hours, there is likely to be an hour's material that needs detailed consideration in the technical rehearsal. You usually have four to eight hours to drill these moments until they are sufficiently prepared for a technical run—the next process. To save time, you drop out those portions in which there is no change to the technical component; this is known as a top-and-tail or cue-to-cue.

Having finished a sequence of cues (which may involve any or all departments), you jump ahead to the stand-by for the next sequence making sure that there is sufficient time within these breaks for presets and the like. There is, however, no point in truncating to such a degree that it would be just as easy to continue the run. Those sections to be dropped should be clearly defined prior to the technical rehearsal. The technical director/stage manager should check with heads of department and with the director, in particular, to ensure that no important component is overlooked. Example: The performers need a "run-in" to a fast sequence for clearly establishing the tempo-rhythm before the technicians join them at pace, and these sections must also be considered as part of the technical rehearsal. But the technical rehearsal is not for testing performance values. Actors should be asked to "mark" their performance; that is, they should deliver at pace and volume, but content (motivation, emotion, feeling) is of minor importance and serves only to exhaust the performer. The form and shape are sufficient for the technical rehearsal, but you will need a complete performance for the technical run to make backstage staff aware of a performer's preparation and follow-through. It's a very different matter doing a fast costume change with a performer who has just been weeping!

As you jump ahead to the next sequence, it's beneficial to the lighting department if the actors give you a speeded-up version of the staging only—like fast-forwarding the tape. You thereby ensure that you have them lit throughout the scene you are cutting by finding those spots where a performer drops out of light. The technical rehearsal is prone to scheduling problems, and it's advisable to push through relentlessly; this at least ensures that the whole show is covered to a minimal standard. Should you finish early, you can go back and redo sticky sequences to imprint them strongly into the minds of the company. With a simple show there may be time to run sections of dialogue; and, if there is one scene that is weak or underprepared, it is the obvious choice.

20.13 Shaping a Complex Cue

How do you clearly convey the fluidity, shape, dynamics, and tempo-rhythm of a cue? How do you reach all those involved without cluttering the process, perhaps giving too much detail to some and not enough to others? Frequently, the technical director will delegate to the lighting designer responsibility for shaping a cue sequence when the major component is lighting. These sequences will usually involve other departments, and the lighting designer must coordinate. Again, unfortunately, there are no rules, so choose the approach that best suits the cue and the individuals involved.

The run-at-it technique is unproductive even when applied to small sequences and should be avoided. Instead, separate the various elements so that they can be absorbed in small, easy-to-comprehend packages that may be expanded to include further complexities. Example: You have a sequence that involves a snap (zero second) visual lighting cue, followed by a fast preset during which sound underpins the onstage action; then a sequential fade to black commencing at a set point in the music and timed to onstage action, followed by scene change and lights up into the next scene. The difficulty for the board operator is the preset, which must finish with accuracy and reliability in time for the next operation to go with sound, with a few moments leeway for those occasions when something goes amiss. If there is any doubt, the lighting designer must do everything possible to simplify the preset. Perhaps it need not be a full preset but an adjustment to an existing state, or you may replot the preset entirely.

Of course, familiarity will improve the speed of the preset, and a good board operator will rehearse such a sequence in the same way that actors rehearse lines; but, unless the task can be achieved at least once during the technical rehearsal, you cannot be sure that it's possible to achieve reliably every performance. Work with the board operator alone for more familiarity with the sequence; and, once the board operator is happy, try the preset with the sound tape rolling so that he or she learns to pace against it. This may never be a conscious process. I can be listening to the radio, quite relaxed—but suddenly I know that something must be done. It takes a moment to realise that the music was used in a show and that my Pavlovian responses are once again being triggered. This degree of familiarity won't be achieved during the technical rehearsal, but the groundwork can be laid.

Now include the performers. Explain the visual component to the board operator, who will then rehearse with the performer. Make sure all actors are familiar with whatever else may be required of them; perhaps they must exit in the blackout and need to locate a beacon in the wings to guide them, or you may need to choreograph the exit to avoid collisions or falls into the orchestra pit. The director or deputy stage manager may organise this while you work with the board operator. Now that everyone is prepared, try the sequence at pace; then listen to comments from all those involved, adjust, and try it again.

In the example above, assume that you were having difficulty getting a clearing cue for the deputy stage manager to bring the lights up after the blackout. The performers were in a perfect position to assess that cue, and they suggested they could commence the dialogue for the next scene in the blackout, which the deputy stage manager could use to cue the board operator. The director's approval was sought and given. To truncate the blackout even further, it was decided that the board operator could take the dialogue itself as a cue, with the deputy stage manager following up with a confirming "Go." This cooperation from the cast came about because they were party to your technical problems and understood what you were trying to achieve for the production. They matched their performance with yours. Had you tried to adjust the sequence through headsets alone, they would have been kept in ignorance, the blackout would have remained far too long, and the phrasing and pace would have dropped so low that the next scene would start at a disadvantage.

But keep things in perspective. In a show with seventy or eighty cues, there may be only four or five moments that benefit from *this very detailed* approach; the remainder can be explained quite well with words and numbers *prior to the attempt then the whole sequence runs as a unit. On occasion you will be unable to find the right words.* Perhaps it's just that those four or five cues are beyond your mastery of language and you need to revert to gesticulation, but sometimes it's the only way to illustrate clearly to all concerned the essence of each cue. Again, whatever works for you will produce the results you know to be necessary.

In the above example the board operator needs to shift attention out of the biobox or away from the desk and onto the stage. It's very difficult at this early uncertain stage, but the process must be commenced—and therein lies the most important responsibility of the lighting designer during the technical rehearsal. At every opportunity you need to associate the board operator with the action onstage. He or she needs to be encouraged to listen to the dialogue, to watch the staging, and to pay less attention to the timing in seconds (as during the plotting) but to match with tempo-rhythms onstage.

The board operator needs a clear understanding of the production's intent for each cue, and this is your responsibility as lighting designer. You cannot expect immediate comprehension, however; this process will continue up to opening. Example: A performer is seated centre delivering a vitriolic description of the villain to her friends at prompt [stg. lft.] while he enters O.P. [stg. rt.] to stand behind her. As she sees the reaction of her friends, the heroine stops, turns to the villain, and pauses; then there is a blackout with, hopefully, a laugh reaction from the audience. The first lighting cue is a subtle isolation to the villain and heroine; the second is the blackout. The shape of the first depends on the performance of the heroine, since you cannot reduce the light on her friends until she has recognised their reaction and is shifting her attention. Your cue begins with the entrance of the villain and continues until the change of focus so that the audience's attention is pulled with that of the heroine across to the villain. There is no way of describing that cue in terms of numbers and cue types. Performers are the only source of accurate information for the board operator; and, even at this early stage, you should remind them that it's likely to change subtly night by night.

It will depend entirely upon the deputy stage manager and board operator whether the blackout creates a belly-laugh or a resounding thud. It's comedy timing that you're looking for: the tirade continues vehemently, then peters out—slow turn with realisation, beat for reaction, black! If the deputy stage manager extends the beat, the audience may be embarrassed; or, if it's cut short, they may not have time to see the reaction that triggers the laugh. If the board operator fumbles or anticipates, the same results occur; but, with a fade instead of a snap out, the moment of comedy can be turned to tragedy or at least to embarrassing sentiment.

It's your responsibility to get this information out of your head and into that of the operator, who will then have a clear image of the intention of each cue and can build performance from now until opening, using that image as a goal.

20.14 Adjusting the States

The processes discussed so far will occupy you for a relatively small percentage of your time during the technical rehearsal; that is not to say that they are less important but that the opportunities for carrying them out are less frequent. Most of your time is spent "seeing the picture for the first time" (see section 19.12); adjusting levels; discussing balance and focus with the director and designer; explaining cue shapes to operators; consulting the technical director/ stage manager regarding timing, repositioning, cues, and the like. Your base of operations remains the production desk, although you, the director, and the set designer will be relatively free to move about the auditorium and to exchange views concerning the stage picture. That way you can clearly define problems before wasting the time of the board operator and others of the company with experimentation.

Once you pinpoint the problem, you need to make some quick decisions: Can the problem be fixed without stopping? How close is the next cue? Is the board operator in the midst of a preset? If you communicate via headsets, will you be cluttering the airwaves, making the deputy stage manager's job impossible?

The technical rehearsal is the first opportunity for the board operator and the deputy stage manager to become familiar with each other and the tempo-rhythm of the show. Plotting adjustments should not interfere with that process or break their concentration. Remember always to ask if there is time, instead of roughly breaking in on headsets; there are other departments besides lighting to be cued on headsets. If the board operator is at the production desk, it's useful to establish a sign language—a simple gesture may tell you what you can do with your interruption. Your delay in taking action may cause friction between you and the director during the technical rehearsal. Having defined a problem and requested a solution, the director sometimes finds it difficult to understand why there cannot be immediate action. He or she can see that the board operator is doing nothing but doesn't realise that the operator is on stand-by from the deputy stage manager and that you must wait your turn.

As lighting designer you must learn to classify problems quickly in three ways:

1. Major problems that must be fixed now and, if necessary, you call stop to do so. These may include moments when the centre of focus is way off or the protagonist is in darkness.

2. Problems of balance, the solutions to which you need to see during the technical rehearsal; however, they may be of insufficient importance for calling a stop. Try to achieve results as the action continues, or take notes and make the adjustment during the next pause when other problems are being fixed.

3. Minor points of colouration and mood that may be a little experimental; it would be to your advantage if they could be included now, but it won't matter if you don't see them until the next run. Note these alterations and "blind-plot" them at the next pause or even at the end of the rehearsal.

The criteria for making these decisions will vary between shows depending on the work load of the operator, his or her experience, and the type of board. Remember that the operator needs time not only to make the alteration but also to record it correctly, and should not be pressured to such a degree that accuracy suffers or cue sheets become a source of errors. You must also keep in mind that there is only a certain amount of detail any individual can absorb at one sitting. Don't expect everything to happen instantly. Look again at the comments in section 19.10 regarding the tendency to leap forward to the final product instead of allowing for development between now and opening.

The Technical Rehearsal

There are sure to be times when you have nothing to do. These periods can be spent constructively away from the production desk. Not only will you begin to wean the board operation away from relying on you, shifting attention to the deputy stage manager, but also you and the set designer must consider the stage from every vantage point. The two of you can have an open, detailed discussion now that you have a product worthy of fine analysis. Examples: The lens of a lantern that you thought hidden can be seen from one corner of the auditorium, and a barndoor or "tophat" must be fitted during trimming. Or a tablecloth seems to be catching more light than the performers seated around it. It needs dyeing, but perhaps you'd prefer that the centre of the cloth remain undipped to retain the bounce off the table centre to assist in underlighting faces. Never forget that a collaboration needs to be worked at. You must engage in a continual exchange of ideas, an occasional difference of opinion, and a great deal of compromise; dispute may not be comfortable, but silence achieves nothing.

20.16 In Summation

You are getting near to completing your design. It needs polish and fine adjustment to force it closer to your original vision, but there is time enough between now and opening night to achieve that. However, a lighting design needs to be performed with assurance and in sympathy with all other elements of the production if it is to be clear to an audience—and it is not within the power of the lighting designer alone to give it that quality! The technical rehearsal marks the beginning of the transfer of your design into the care of the lighting crew, and you must encourage that process so that, by the time of opening, you are no longer important to the smooth operation of the show.

CHAPTER 21

Dress Rehearsal and Technical Runs

The design is almost out of your hands; while there is some adjusting, trimming, and fine-tuning to be done, your principal task prior to opening is to make yourself redundant. Your vision must be passed on to the performance staff, who must be encouraged to make the show uniquely their own, within parameters. For many lighting designers this is a difficult period. Some dump the entire weight of the design onto the staff and disappear into a corner, where they suffer none too silently. Others, finding it extremely difficult to let go, continue trimming and altering to retain control over their creation. Neither approach is helpful to the production or to your staff, and this chapter will discuss ways to transfer your design to, in particular, the board operator. This is not to say that others of your staff are to be ignored; rather, the detailed example of the board operator contains the essence of your responsibilities to the entire department.

21.2 Attendance at Note Sessions

During the time from now to opening you may spend as much time in note sessions as you do running the show. These sessions are frequently perceived as nothing more than a necessary chore, but they are your principal means of continuing interdepartmental collaboration.

The structure of notes sessions will vary between companies. One extreme comprises a single event that everyone attends and all notes are given in sequence—the majority will be for performers and may be quite personal, while only rare reference is made to technical departments. At the other extreme, no combined session is held; all heads of departments conduct their own. It's assumed that interaction between departments has been achieved through discussions at the production desk. This may not be the case, and other departments will be kept in ignorance until confronted with changes at the next run.

The best compromise is a combined session immediately following the run, at which all departments are represented, to discuss gross details and major changes. This is followed at a convenient time by departmental sessions to consider fine detail, together with specific departmental problems. The head of a department must ensure that any relevant information arising at these meetings is passed on before the next run. Whatever format you use, you must find ways of continuing the development of the show up to opening with particular emphasis on the following (sections 21.2.1 to 21.2.4):

21.2.1 Matching the Production Concept

In the past months those involved in the original production concept meetings have travelled a large circle. They started with a single idea, then went their various ways to achieve their departmental contribution. As opening draws near, they are intent upon returning to the same point of departure. It's not easy; there may be failures in certain areas that need to be compensated for in others. Examples: If the visual impact of one important scene is less than anticipated perhaps the costume designer can assist your lighting with the addition of a vibrant shawl; or, if the staging has not achieved the degree of focus intended, you alter the balance artificially with highlights. You need to use all skills available to squeeze from the production a clear statement of the concept.

21.2.2 Dialogue with Performers

At every opportunity you need to clarify the interaction between performers and lighting. You can best accomplish this by continuing the dialogue you established during the technical rehearsal.

If some actors continue to have trouble finding their light, you may be able to assist by allowing them time onstage under lighting to experiment with the problem at their own pace. Sometimes performers will take exception to receiving notes from a lighting designer; they don't appreciate the necessity for interaction and consider that an electrician "cannot possibly know about make-up!" Try taking a devious route; perhaps the designer has a better rapport with these performers and will be the channel for your achieving results. Be careful, though, when using this approach; the intermediary needs to be clear regarding both the problem and solution, and the performer must not feel manipulated.

21.2.3 Two Designers—One Product

I have found it both pleasant and educational to work with one set designer in particular. He insists on stage time alone just prior to opening with nothing more than worklights. When we first worked together, I was puzzled and contrived to sneak in to watch him at work. His tools were a pot of black paint and a fine brush; with a dash here and a dab there he was fine-tuning his design to match the end-results achieved by the lighting department. His argument went like this: In the early stages of production the workshop demands precise detail from the designer before starting construction, while the lighting department remains the flexible partner. However, once the lighting is trimmed to the performance, the set designer is able to take the process one step further and—as this one did with light and shade produced from the pot of black paint—to blend the two designs. Example: A cushion was catching light and upstaging performers. Using the paint, Tom added texture that was in the style of the production and yet reduced reflected light to a suitable level. In the original design specifications the cushion was vaguely textured; but, until Tom had seen it under performance lighting, he was unsure to what degree it needed to be broken down.

Not every team will work in this fashion, but each must discover a method that allows both individuals freedom within their own area of responsibility yet combines to a common end-result.

21.2.4 Adjusting the Picture

You will need to continue fine adjustments of intensity and balance to create the best picture possible for the whole audience, regardless of position in the auditorium. On occasions when at last I've found time to check the picture from the dress circle [balcony], I've been gripped by a sense of panic because the show looks entirely different. The cyclorama, so apparent from the stalls [orchestra seating], fades into the background, and the stage floor dominates the stage.

In situations like this you need to balance and rebalance from every aspect to reach a compromise that satisfies the designer, the director, and you, the lighting designer. Your goal is to keep the production concept and performers in the foreground with a background that complements and adds appropriate dimension. This will be achieved largely by notes and blind-plotting, since the deputy stage manager must have primary use of the headset systems, so that all concerned gain a sense of the show's flow. It's important that both the deputy stage manager and operator have this sense of flow prior to opening and are confident of their mastery of the show. To assist them even further, the lighting designer should try to engineer at least one run immediately prior to opening where the cue sheets receive no alterations; this helps to build confidence since all documentation has been proven under performance conditions.

21.3 Trimming

During this period you will need to arrange stage time (not necessarily with exclusive use of the stage) to trim the rig; that is, to adjust those lanterns [instruments] that are not achieving the required results.

A piecemeal approach to trimming is uneconomic; it's better to allow your list to grow to a reasonable size before you attack all the problems in a session similar to the focus, though this may require you to explain to the others of the production team the reasons for the delay. But be sure that the director and set designer have an opportunity to view an alteration under performance conditions prior to opening. What the lighting designer considers to be a "fine trim" may be viewed by the director as a major alteration. Ideally, you should arrange for all alterations to be completed prior to the final dress rehearsal.

Keep the head electrician informed of what's contained in the list so that he or she can prepare before the event in much the same way as the rig and focus were prepared for. Thus, the replacement lanterns, colour, appropriate ladders, and tools will be available, but, what is more important, there will be a detailed, systematic approach so that stage time will be used effectively.

Take care! Once a circuit has been adjusted, bring up the cue state to check that the changes haven't caused "damage" elsewhere. While shifting a lantern to fill one hole, you may create another in a position previously well covered, or you may accidentally destroy a portion of the picture that is most pleasing.

21.4 Major Redesign

What action should you take when a major proportion of your design doesn't work?

As always, your principal enemies are time and money. Because it's not easy to admit a major mistake, you may try to force a solution from the original design so that the money and effort already expended are not wasted. But when you eventually admit that more drastic action must be taken, you may have left yourself with no time to effect the changes.

Your major support will be the head electrician, who is often the only one able to match your concern for professional standards and has an advantage over you, since, from the plotting [dry tech.] onwards, he or she has remained in the background and may have gained an objective overview that you are denied. It is the head electrician who may have seen the problem developing and could have already found a solution, which the pressure of the moment obscures from you.

Early recognition of the problem is only half the battle; the solution needs to be feasible in terms of time, money, and personnel. A plan of execution must be formulated that least disrupts the continuing rehearsal process; without it any desperate attempt at a solution will cause as many problems as it solves.

Convene a special production meeting at which the production manager and director in particular can assess both the likelihood of success and the unsettling influence of last-minute alterations on the company. A marvelous solution is worthless if your operators and/or cast are unable to assimilate it before they are exposed to the stress of an audience. It's often better to favour simplicity; merely illuminate the stage and allow the performers to carry the moment rather than risk chaos.

21.5 Entrusting Your Design to the Board Operator

It's to the board operator that you must entrust the heart of your design. When considering that process in detail, remember that you must lavish the same attention on the dome operators, floor lighting person, and so on, so that a complete team is created. In the process ensure that you replace yourself as head of that team with the stage manager and head electrician, who are charged with maintaining standards throughout the run. To exclude them from the process would be to invite distortion of the design; they must maintain standards as they understand them; but, if you depart before imparting information clearly, those left behind will be obliged to interpret your intention in the light of their own experience.

The process of developing operators who are adept at shaping lighting changes that enhance the production is frequently a rewarding exercise. To mould an understanding in the mind of another, as opposed to dictating a result, encourages new creative forces that frequently exceed your expectations. (I far prefer to see a final performance that is still vibrant and interesting than a lifeless carbon copy of what I dictated.)

21.6 What Makes a Good Board Operator?

It's rare for a lighting designer to have the choice of board operator. Generally, you must accept the individual who "comes with the house" and who thus has experience with the board and is at home in the theatre. Hence, with every new show you must make a quick assessment: how to capitalise on the operator's strengths and how to improve weaknesses. All designers will have their own list of qualities against which to judge a board operator, but the qualities listed below encompass most:

21.6.1 Accuracy and Speed

These were the qualities manufacturers recognised in computers that made them so attractive for lighting control, but computerisation is merely an aid to the operator; the machine can be no better than the individual controlling it.

21.6.2 Reliability and Precision

You rely upon the operator to record the lighting plan [plot] precisely and to reproduce it at each performance. The operator's reliability must also be a behavioural quality; you need him or her on time and sober every night.

21.6.3 Sensitivity to Performance

A board operator needs to assess performances nightly, matching the lighting operation to the slight differences and variations perceived onstage. When mechanical failure occurs, the operator must be able to improvise with what remains to create as nearly as possible the original stage picture.

21.6.4 An Ear for Rhythm

Many good board operators have musical training, which is indicative of their need for an appreciation of tempo-rhythm in music, dialogue, and movement. It enables them to blend with other performers, take visual cues, or blend with a phrase of music.

21.6.5 Understanding of Equipment

All board operators need a keen sense of the equipment under their control, both the permanently installed equipment and that rigged specifically for the show. They quickly recognise what circuit has failed or how the board is misbehaving so that they can accurately define faults for the maintenance technicians.

21.6.6 Concentration and Consistency

Particularly with a long-running show the board operator's powers of concentration must be such as to shut out distractions. The same standard of performance must be delivered for the 139th matinee as much as for opening night.

21.6.7 Direct Eye-to-Hand Transfer

There is a quality in good operators that enables them to translate the stimulus received by their eye directly into sympathetic manual responses without the obvious intrusion of intellect. Examples: The follow-spot must appear as if it is motivated by the performer, and a front-of-house fade-up should feel motivated by the rising curtain. Very often an onstage performer is criticised because "you can see the wheels turning" and is praised for the apparent ease and lack of effort required to create the illusions. These same qualities are required of a good board operator.

21.6.8 A Delight in Subtleties

Like most backstage performers board operators rarely have the satisfaction of direct approval: appreciation in the form of applause. They need to gain satisfaction from knowing that tonight's performance was as good, if not better, than last night's. This is all that is allowed professional backstage performers, and they must be encouraged to take pride in their professionalism.

21.7 Drilling Sessions

The board operator has less than one week to achieve results equivalent in size and difficulty to a "supporting artist." Unfortunately, runs and dress rehearsals alone are not always sufficient to perfect operation; these may increase the operator's awareness of the rate and shape of performance, but the pressure of time doesn't allow for drilling and experimentation. In order to build confidence and ability, the board operator needs coaching, encouragement, and objective criticism. It's unlikely you can afford time during runs to drill particular sequences as you did in the technical rehearsal; therefore, you must allocate time within the production schedule. For difficult sequences the lighting designer may request the services of the entire company for ten minutes at the end of a run, or, just prior to the final dress rehearsal, a director may devote an entire call to fine-tune particular elements. However, these sessions are expensive in work hours and are not always possible within the schedule. You must invent ways within your department that give the board operator sufficient rehearsal without the services of the company.

Generally, the deputy stage manager and sound operator are happy to assist and frequently welcome the opportunity to consolidate their own work, while performers will often devote time when a particularly difficult sequence involves them. Each of these generous offers will assist in reproducing performance conditions, but it will probably fall to you and the head electrician to read the bulk of the performer's lines and accurately reproduce staging (a tape recording of an earlier run is also useful). These sessions can be fun, since they are usually a mixture of concentrated effort and inspired idiocy; however, the objective is to allow the board operator to strengthen a grasp of the show.

Until operators gain confidence and appreciate that they have the latitude to shape a cue themselves, they will continue to "do it as he told me." Fortunately, the beat of the musical director or the pace of a performer is nowhere near as rigid as that. You should encourage the operator to do what feels "right" for the moment, and only then will the lighting design become part of the production instead of something superimposed over its framework. For years board operators have been exhorted to reproduce their performance accurately, and you may find them tentative when they are first introduced to this new concept of "feel it." They prefer the distant and uninvolved "stop-watch" function, since its results can be precisely verified. Often, they need reassurance that they have the ability and require only a sense of freedom to release it. They need convincing that there is no right or wrong, only better and not-so-good. Most important of all, they need to be sure they have your confidence.

21.8 Eyes Onstage

Perhaps the most important habit you can instill in the board operator during drilling sessions is to gaze concentratedly onstage, not within the biobox (see section 20.13). I recently saw a performance in which it was obvious that the cues were one step ahead for the entire act! Obviously, an automatically sequenced computer board was being used; and, because of some inaccuracy of preset or operation, the operator took one step ahead and remained there the entire seventy-five minutes! How an operator or deputy stage manager could allow such negligence to occur is beyond me. I don't refer to the initial mistake but to the fact that it was not perceived and corrected immediately. Evidently, the board operator never looked at the stage, and the deputy stage manager was buried deep in the prompt copy, completely unaware of what was happening. Both should be able to recognise every state in the show from their difference vantage points. The operator is in a better position front-of-house to see gross mistakes (for example, fader missing from the preset), whereas the deputy stage manager, who can see the individual lanterns, may be able to identify specific problems. While they don't need to learn the states parrot fashion, they do need to be very aware of what is "normal" so that, instinctively realising when something is amiss, they go searching for it. Once they've defined the problem, they can take action to rectify the situation without further disturbing the audience (see section 21.10).

21.9 The Doomsday Approach

During drilling sessions it's useful to point out to the board operator those lighting states that are risky and to encourage them to predict solutions to problems before they arise. Example: You may isolate to a single spot on the protagonist, dropping the remainder of the stage to low levels. What happens if the dimmer controlling that lantern blows a fuse? Unless the operator is quick, the central argument of the script may be played in black. If you can warn operators of this likelihood and encourage them to "imagine the worst," then the reaction time between occurrence and solution is likely to be reduced and the damage minimised. The board operator must be quite definite in the choice of alternate dimmer, picking one downstage that will guide the performer to the solution chosen. Your preparations need to instill awareness—not panic—so that board operator and performer work together.

Similarly, at about this time it is your responsibility, along with the board operator, to establish stand-by matrix states when working on a computer board. This device uses mechanical means to substitute for the memory of a computer board when, for any reason, it fails. On most machines about ten separate states can be set up; you should detail those settings that will be most useful to the operator, as in the following example:

Matrix 1   Scene change and preset; the state of cue 15; used as required.

Matrix 2   Full up state, daylight; the state of cue 6; used majority act 1, commencement act 2, and curtain calls.

Matrix 3   Full up state, moonlight; the state of cue 31; used act 2/sc. 4 and sc. 6 and crossfades with matrix 2 for sunsets.

Matrix 4   P.S. [stg. lft.] bias, daylight; the state of cue 23; used to highlight action prompt side act 1.

Matrix 5   O.P. [stg. rt.] bias, moonlight; the state of cue 42; used to highlight action O.P. act 2 and balance matrix 4.

Matrix 6   Finale act 1; the state of cue 36.

Matrix 7 Finale act 2; the state of cue 73.

Matrix 8 Special effects state, fire sequence act 2/sc. 4; state of cue 62.

Matrix 9 Special effects state, water sequence act 2/sc. 5; state of cue 67.

Matrix 10 Lantern check; all faders at 100 percent; a usual setting to allow for checking the rig preshow.

Using this detail the board operator will be able to continue the performance under less than ideal conditions, but at least the audience will not be deprived of their entertainment. The matrix must be established during the rehearsal period before you play to your first audience; it's too late to think about it once failure has occurred. The operator should not have to chase the lighting designer for the information; it's your responsibility!

21.10 Mistakes

Even professionals have occasional lapses and aberrations of memory during the rehearsal period; later in the run inattention will be an added cause. Unfortunately, mistakes in lighting are most obvious; if an actor transposes words, few in the audience even notice, and the other performers can generally cover; but lighting transpositions (for example, 40 at 50 percent instead of 50 at 40 percent) blaze across the stage for all to see—and for those in the production to shout about!

A lighting designer must be prepared to act as a cushion between the shouters and operators. There's no purpose in making excuses, but you can help everyone get the seriousness of the mistake into proportion and get on with the show. When the same mistake reoccurs, perhaps then it's time for severity—but the older I get, the more I realise that shouting is of more benefit to the shouter than to the production. Whether the problem is due to equipment failure or to a mistake in operational detail, panic achieves nothing. Instead, the board operator should analyse the seriousness of the mistake before deciding on a course of action. Having never seen the show before, the spectators don't know what is supposed to happen; however, if a light fades up, then snaps out, and then another snaps in to replace it, of course they're going to recognise it as a mistake. The giveaway is the obvious panic—not the choice of circuits. Example: If a red streak textures the cyclorama accidentally, the board operator must make lightning judgements: Are the actors in light? Is there time for corrections? Am I likely to ruin the next sequence if I take time now to correct the mistake?

If actors are lit and the audience is able to comprehend the action onstage, the mistake may be better left or very gently eased out—the effect may even appeal to those who like a surreal touch to their lighting! If, however, performers are without sufficient light, the first priority of the operator is to get light to them fast, but without drawing undue attention. If it's a mistake that will take a considerable time to correct, a full wash of acting areas will allow the performance to continue while the state-of-the-board sheets are used to correct the fault; then the action can be picked up four or five cues hence.

Frequently house rules exclude all visitors from the biobox unless approved by the head electrician—and this also applies to the lighting designer. Its purpose is to prevent frantic lighting designers or directors from bursting in during the middle of a performance to demand that the operator fix a mistake immediately. Such behaviour does little to assist the board operator and frequently has the opposite effect. You must allow stage management and operators to handle performance problems in the best way they know without interference, for you will shortly be leaving the production. You may not agree with the steps they take to solve the difficulties, in which case you can point out the alternative afterwards; but you must trust them to care for the show to the best of their abilities.

21.11 Opening-Night Nerves

During recent chapters the term *opening night* or *opening* has been used increasingly. It's difficult to maintain a sense of proportion with this relentless build of apprehension, try as you may to play down the importance of the occasion. The unfortunate overemphasis given to opening contributes to the impression that a paying audience later is somehow less important than the critics and invited guests of opening night. This provokes a reaction performance that generally occurs on the night after opening; the adrenaline has gone, everyone is tired, and performance standards suffer. The resulting pressure on crew and performers to do well on opening night can be disastrous, and the lighting designer and head electrician will need to counteract that influence in whatever way seems appropriate. There are some maxims that might help you and a nervous crew:

1. The dress rehearsal, when your professional colleagues are likely to be in attendance, is certain to be a more discerning audience. This helps get nerves over before opening.
2. The best way to influence your opening night audience is to entertain them, just as you would any other audience.
3. The best performance must be closing night; until then each performance should be minimally better than the last.
4. Those VIP's in the opening audience, who are held in such awe, are just as human as you are.

21.12 Returning the Lighting Desk to the Biobox [Lighting Control Booth]

When should the operator leave the production desk and return the lighting control desk to the biobox [lighting control booth]? Remember that the view from the biobox is utterly different and that the transfer will be disorienting for the board operator. There will be no improvement while adjusting to the new surroundings and trying to associate a cyclorama-dominated view of the stage from the production desk with the new aspect from the back of the circle [balcony], where the stage floor fills the picture. The transfer needs to occur in time for the operator to settle and adjust before opening. A good time for this is the run prior to the final dress rehearsal so that the operator is not doubly affected by the shift and the first audience.

21.13 Cue Sheets

Having drilled and rehearsed the show, you now have a competent and well-prepared operator, who is attuned with, and sensitive to, performances—but who might get run over by a bus on the way to the final dress rehearsal! Now you know why cue sheets must remain with the board and why you write cue sheets so that anyone with a basic knowledge of the show and board can step in at short notice to deliver a reasonable performance. Cue sheets that are so unique only one person can read them are dangerous.

Normally, the head electrician would be first choice as understudy; the stand-by operator for the theatre would be another. (This individual will have trained on the board and been used to relieve the permanent employee for annual leave, and so on.) An understudy who has not been closely associated with the development of the production should be invited to become familiar with the cue sheets and the show.

One final suggestion concerning cue sheets: The lighting designer should try to give the board operator at least one run before opening without alterations. This ensures that any rewritings are given a proof-run, and the operator can be confident that they are correct.

21.14 Updating Records

As you draw to the end of the rehearsal process, you should update all documentation (sections 21.14.1 to 21.14.3) and ensure that copies are retained in company records. In this way you safeguard the standards you have established for the production and make reproduction or transfer to another theatre easy.

21.14.1 The Plan [Plot]

It's rare for the lighting designer to redraw the plan [plot] completely; usually you clearly indicate changes on the original transparency; or, if you prefer to work in pencil, changes are even easier. A copy should then be made for the head electrician, since the original master is likely to be well-worn by now. A second copy goes to the stage manager for inclusion in the prompt copy, which forms the basis of company records of the show.

Dress Rehearsal and Technical Runs

21.14.2 State-of-the-Board and Cue Sheets

Copies of the up-to-date state-of-the-board sheets or computer print-out, together with detailed cue sheets, must be included in the prompt copy for record purposes and also to safeguard against loss from the biobox. You will also retain a copy of state-of-the-board sheets for your personal records.

21.14.3 Lantern Schedule

The head electrician will generally have kept the lantern schedule updated, but, if not, work with him on the document when you deliver the replacement master plan.

Note. After the plotting [dry tech.] session the cue synopsis becomes redundant, and there is no advantage in updating it, since it has been replaced by detailed documents of execution (for example, plan, cue sheets, and the like).

21.15 *Final Dress Rehearsal*

Often, management will arrange an invited audience at the final dress rehearsal, comprising family, friends, and perhaps taxi-drivers and local nurses. (You should arrange invitations for those casual workers who worked the rig and focus but are no longer associated with the production; they may enjoy seeing the results of their work.)

Prior to this event a meeting, however brief, should be arranged between the director, set designer, production manager, and lighting designer to assess the state of the production, to see if more could be done before opening, and to determine what is feasible to achieve under the circumstances. You've all attempted to realise the production concept with varying degrees of success, and basically it's too late now to do anything but tidy up. Those few changes that are decided upon should be executed before the final dress rehearsal so that everyone has a chance to see the effect in performance before opening night. Perfection is rare in this profession; as long as you give it your best shot, there's nothing to be gained from recriminations or regrets. Whatever your sense of achievement, you must continue to support those people to whom the weight of performance has shifted. Don't allow your feelings to drag them down or to form inflated expectations. Either result can damage the chances of the show's success.

At the final dress rehearsal you may find, for instance, that components of the rig you've agonised with and eventually compromised away jump to the foreground once again, and tiny blemishes take on enormous proportions. Your sensitivities are raised to greater heights than ever by the presence of an audience.

Don't panic! Instead, analyse the problem quietly: Is there, or was there ever, a solution? Is there time available to carry out improvements? Most important of all, are you overreacting? If you change, how upsetting is it going to be for the cast and crew?

You are being forced for the last and, perhaps, most painful time to compare the results you have achieved with your original vision. It's not a time for lamentations but for good analytic craftmanship; you must take responsibility for the compromises that circumstances forced upon the design, but you must not allow the painful and seemingly obvious failures to cancel out the many small successes. Probably the last important skill for you to develop as lighting designer is your ability to blend with an audience; through their eyes see your production for the first time. Members of an audience are encouraged to become a large, amorphous body that thinks and feels in unison; if you are able to feel with them, you may be able to finish the final dress rehearsal with an honest and objective assessment of the production. If you find yourself, and those beside you, leaning forward in expectation, you may be able to say that the efforts of the production team have been successful and, particularly, that the performance staff has clearly comprehended your intention and has brought it successfully to fruition.

On completion of the final dress rehearsal, give brief notes to the whole lighting team, making sure that you ignore none, before getting them off home to relax before the stress of opening. Don't keep them long (they have family or friends in the audience), and be sure to balance the positive and the negative in your criticism.

21.16 In Summation

Now that you have developed a group of individuals into a cohesive performance staff confident and free enough to continue developing and supporting the production, then—and only then—do you have a completed design. Congratulations! It's been a long grind, and, whether the results meet your expectations or not, your successful completion of the process is, in itself, sufficient cause for congratulations.

CHAPTER 22

Opening Night

However difficult and uncomfortable openings may be for you, if you value the associations you have made with the management, company, and, in particular, the lighting crew, you need to be supporting them in the successes and failures of the evening. Since you are little more than a patron for the evening, sit back, enjoy the excitement, and join in the applause.

Some styles of theatre demand curtain calls as part of the genre, but I often wonder what they achieve. Having struggled to see through my tears Mimi dying so beautifully in *La Bohème*, it does nothing for my further enjoyment of the show to see her, large as life, taking curtain calls. Fortunately, lighting people stay in the background, and it's unlikely they will ever be confronted with this unresolved dilemma.

22.2 Criticism

I remember one show where the lighting for a particular scene was given a rave review, but there was not a single lantern [instrument] burning—it was lit from top to bottom with real candles, an effect that, unfortunately, the fire department will rarely allow these days. I found it a matter of concern that the reviewer was evidently unable to notice the difference.

Critics today are not perceived as experienced individuals who have an opportunity to present their viewpoint to the public. Rather, they are frequently seen by practitioners and audience alike as reflectors of public taste who speak with the unimpeachable authority of the media. As a professional, you must not allow yourself to be distracted by this publicity machinery and trapped into "playing the audience."

Take the analogy of a dancer: what draws the admiration of the audience is the apparent ease with which fantastic movements are made. It seems that lighting designers who draw attention to the skills involved in their creation are like dancers who continually point out to the audience the difficulty of the choreography. Instead, they should channel their efforts into building the standard of the whole product and rely upon the acumen of the critics to realise how skillfully this has been achieved. This is the basis of the argument that theatre critics should know as much about the profession as possible.

So, when criticisms are published, keep the good ones for your folio. Don't let the bad ones dim your enthusiasm, but be open enough to learn from anyone whose opinion is based on professional standards.

22.3 Murphy's Law of Opening Night

Theatre people are superstitious; they have all sorts of silly rules about whistling in the dressing rooms, and about never referring to *Macbeth* by title but rather as "that Scottish play." Among their superstitions is Murphy's Law of Opening Night, which states that, if ever anything is to go wrong, it will be this night. A doorknob that has survived the rigours of the rehearsal process successfully will choose tonight to come off in the actor's hand, trapping him onstage with no means of exit, or dimmers will pulse for no reason, making little flashes of lightning across the cyclorama during every blackout.

Despite anyone's tendency to blame these occurrences on Fate or Murphy, you can prevent most of them simply by attending to routine preshow checks and by not allowing the excitement of opening night to distract you. You may arrive at the theatre in time to satisfy yourself that everything that can be predicted to go wrong is checked; it's no longer your responsibility to carry out these checks, but your presence may ensure that detail is attended to soberly. At all costs you must not appear to be looking over the shoulder of the head electrician; rather, make prior arrangements to attend in support. It's unlikely that he or she alone will be able to check every detail and may welcome an extra pair of eyes unobtrusively watching.

22.4 Nervousness

If you're a nervous type, try not to let it show during any contact you have with the performance staff prior to the show; they are likely to have sufficient nervous energy of their own. Instead, continue the battle against opening-night nerves (section 21.11), and try to instill confidence in each individual—not foolhardiness, but confidence. Nerves, generally a result of self-consciousness, are not the same as performance adrenaline; they come from a state of mind that makes you unreasonably worried about yourself. If some members of the lighting crew are having difficulty controlling their nerves, you may be able to help by giving them something new—not too difficult but demanding reasonable concentration—with which you can challenge them to come out of themselves and consider more the well-being of the production.

22.5 Surviving the Show

Halfway through the first act, you're just beginning to relax and enjoy the performance when something disastrous happens. What should you do? Absolutely nothing. Have faith! Your crew members are trying their best, and there's nothing you could do that they aren't doing; remember, tomorrow you'll be gone and they'll manage to cope then, too. Find out what happened later if you can't guess from the evidence onstage. Commiserate with the operator and offer congratulations on the display of skills that found a solution while drawing least attention to the mistake. There's nothing you can say in the form of a note than an operator hasn't already said to himself (or herself) with more invective. This is theatre, not film, and there's always another performance in which to make amends.

22.6 Obligations

Your leave-taking from the crew is not a time for heartfelt insincerity—glowing comments that have little or no value since they are motivated by the occasion, rather than need. It's better that you deliver encouragement earlier in the rehearsal process, when stress and tension are at their highest; a moment of praise or congratulation then will be far more appreciated and beneficial than during the flood of compliments that generally follow an opening. Instead, impress upon crew that openings are merely the first step in a long, gradual improvement that will continue until closing night.

Many more managements are choosing to open the after-show party to both cast and crew or, alternatively, to supply refreshments in the greenroom for the backstage crew. You may be in a position to jog the memory of management on your crew's behalf; in any event, try to ensure that something suitable is supplied—giving champagne to those who are more likely to appreciate beer is an inappropriate gesture. I have learned to become a little wary of opening-night parties; they can be extraordinarily boring, and people tend to drink a little too much to compensate. On rare occasions this may supply the fuel for "honest criticism," which can quickly degenerate into a gripe session. I prefer to make my farewells, then fade quietly away. But don't forget to take your final cheque with you!

CHAPTER 23

The Run—
Continued Involvement
of the Lighting Designer

With the rise of the curtain on opening night your contractual obligations as a free-lance lighting designer are over, but many believe that your professional and social obligations continue for the length of the run. If you're free-lance and are never again seen at the production, the staff and crew won't think badly of you; they realise that your next pay cheque demands your travelling on to new productions. On the other hand, for a staff/house designer never to be seen at performances would be perceived as negligence or, at best, insensitivity. You challenged the staff and crew not only to deliver nightly a performance that serves the mechanics of the show but also to develop with the production as it matures; they will have difficulty accepting this responsibility without your support and encouragement.

The lighting profession has developed a tradition of training that requires you to pass on your knowledge and to make every member feel responsible for becoming part of this information chain. The system can be likened to an informal apprenticeship, which takes as many forms as there are members. The obligations for your further involvement during the run are closely associated with this tradition. You need to follow up what you have begun, to see how the production and the confidence of personnel matures, and, in the process, to check on your own development. Some time away from the product will improve your objectivity and allow you to judge more truly the quality of your own work.

23.2 Follow-up Attendances

The amount of time you spend on this process need not be great; you may not need to see a complete show, perhaps just a difficult act occasionally. The rules of conduct mentioned before still apply (such as not entering the biobox [lighting control booth] without the permission of the head electrician). Get a message to both the stage manager and head electrician before your visits; first, it's a matter of ethics, and, second, you want to check if there is anything in particular you should watch to assist anyone in carrying out responsibilities better. Remember that free-lancers are no longer under contract to management and won't be covered by worker's compensation backstage. Generally, these rules will be overlooked and you'll be welcomed, but a free-lancer is wise to investigate such coverage through private insurance.

The foundation of your continued influence is the documentation you left behind: plan [plot], state-of-the-board sheets, lantern [instrument] schedule, and cue sheets; your sole purpose in attending is to check that these parameters are maintained, within the latitude for development you established. You must be careful not to engage in redesign if what you see is not to your liking. The design was completed on opening night, and you have no authority to change details without particular reference to the director and permission from management.

Any notes you give after the performance should be of the broader style suggested in section 21.11. You may be able to praise certain areas of development and point out how another cue may be developed in the same way. Clearly indicate when a cue differs from the original concept; this note may need to be given in the presence of the stage manager and/or head electrician so that discussion can ensue regarding the changes and the manner in which they occurred. Remember, you asked for and encouraged improvements; any misinterpretations may have been caused by your lack of clarity.

23.3 Change versus Developments

When you find radical change to the operation and/or rig, speak to whomever authorised the change and ask the purpose. Almost certainly, the reasons will be valid; perhaps the colour change was necessary since the original colour was no longer available, or staging may have altered and the operation had to be varied to match it. The "change" may have also been simply a one-off mistake tonight.

Changes can be authorised only by the stage manager, who is charged with maintaining the show as it was originally produced. If you believe that changes were unnecessary or should have been effected in a different manner, you will need to discuss alternatives with the stage manager, who is the authority you are now concerned with. To alter the stage manager's decisions may be seen as undermining his or her position in the company.

More often, changes are the result of gradual deviation away from the original concept over time. When the operator is reminded of the original cue shape, the usual response is: "I knew there was something wrong with that cue; I've been trying to find it again. . . ." Before you arbitrarily reverse changes, carefully analyse them; there may be valid cause for "gut reaction" changes the board operator has effected. Maybe the original concept was flawed, and the operator has been following instinct in an attempt to find a way around the difficulty.

Rarely, you may find that an onstage lantern has been shifted—perhaps a performer needed room to prepare an entrance. In such a case, point out the alterations to the stage manager so that he or she is seen to exercise authority in the eyes of both the floor lighting person and the performer. A compromise will surely be found.

Before departing, ensure that the stage manager and head electrician know how to contact you and that they feel free to do so when necessary. It's their job to maintain the show, but you should remain available as a reference and support when needed.

23.4 Transfer and/or Re-production

There is a tendency among managements to offer a low fee to a lighting designer for the transfer of a show to another theatre or for a return production in the same theatre. "But you've done it before," they cry. To come to a fair resolution, go back to the schedule in chapter 2 and revise it for either transfer or re-mounting. Estimate the number of hours involved to achieve the task successfully; then charge according to the hours spent as a proportion of the original fee.

When you transfer to another theatre, virtually everything from two weeks prior to the opening night must be repeated anew. Every detail concerning choice and placement of equipment must be reconsidered from basic principles; most of the theatre familiarisation and intelligence must be gathered once again; the operator's staff and control equipment will almost certainly be different and will need to be blended into the production. About all you save is the time spent formulating the production concept, but, even then, there may be some cause for reconsideration. I remember a *Figaro* that transferred to an open-air performance at which dinner was served during the sunset interval [intermission] break. The lighting concept had to be reconsidered to include available light, to augment it as necessary, and to take over for the night scenes after the interval— a completely different design!

Generally, you try to adapt available equipment to match as closely as possible the results previously achieved; there may be some improvement but also many compromises. Because other members of the production team often have difficulty understanding the reasons for the losses, you must take care when explaining why results differ from the original. Example: You could be asked to duplicate front-of-house lighting without the benefit of an orchestra bar, with entirely different angles, and with box booms that have limited access to the stage; you need to devise new solutions that don't require knocking holes in walls or hanging extra bars in impossible positions.

Re-mounting a production in the same theatre is considerably easier. Your schedule in chapter 2 picks up about one and one-half weeks prior to opening, and you can use a shorter production week (see chapter 16). Given resources of personnel, facilities, and equipment many major companies operate a daily change of repertoire, though special skills are involved that are beyond the scope of this section. You may need to spend additional time with the operators and crew when they differ from those who serviced the original production (it's for this reason that companies involved in repertoire work benefit greatly from computer-assisted operation). You must appreciate that their personalities and body-rhythms vary, and you cannot expect precisely the same shape and feel to every cue. Since they tend to adapt cues to match their own perceptions, you should be prepared to rephrase, reexplain, perhaps even reconsider, to suit the new personality.

In the interim between the original production and re-mounting, your tastes will have changed, and what you see this time onstage may shock you. Be careful not to plot all over again; you may have time to make slight variations, but a major reconception will be out of the question. Also, in the interim, the solution to a vexing problem in the original production may present itself. It's advisable to rig the original circuits as well, just in case your brilliant new insight is an absolute disaster.

To what degree the original documentation will be of use will depend on whether you are transferring or simply re-mounting. In the latter case, of course, much of the paperwork will be unchanged. The necessity for retaining copies yourself or within management (prompt copy) is obvious.

23.5 Bump-outs [Load-outs]

I enjoy bump-outs, the process of getting the show out of the theatre on completion of its run and restoring the facilities to "mint" condition. Most people, though, consider them a dreadful chore; the cast has gone to a party, for the most part management has disappeared, and the crew is left to get on with the work as quickly as possible. The attendance of the lighting designer may help to make the electrics crew feel less lonely, so try to be there, if at all possible. Of course, in a union house it can be only a social visit, but in a nonunion house an extra pair of hands will probably be welcome (though you must ensure that the organisation and authority rests with the stage manager and head electrician). Occasionally, in a nonunion house or on an arts council tour, a group of performers will offer to lighten the load. If so, the supervisor needs to maintain control over the extra hands so as to avoid accident or damage that can be caused by more enthusiasm than skill.

The purpose of the bump-out is to return all departmental equipment and facilities to a state in which you would like to have found it, though not necessarily the state that you did! You must service any equipment that you know to be defective, clean out all work areas, and see that all lanterns are in standard condition. Remember the prerig preparations discussed in section 17.5? You won't have time to do all of that, but it's the ideal to which you should be aiming. Pay particular attention to storage so that no damage can occur between your departure and the arrival of the next lighting team.

Because of the late hour and the nature of the chore (often bump-outs immediately follow the final performance despite overtime rates), attention to detail is often neglected, and safety precautions taken during rigging are forgotten. This tendency must be curbed by the supervisor so that the end of the run is not marred by a nasty accident.

To encourage your own development, you should arrange two informal meetings: the first with the production team and the second with the head electrician and staff. Try to have them near the end of the run, preferably after the bump-out, so that they encompass the entire process of lighting the show. Any lighting designer can learn only from experience and needs to ensure that an assessment is as objective as possible. Your colleagues on the project are the only ones who can confirm your judgement or, perhaps, suggest alternative approaches that you may consider in the future.

I particularly value the opinion of the head electrician, who has seen many shows pass through that theatre and is in a perfect position to judge the integrity of your work. Try not to appear as if you are seeking acclaim; in the same vein, you must be prepared to accept a degree of adverse criticism. That is exactly the treatment you have been handing the staff and your colleagues throughout the process, and it's fair that they get at least one chance of returning the compliment.

CHAPTER 24

In Conclusion

In conclusion let me draw your attention once again to Jean Rosenthal's book *The Magic of Light* (see Bibliography) and, in particular, to the quotation from it in chapter 3 concerning collaboration. When I first read that book, I was excited by a philosophy for lighting the stage that I believed many of us practiced but that had never before been expounded. In part, this book has been an attempt to expand upon the spirit of Rosenthal's argument and to illustrate how one lighting designer attempts to work within the parameters she formulated.

While auditioning prospective students, I found that our field seems to be the glamourous younger sister of the technical family. Inexperienced individuals—a kid at school or someone at the community theatre—plug in a light or push a fader and are dazzled by the power in their fingers. Often encouraged with false expectations of a career, they dash off to find a course and are frustrated when they discover that there are so few rules and even fewer guidelines, since each practitioner has acquired over a period of time an appreciation of the basic tools of lighting by close association and practice. This frustration extends beyond the student professional to the semiprofessional, amateur, and even schoolteachers who cannot afford three years of study. All require access to something more than a nuts-and-bolts discussion of equipment, something that they can use as a guide to the whole process of lighting—a map that steers them from first reading to opening night.

All these reasons made me decide to write this book. I wanted to talk of lighting in terms that all theatrical people would find accessible and to describe commercial approaches to lighting in a clear, concise fashion to give insight into purpose and practicalities. I wanted to talk with fledgling lighting designers so that they could glean something on which to start building a body of experience but, at the same time, would comprehend the complexities of the subject.

24.2 Further Advancement: Folios and Agents

At best, the material contained within this volume can only be a start. I've indicated throughout great gaps in basic theory and detail (such as basic electricity, detailed knowledge of lighting boards and lanterns [instruments], and safety procedures) that I have assumed you already know; if not, you must pursue them elsewhere. The books and magazines listed in the Bibliography indicate areas of further study, but that list is limited; you will need to search out avenues where practical experience has indicated that you lack skill. However, study alone will be insufficient; practise must form the core of your further education. You cannot learn your craft from a book; you need to get your fingers burnt (literally!) if you are to comprehend not only the theory but also the practical application— how you adapt to match your unique conception.

As you amass experience, keep a concise record (productions, dates, places, basic documentation, critical reviews, and colour photographs) that will form the body of a folio. Then you will have a complete record of your experience that can be easily absorbed by prospective employers/agents. The folio need not be overloaded with masses of detail; rather, it should succinctly illustrate your craftsmanship and those qualities within your work that make you unique. Those are the qualities that make you employable over a run-of-the-mill designer or suit you to a particular task. At all times carry with you a résumé; it need be no more than a page that gives personal contact details and the bare bones of your experience in reverse order (most recent first); it's your version of a calling card.

Obtaining an agent to represent you is frustrating; you can't get an agent without experience, and you can't gain experience unless you find work. Your folio will eventually become the lever that will gain you access, but it needs to be sufficiently robust to prove to the agent that you're worth representing. This won't happen overnight; for some time yet you will need to hustle your own bookings whenever opportunity presents, and this same kind of determination will catch the attention of your future agent.

24.3 My Corner Baker

During the writing of this book I frequently found the need to duck down to the corner baker for some sustenance and that surge of energy I get from something sticky and sweet. My baker and I got to know each other a little, and, when he discovered that I was a lighting designer for the stage, he said: "So, you light the drama. You must see things differently from the rest of us."

My ego found the implications flattering; it was pleasing to be treated as a specialist, as somebody with a unique insight. However, if we extend and reverse the assessment he made, it would mean that my baker has a taste different from everyone else's—and that does not explain why I am frequently forced to stand in line for his produce. If his taste is so different, how can it be popular? The evidence implies that his taste and the goodies he manufactures with it have a common touch, and it is simply the method in which he applies his skill that makes him a craftsman of extraordinary quality.

I must, therefore, reluctantly, reject the compliment of my friend. If you, too, are to echo and play upon the theatrical tastes of your audience, you must first understand the general public's perception of light and use your skills to expand and heighten that perception to become entertainment of rare taste and quality. I look forward to joining with each of you in that continuing quest that will occupy us for the rest of our careers.

Bibliography

Lighting

Bentham, Frederick. *The Art of Stage Lighting*. 2d ed. New York: Theatre Art Books, 1976.

McCandless, Stanley. *A Method for Lighting the Stage*. New York: Theatre Arts Books, 1958.

Palmer, Richard H. *The Lighting Art*. Englewood Cliffs, NJ: Prentice-Hall, 1985.

Pilbrow, Richard. *Stage Lighting*. New York: Van Nostrand Reinhold, 1970.

Reid, Francis. *Lighting the Amateur Stage*. Rank Strand *Tabs*, Supplement Nos. 1 & 2. (See Magazines section for TABS details.)

————. *The Stage Lighting Handbook*. New York: Theatre Arts Books, 1976.

Rosenthal, Jean, and Lael Wertenbaker. *The Magic of Light*. Boston: Little, Brown, 1972.

Sellman, Hunton D., and Merrill J. Lessley. *Essentials of Stage Lighting*. 2d ed. Englewood Cliffs, NJ: Prentice-Hall, 1982.

Stoddard, Richard. *Stage Scenery, Machinery, and Lighting: A Guide to Information Sources*. Detroit: Gale Research Co., 1977.

Streader, Timothy, and John Williams. *Create Your Own Stage Lighting*. Englewood Cliffs, NJ: Prentice-Hall, 1985.

Varley, Helen, ed. *Colour*. (Edited and designed by Marshall Editions Limited.) Los Angeles: Knapp Press, 1980.

Warfel, William B. *A Handbook of Stage Lighting Graphics*. Drama Books, 1974.

Warfel, William B., and Walter R. Kalppert. *Color Science for Lighting the Stage*. New Haven: Yale University Press, 1981.

Associated Skills

Bowman, Ned A. *Shop Cook Book: The Handbook of Technical Practice for the Performing Arts*. New York: Scenographic Media, 1972.

Corson, Richard. *Stage Makeup*. 7th ed. Englewood Cliffs, NJ: Prentice-Hall, 1986.

United Nautical Publishers. *The Colour Book of Knots*. New York: Macmillan, 1982.

Historic Background

Penzel, Frederick. *Theatre Lighting Before Electricity*. Middletown, CT: Wesleyan University Press, 1978.

Rees, Terence. *Theatre Lighting in the Age of Gas*. London: Society for Theatre Research, 1978.

Theoretical Background

Lounsbury, Warren C. *Theatre: Backstage from A to Z*. Seattle: University of Washington Press, 1984.

Mason, Peter. *The Light Fantastic*. Melbourne, Australia: Penguin, 1981. (also on audio cassette—Australian Broadcasting Commission)

Magazines

Tabs (Rank Strand). F. Reid, ed. P.O. Box 51 Great West Road; Brentford, Middlesex TW8 9HR, U.K.

Theatre Crafts. P. MacKay, ed. P.O. Box 630, Holmes, Pennsylvania 19043–9930, U.S.A.

Index